ESSENTIALS OF FINANCE

Artusard Renault

Essentials of Finance

Artusard Renault

Published by Artusard Renault, 2025.

ESSENTIALS OF FINANCE

First edition. August 8, 2025.

ISBN: 979-8231385584

Written by Artusard Renault.

Chapter 1

Finance Defined

Finance is the set of activities dealing with the management of funds. More specifically, it is the decision of collection and use of funds. It is a branch of economics that studies the management of money and other assets.

The field of ***finance*** refers to the concepts of time, money and risk and how they are interrelated. The term "finance" may thus incorporate any of the following:

- The study of money[1] and other assets[2]
- The management and control of those assets
- Profiling and managing project risks
- The science of managing money
- The industry that delivers financial services
- As a verb, "to finance" is to provide funds for business[3] or for an individual's large purchases (car, home, etc.).

Money is anything that is generally accepted as payment for goods and services and repayment of debts. The main uses of money are as a medium of exchange, a unit of account, and a store of value. Some authors explicitly require money to be a standard of deferred payment.

The term price system is sometimes used to refer to methods using commodity valuation of money accounting systems.

Money includes both currency, particularly the many circulating currencies with legal tender status, and various forms of financial deposit accounts, such as demand deposits, savings accounts, and

1. http://en.wikipedia.org/wiki/Money
2. http://en.wikipedia.org/wiki/Asset
3. http://en.wikipedia.org/wiki/Business

certificates of deposit. In modern economies, currency is the smallest component of the money supply.

Money is used as an intermediary for trade, in order to avoid the inefficiencies of a barter system, which are sometimes referred to as the 'double coincidence of wants[4] problem'. Such usage is termed a *medium of exchange.*

Unit of account

A *unit of account* is a standard numerical unit of measurement of the market value of goods, services, and other transactions. Also known as a "measure" or "standard" of relative worth and deferred payment, a unit of account is a necessary prerequisite for the formulation of commercial agreements that involve debt.

- Divisible into small units without destroying its value; precious metals can be coined from bars, or melted down into bars again.
- Fungible[5]: that is, one unit or piece must be perceived as equivalent to any other, which is why diamonds[6], works of art[7] or real estate[8] are not suitable as money.
- A specific weight, or measure, or size to be verifiably countable. For instance, coins are often made with ridges around the edges, so that any removal of material from the coin (lowering its commodity value) will be easy to detect.

To act as a *store of value*, a commodity, a form of money, or financial capital[9] must be able to be reliably saved, stored, and

4. http://en.wikipedia.org/wiki/Double_coincidence_of_wants

5. http://en.wikipedia.org/wiki/Fungibility

6. http://en.wikipedia.org/wiki/Diamond

7. http://en.wikipedia.org/wiki/Art

8. http://en.wikipedia.org/wiki/Real_estate

retrieved — and be predictably useful when it is so retrieved. Fiat currency like paper or electronic currency no longer backed by gold in most countries is not considered by some economists to be a store of value.

Liquidity describes how easily an item can be traded for another item, or into the common currency within an economy. Money is the most liquid asset because it is universally recognized and accepted as the common currency. In this way, money gives consumers the freedom to trade goods and services easily without having to barter.

Liquid financial instruments are easily tradable[10] and have low transaction costs[11]. There should be no — or minimal — spread[12] between the prices to buy and sell the instrument being used as money.

Types of money

In economics, money is a broad term that refers to any instrument that can be used in the resolution of debt. However, different types of money have different economic strengths and liabilities. Theoretician Ludwig von Mises[13] made that point in his book *The Theory of Money and Credit*[14], and he argued for the importance of distinguishing among three types of money: commodity money, fiat money, and credit money. Modern monetary theory also distinguishes among different types of money, using a categorization system that focuses on the liquidity of money.

---

9. http://en.wikipedia.org/wiki/Financial_capital
10. http://en.wikipedia.org/wiki/Tradable
11. http://en.wikipedia.org/wiki/Transaction_cost
12. http://en.wikipedia.org/wiki/Bid/offer_spread
13. http://en.wikipedia.org/wiki/Ludwig_von_Mises
14. *http://en.wikipedia.org/wiki/The_Theory_of_Money_and_Credit*

Commodity money

Commodity money value comes from the commodity out of which it is made. The commodity itself constitutes the money, and the money is the commodity. Examples of commodities that have been used as mediums of exchange include gold[15], silver[16], copper[17], rice[18], salt, peppercorns, large stones, decorated belts, shells, alcohol, cigarettes, cannabis, candy, barley[19], etc. These items were sometimes used in a metric of perceived value[20] in conjunction to one another, in various commodity valuation or Price System[21] economies. Use of commodity money is similar to barter, but a commodity money provides a simple and automatic unit of account[22] for the commodity which is being used as money.

Representative money

Representative money[23] is money that consists of token coins[24], other physical tokens such as certificates, and even non-physical "digital certificates" (authenticated digital transactions) that can be reliably exchanged for a fixed quantity of a commodity such as gold[25], silver[26] or potentially water[27], oil[28] or food[29]. Representative money thus

15. http://en.wikipedia.org/wiki/Gold

16. http://en.wikipedia.org/wiki/Silver

17. http://en.wikipedia.org/wiki/Copper

18. http://en.wikipedia.org/wiki/Rice

19. http://en.wikipedia.org/wiki/Barley

20. http://en.wikipedia.org/wiki/Value

21. http://en.wikipedia.org/wiki/Price_System

22. http://en.wikipedia.org/wiki/Unit_of_account

23. http://en.wikipedia.org/wiki/Representative_money

24. http://en.wikipedia.org/wiki/Token_coin

25. http://en.wikipedia.org/wiki/Gold

26. http://en.wikipedia.org/wiki/Silver

27. http://en.wikipedia.org/wiki/Water

stands in direct and fixed relation to the commodity which backs it, while not itself being composed of that commodity.

Credit money

Credit money[30] is any claim against a physical or legal person that can be used for the purchase of goods and services. Credit money differs from commodity and fiat money in two ways: It is not payable on demand (although in the case of fiat money, "demand payment" is a purely symbolic act since all that can be demanded is other types of fiat currency) and there is some element of risk that the real value[31] upon fulfillment of the claim will not be equal to real value expected at the time of purchase.

This risk comes about in two ways and affects *both* buyer and seller.

First, it is a claim and the claimant may default (not pay). High levels of default have destructive supply side effects. If manufacturers and service providers do not receive payment for the goods they produce, they will not have the resources to buy the labor and materials needed to produce new goods and services. This reduces supply, increases prices and raises unemployment, possibly triggering a period of stagflation. In extreme cases, widespread defaults can cause a lack of confidence in lending institutions and lead to economic depression[32]. For example, abuse of credit arrangements is considered one of the significant causes of the Great Depression[33] of the 1930s.

---

28. http://en.wikipedia.org/wiki/Petroleum

29. http://en.wikipedia.org/wiki/Food

30. http://en.wikipedia.org/wiki/Credit_money

31. http://en.wikipedia.org/wiki/Real_value

32. http://en.wikipedia.org/wiki/Economic_depression

33. http://en.wikipedia.org/wiki/Great_Depression

The second source of risk is time. Credit money is a promise of *future* payment. If the interest rate on the claim fails to compensate for the combined impact of the inflation[34] (or *deflation*[35]) rate and the *time value of money*[36], the seller will receive less real value than anticipated. If the interest rate on the claim overcompensates, the buyer will pay more than expected.

Over the last two centuries, credit money has steadily risen as the main source of money creation, progressively replacing first commodity and then representative money.

A particular problem with credit money is that its supply moves in line with the *business cycle*[37]. When lenders are optimistic, notably when the debt level is low, they increase their lending activity which creates new money. This may also trigger inflation and *bull markets*[38]. When creditors are pessimistic (for instance, when debt level is perceived as too high, or unwise lending activity in the past has resulted in situations where defaults are expected to follow), then creditors reduce their lending activity and money becomes "tight" or "illiquid." Bear markets[39], characterized by bankruptcies and market recessions, may follow.

Fiat money

Fiat money is any money whose value is determined by legal means, rather than the strict availability of goods and services which are named on the representative note.

Fiat money is created when a type of credit money (typically notes from a central bank, such as the Federal Reserve System[40] in

34. http://en.wikipedia.org/wiki/Inflation_rate
35. *http://en.wikipedia.org/wiki/Deflation*
36. *http://en.wikipedia.org/wiki/Time_value_of_money*
37. *http://en.wikipedia.org/wiki/Business_cycle*
38. *http://en.wikipedia.org/wiki/Bull_market*
39. http://en.wikipedia.org/wiki/Bear_market

the U.S.) is declared by a government act (**fiat**) to be acceptable and officially-recognized payment for all debts, both public and private. Fiat money may thus be symbolic of a commodity or a government promise, though not a *completely specified amount* of either of these. Fiat money is thus not technically fungible or tradable directly for fixed quantities of anything, except more of the same government's fiat money.

Fiat moneys usually trade against each other in value in an international market, as with other goods. An exception to this is when currencies are locked to each other, as explained below. Many but not all fiat moneys are accepted on the international market as having value.

Those that are trade indirectly against any internationally available goods and services [7][41]. Thus the number of U.S. dollars[42] or Japanese yen[43] which are equivalent to each other, or to a gram of gold metal, are all market decisions which change from moment to moment on a daily basis. Occasionally, a country will peg the value of its fiat money to that of the fiat money of a larger economy: for example the Belize dollar[44] trades in fixed proportion (at 2:1) to the U.S. dollar, so there is no floating value ratio of the two currencies.

Representative, credit, and fiat money all provide solutions to several limitations of commodity money. Depending on the laws, there may be little or no need to physically transport the money — an electronic exchange may be sufficient. Other types of moneys have as their sole use to be medium of exchange, so their supply is not

---

40. http://en.wikipedia.org/wiki/Federal_Reserve_System

41. http://en.wikipedia.org/wiki/
Money#cite_note-Mises-6_01abfc750a0c942167651c40d088531d_cite_note-Mises-6

42. http://en.wikipedia.org/wiki/U.S._dollar

43. http://en.wikipedia.org/wiki/Japanese_yen

44. http://en.wikipedia.org/wiki/Belize_dollar

limited by competing alternate uses. Credit and fiat monies can be created without limit in theory, so there is no limit on trade volumes.

Fiat money, if physically represented in the form of currency (paper or coins) can be easily damaged or destroyed. However, here fiat money has an advantage over representative or commodity money, in that the same laws that created the money can also define rules for its replacement in case of damage or destruction. For example, the U.S. government will replace mutilated federal reserve notes (U.S. fiat money) if at least half of the physical note can be reconstructed, or if it can be otherwise proven to have been destroyed. By contrast, commodity money which has been destroyed or lost is gone.

Paper currency is especially vulnerable to everyday hazards: from fire, water, termites, and simple wear and tear. Currency in the form of minted coins is more durable but a significant portion is simply lost in everyday use. In order to reduce replacement costs, many countries are converting to plastic currency. For example, Mexico has changed its twenty and fifty peso notes, Singapore its $2, $5, $10 and $50 bills, Malaysia with RM5 bill, and Australia and New Zealand their $5, $10, $20, $50 and $100 to plastic, both for the increased durability and because plastic may be easily specifically constructed for each denomination, thus making it impossible for counterfeiters to "lift" or raise the value of a bill by using the material of a bill of lesser value as a primary source to make a counterfeit note of higher value.

Some of the benefits of fiat money can be a double-edged sword. For example, if the amount of money in active circulation outstrips the available goods and services for sale, the effect can be inflationary. This can easily happen if governments print money without attention to the level of economic activity, or if successful counterfeiters flourish.

A criticism of credit and fiat moneys relates to the fact that their stabilities are highly dependent on the stability of the legal system backing the currency: should the legal system fail, so will the value of any type of money that depends on it. However, this situation is typical of the maintenance of the value of any promissory note system: if a guarantor creates money or wealth by means of any legal *promise* to provide goods or services in the future (as is the case with both credit and fiat type moneys), then any failure of a legal system which backs up the rights of the debt-holder to collect on the promise, will act to jeopardize the value of future promises.

A common characteristic of fiat money is inflation[45]*. From 1944-1971 gold*[46] *was the base currency*[47] *underpinning the Bretton Woods system*[48] or gold standard[49] which functioned as the worldwide monetary system[50].

Money supply

The money supply is the amount of money within a specific economy available for purchasing goods or services. The supply in the US is usually considered as four escalating categories M0, M1, M2 and M3. The categories grow in size with M3 representing all forms of money (including credit) and M0 being just base money (coins, bills, and central bank deposits). M0 is also money that can satisfy private banks' reserve requirements. In the US, the Federal Reserve[51] is responsible for controlling the money supply, while in the Euro area[52] the respective institution is the European Central

---

45. *http://en.wikipedia.org/wiki/Inflation*

46. *http://en.wikipedia.org/wiki/Gold*

47. *http://en.wikipedia.org/wiki/Currency*

48. *http://en.wikipedia.org/wiki/Bretton_Woods_system*

49. http://en.wikipedia.org/wiki/Gold_standard

50. http://en.wikipedia.org/wiki/Monetary_system

51. http://en.wikipedia.org/wiki/Federal_Reserve

Bank[53]. Other central banks with significant impact on global finances are the Bank of Japan[54], People's Bank of China[55] and the Bank of England[56].

When gold is used as money, the money supply can grow in either of two ways. First, the money supply can increase as the amount of gold increases by new gold mining at about 2% per year, but it can also increase more during periods of gold rushes and discoveries, such as when Columbus discovered the new world and brought gold back to Spain, or when gold was discovered in California in 1848. This kind of increase helps debtors, and causes inflation, as the value of gold goes down.

Second, the money supply can increase when the value of gold goes up. This kind of increase in the value of gold helps savers and creditors and is called deflation, where items for sale are less expensive in terms of gold. Deflation was the more typical situation for over a century[57] when gold and credit money backed by gold were used as money in the US from 1792 to 1913.

Monetary policy

Monetary policy is the process by which a government[58], central bank, or monetary authority manages the money supply[59] to achieve specific goals. Usually the goal of monetary policy is to accommodate economic growth in an environment of stable prices. For example, it is clearly stated in the Federal Reserve Act[60] that the

---

52. http://en.wikipedia.org/wiki/Euro_area

53. http://en.wikipedia.org/wiki/European_Central_Bank

54. http://en.wikipedia.org/wiki/Bank_of_Japan

55. http://en.wikipedia.org/wiki/People%27s_Bank_of_China

56. http://en.wikipedia.org/wiki/Bank_of_England

57. http://en.wikipedia.org/wiki/Century

58. http://en.wikipedia.org/wiki/Government

59. http://en.wikipedia.org/wiki/Money_supply

Board of Governors[61] and the Federal Open Market Committee[62] should seek "to promote effectively the goals of maximum employment, stable prices, and moderate long-term interest rates."

A failed monetary policy can have significant detrimental effects on an economy and the society that depends on it. These include hyperinflation[63], stagflation[64], recession[65], high unemployment[66], shortages of imported goods, inability to export goods, and even total monetary collapse and the adoption of a much less efficient barter economy. This happened in Russia, for instance, after the fall of the Soviet Union[67].

Governments and central banks have taken both regulatory and free market approaches to monetary policy. Some of the tools used to control the money supply include:

- changing the rate[68] at which the government loans or borrows money
- currency purchases or sales
- increasing or lowering government borrowing
- increasing or lowering government spending
- manipulation of exchange rates[69]
- raising or lowering bank reserve requirements
- regulation or prohibition of private currencies

---

60. http://en.wikipedia.org/wiki/Federal_Reserve_Act

61. http://en.wikipedia.org/wiki/Board_of_Governors

62. http://en.wikipedia.org/wiki/Federal_Open_Market_Committee

63. http://en.wikipedia.org/wiki/Hyperinflation

64. http://en.wikipedia.org/wiki/Stagflation

65. http://en.wikipedia.org/wiki/Recession

66. http://en.wikipedia.org/wiki/Unemployment

67. http://en.wikipedia.org/wiki/History_of_the_Soviet_Union_(1985-1991)

68. http://en.wikipedia.org/wiki/Interest_rate

69. http://en.wikipedia.org/wiki/Exchange_rate

- taxation or tax breaks on imports or exports of capital into a country

For many years much of monetary policy was influenced by an economic theory known as monetarism. *Monetarism*[70] is an economic theory which argues that management of the money supply should be the primary means of regulating economic activity. The stability of the demand for money prior to the 1980s was a key finding of Milton Friedman[71] and Anna Schwartz[72] supported by the work of David Laidler[73], and many others.

The nature of the demand for money changed during the 1980s owing to technical, institutional, and legal factors and the influence of monetarism has since decreased.

Barter

The use of barter[74] like methods may date back to at least 100,000 years ago. (Barter is defined as "a trade or exchange of goods or services without using money." Its origins are traced back to the dawn of mankind. Early bartering was done on a one-on-one basis and is still used today between some individuals and businesses on an informal basis. However, Modern Barter and Trade has moved beyond the old one-on-one barter

---

70. *http://en.wikipedia.org/wiki/Monetarism*

71. http://en.wikipedia.org/wiki/Milton_Friedman

72. http://en.wikipedia.org/wiki/Anna_Schwartz

73. http://en.wikipedia.org/wiki/David_Laidler

74. http://en.wikipedia.org/wiki/Barter

concept by practicing third party barter whereby the buyer is not obligated to purchase from the seller and vice versa. Rather, in Modern Barter and Trade, a barter exchange operates as a broker and banker and trade credits are used as a unit of exchange to facilitate trading among multiple companies and individuals. Modern trade and barter has developed into a sophisticated tool to help businesses increase their efficiencies by monetizing their unused capacities and excess inventories.

The worldwide organized barter exchange and trade industry has grown to be an 8.0 billion dollar a year industry and is used by hundreds of thousands of businesses and individuals as a mechanism to increase their revenues, preserve cash flows and market themselves to new buyers. The modern barter and trade industry operates to improve the overall economy by injecting additional commerce into the system and thereby improving the financial strength of all of its participants. The advent of the internet, and sophisticated relational database software programs has further advanced the barter industry's growth financial credibility. Barter offers a tremendous opportunity for entrepreneurs that understand economics, sales, banking and customer service.

The U.S. government officially recognized barter exchanges as third party record keepers in 1982 with the passage of the Tax Equity & Fiscal Responsibility Act which also required all barter exchanges to classify their members' barter sales as reportable income to the IRS via an annual 1099-B filing. Organized barter has grown throughout the world to the point now where virtually every country has a formalized barter and trade network of some kind.)

In the past, goods were exchanged on a one-on-one basis with the intent that the value of the goods traded was of relatively equal value. Prior to the establishment of currencies, barter was the most accepted form of commerce. The equality of the value in a one-on-one barter is often an issue.

In 1626 Peter Minuet traded $24 worth of beads, knives and kettles for Manhattan Island - clearly Peter got the benefit of the bargain on that transaction. Barter is still practiced informally on a one-on-one basis everyday on a global basis. Organized barter networks have developed to permit third party bartering which in effect eliminates the concern over unequal one-on-one trading. The barter exchange operates as a broker and bank and each participating member has an account which is debited when purchases are made, and credited when sales are made in trade or barter dollars.

Trade Exchanges

A trade or barter exchange is a commercial organization that provides a trading platform and bookkeeping system for its members or clients. The member companies buy and sell products and services to each other using an internal currency known as barter or trade dollars. Modern Barter and Trade has evolved considerably to become an effective method of increasing sales, conserving cash, moving inventory, and making use of excess production capacity for businesses around the world. Businesses in a barter earn trade credits (instead of cash) that are deposited into their account. They then have the ability to purchase goods and services from other members utilizing their trade credits - they are not obligated to purchase from who they sold to, and vice versa. The exchange plays an important role because they provide the record-keeping, brokering expertise and monthly statements to each member.

Commercial exchanges make money by charging a commission on each transaction either all on the buy side, all on the sell side, or a combination of both. Transaction fees typically run between 8 and 15%. It is estimated that over 500,000 businesses in the U.S. are involved in a barter exchange activities. There are approximately 500 commercial and corporate barter companies serving all parts of the world. There are two industry groups, the National Association of Trade Exchanges (NATE) and the International Reciprocal Trade Association (IRTA). Both offer training and promote high ethical standards among their members. Moreover, each has created it own currency through which its member barter companies can trade. NATE's currency is the known as the BANC and IRTA's currency is called Universal Currency (UC).

Exchange systems provide new sales and higher volumes of business, conserving cash for essential expenditures, exchange of unproductive assets for valuable products or services, reduction of unit costs, and opening new outlets for excess inventory and unused capacity. Reciprocal trade finance enables a firm to buy using its incremental cost of production. So long as incremental revenue exceeds incremental cost, it is worth it for a firm to trade using a barter exchange.

There are multiple reasons to use a good barter exchange:

- Increased purchasing power
- Increased revenue
- Preserving Cash
- More clients (both from the barter exchange and from cash-business referrals from barter clients)
- Better cash flow
- Greater marketing opportunities
- Improved efficiency

Unless a business has more work than it can handle, barter is a 'no-brainer' for any company. A business has all its fixed costs (rent, salaries, insurance, vehicles, workers' comp, machinery, etc.) whether it has two hundred customers or five hundred, if a business can take down time or inventory that is costing money and turn it into new revenue, it's a slam dunk. The major benefit to companies is that they get to leverage their cost of goods.

Organized barter companies also have many more benefits over conventional advertising methods since they are much more proactive. Barter members call into the exchange brokerage with things they need and the brokers match those needs with other members that can fill them. There are usually fees to join, but compared to a print advertisement for example, you only pay to join once and then most exchanges are 'pay per use'.

The first exchange system is the Swiss WIR Bank. It was founded in 1934 as a result of currency shortages after the stock market crash of 1929. "WIR" is both an abbreviation of Wirtschaftsring and the word for "we" in German, reminding participants that the economic circle is also a community. Only SME can join WIR. Its purpose is to encourage participating members to put their buying power at each other's disposal and keep it circulating within their ranks, thereby providing members with additional sales volume.

WIR has grown to 62,000 members, trading approximately the value of 3 billion Swiss Franc. The offering of goods and services for WIR is promoted by the fact that every official participant is obligated to accept payment in WIR for at least 30% of the first 2000 francs of the selling price, and every loan holder must amortize his/her debt by selling goods/services for WIR.

Corporate Barter

Corporate Barter is another sector of the barter and trade industry. It focuses on larger transactions, which is different from a traditional, retail oriented barter exchange. Corporate barter exchanges typically use media and advertising as leverage for their larger transactions. It entails the use of a currency unit called a "trade-credit". The trade-credit must be known and guaranteed (contract to eliminate ambiguity and risk).

Swapping

Swapping is the increasingly prevalent informal bartering system in which participants in Internet communities[75] trade items of comparable value on a trust basis.

While swapping is an excellent way to find and obtain items that are inexpensive, it relies upon honesty. A dishonest participant might arrange a swap, and then never complete their end of the transaction, thus getting something for nothing. This practice is called *swaplifting*, a pun[76] on *shoplifting*[77]. The victim's recourse is often limited to shunning[78] the swaplifter, or taking him to small claims court[79].

75. http://en.wikipedia.org/wiki/Internet_communities

76. http://en.wikipedia.org/wiki/Pun

77. *http://en.wikipedia.org/wiki/Shoplifting*

78. http://en.wikipedia.org/wiki/Shunning

Complex business models based on the concept of barter are today possible since the advent of Web 2.0[80] technologies.

In the other word Barter means: The act of trading goods and services between two or more parties without the use of money. Bartering benefits companies and countries that see a mutual benefit in exchanging goods and services rather than cash, and it also enables those who are lacking "hard currency" to obtain goods and services. To make up for a lack of hard currency, Thailand[81]'s township[82], Amphoe Kut Chum[83], once issued its own local scrip[84] called *Bia Kut Chum*: Bia[85] is Thai[86] for cowry[87] shell, was once 1⁄6400 Baht, and is still current in metaphorical expressions. Running afoul of national currency laws, the community changed to barter coupons[88] called *Boon*[89] Kut Chum that bear a fixed value in baht, which they swap for goods[90] and services[91] within the community[92].

---

79. http://en.wikipedia.org/wiki/Small_claims_court
80. http://en.wikipedia.org/wiki/Web_2.0
81. http://en.wikipedia.org/wiki/Thailand
82. http://en.wikipedia.org/wiki/Township
83. http://en.wikipedia.org/wiki/Amphoe_Kut_Chum
84. http://en.wikipedia.org/wiki/Scrip
85. http://en.wikipedia.org/wiki/Thai_baht
86. http://en.wikipedia.org/wiki/Thai
87. http://en.wikipedia.org/wiki/Cowry
88. http://en.wikipedia.org/wiki/Coupon
89. *http://en.wikipedia.org/wiki/Merit_(Buddhism)*
90. http://en.wikipedia.org/wiki/Goods
91. http://en.wikipedia.org/wiki/Service_(economics)
92. http://en.wikipedia.org/wiki/Community

Tax implications

In the United States, the sales a barter exchange makes are considered taxable revenue by the IRS and the gross amount of a barter exchange member's sales are reported to the IRS by the barter exchange via a 1099-B form. The requirement for barter exchanges to report members sales was enacted in the Tax Equity & Fair Responsibility Act of 1982. According to the IRS, "The fair market value of goods and services exchanged must be included in the income of both parties." Other countries do not have the reporting requirement that the U.S. does concerning proceeds from barter transactions. However, if you barter for goods and/or services, you are taxed not more or less than if it were a cash transaction. In other words, it is handled the same way as a cash transaction regarding taxation. If you bartered for a profit, you pay the appropriate tax, if you generated a loss in the transaction, you have a loss. Bartering for business is also taxed accordingly as business income or business expense

Trading in red ochre[93] is attested in Swaziland[94], shell jewellery in the form of strung beads also dates back to this period, and had the basic attributes needed of commodity money[95]. To organize production and to distribute goods and services among their populations, before market economies[96] existed, people relied on tradition, top-down command, or community cooperation. Relations of reciprocity[97], and/or redistribution, substituted for market exchange.

The Shekel[98] referred to an ancient unit of weight and currency. The first usage of the term came from Mesopotamia[99] circa 3000 BC.

93. http://en.wikipedia.org/wiki/Red_ochre
94. http://en.wikipedia.org/wiki/Swaziland
95. http://en.wikipedia.org/wiki/Commodity_money
96. http://en.wikipedia.org/wiki/Market_economies
97. http://en.wikipedia.org/wiki/Reciprocity

and referred to a specific mass of barley[100] which related other values in a metric[101] such as silver, bronze, copper etc. A barley/shekel was originally both a unit of currency[102] and a unit of weight... just as the British Pound was originally a unit denominating a one pound mass of silver.

According to Herodotus[103], and most modern scholars, the Lydians[104] were the first people to introduce the use of gold and silver coin. It is thought that these first stamped coins[105] were minted around 650-600 BC. A stater coin was made in the stater (trite) denomination. To complement the stater, fractions were made: the trite (third), the hekte (sixth), and so forth in lower denominations.

The name of Croesus[106] of Lydia[107] became synonymous with wealth in antiquity. Sardis[108] was renowned as a beautiful city. Around 550 BC, Croesus contributed money for the construction of the temple of Artemis at Ephesus, one of the Seven Wonders of the ancient world[109]

The word "money" is believed to originate from a temple of Hera[110], located on Capitoline[111], one of Rome's seven hills. In the

---

98. http://en.wikipedia.org/wiki/Shekel
99. http://en.wikipedia.org/wiki/Mesopotamia
100. http://en.wikipedia.org/wiki/Barley
101. http://en.wikipedia.org/wiki/Metrics
102. http://en.wikipedia.org/wiki/Currency
103. http://en.wikipedia.org/wiki/Herodotus
104. http://en.wikipedia.org/wiki/Lydians
105. http://en.wikipedia.org/wiki/Coins
106. http://en.wikipedia.org/wiki/Croesus
107. http://en.wikipedia.org/wiki/Lydia
108. http://en.wikipedia.org/wiki/Sardis
109. http://en.wikipedia.org/wiki/Seven_Wonders_of_the_ancient_world
110. http://en.wikipedia.org/wiki/Hera
111. http://en.wikipedia.org/wiki/Capitoline

ancient world Hera was often associated with money. The temple of Juno Moneta[112] at Rome was the place where the mint of Ancient Rome was located. "Juno" etymology may be derived from the Etruscan goddess Uni[113] (which means "the one", "unique", "unit", "union", "united") and "Moneta" either from the Latin word "monere" (remind, warn, or instruct) or the Greek word "moneres" (alone, unique).

---

112. http://en.wikipedia.org/wiki/Juno_Moneta

113. http://en.wikipedia.org/wiki/Uni_(mythology)

Chapter 2

Working Capital Management

Working Capital defined

Working capital ordinarily means the excess of current assets over current liabilities. The term is used to indicate the total current assets, in which case the excess of current assets over current liabilities is referred to as net working capital.

There are two types of working capital: permanent working capital and permanent working capital. The first, represents a fixed sum equal to the minimum working capital requirements at any time of the year. The second, consists of the variable amount of working capital, the sum depending upon the seasonal activity and the emergency and extraordinary needs of the business,

Working capital means the firm's holdings of current, or short-term, assets such as cash, receivables inventory, and marketable securities. This refers to academic literature,i.e.,total current or circulating assets because of their cyclical nature. Cash is initially employed to purchase inventory which is in turn on credit and results in accounts receivables. Receivables become cash-part of which is reinvested in additional inventory and part (i.e., the amount above cost) going to profit or cash throw-off.

Corporate executives devote a considerate amount of attention to the management of working capital. An examination of the components of working capital . An examination of the components of working capital is helpful because of the preoccupation of management with the proper combination of assets and acquired funds, concerted efforts are made to ensure the ability of the firm to meet the short-term obligations. The management must be concerned with proper financial structure, these and other funds must be raised judiciously. This provides a theoretical framework in the risk/return trade-off of various approaches, applied in the firm's working capital management.

Concept of Working Capital

Working capital refers to the amount of funds tied up at any stage of the cycle, from the time funds are initially committed to the time they are collected. These funds change in form ranging from cash (awaiting use for the purchase of day goods) in preparing a balance sheet at any point in time. In accounting definition, working capital is the total current assets investment of the company at any given time. Working capital is normally at its lowest points at the start of the cycle when goods are purchased and at the end, when you paid your financing source. The peak of the working capital investment comes when all the inputs have been expended and the finished product is ready for market.

There are two possible interpretation of working capital concept;

a. Balance Sheet Concept

The balance sheet concept is represented by the excess of current assets over current liabilities and is the amount normally available to finance current operations.. It is also used as synonym for gross or total current assets. The excess of current assets over current liabilities is called the net working capital or net current assets. This view about working capital is supported by known economists. They feel that current assets should be considered as working capital as the whole of it helps to earn profits; and the management is more concerned with the total current assets as they constitute the total funds available for operational purposes..

The conventional definition of working capital in terms of the difference between the current assets and the current liabilities somewhat confusing. Working capital is really what a part of long-term finance is locked in and used for supporting current activities. The larger the amount of working capital so derived, greater the proportion of long-term capital sources siphoned off to short-term activities. It is difficult to say whether this is right or wrong. Apparently, when firms are warned about tight working capital situation, the logic of the above definition would perhaps indicate diversion of long-term finances for short-term purposes Liquidation of debtors and inventory into cash would also keep the level of working capital unchanged.

A relatively large amount of working capital according to this definition may produce a false sense of security at a time when cash resources in the absence of adequate profits. Again, under the conventional method, cash enters into the computation of working capital. But it may have been more appropriate to exclude cash from such calculations because one compares cash requirements with current assets less current liabilities. The implication of this in conventional working capital computations is that during the financial period current assets get converted into cash which, after paying off the current liabilities, can be used to meet other operational expenses. The paradox, is that such current assets as are relied upon to yield cash must themselves to be supported by long-term funds until they are converted into cash.

a. Operating Cycle –Concept - A company's operating cycle typically consists of three primary activities: purchasing

> resources, producing the product, and distributing (selling) the product. These activities create funds flows that are both unsynchronized and uncertain. They are unsynchronized because cash disbursements (for example, payments for resource purchases) usually take place before cash receipts) example, collection of receivables.)

> They are uncertain because future sales and costs, which generate the respective and disbursements, cannot be forecasted with complete accuracy . If the firm is to maintain liquidity and function properly, it has to invest funds in various short-term assets (working capital) during this cycle. It has to maintain a cash balance to pay the bills as they come due. In addition, the company must invest in inventories to fill customer orders promptly.

Illustrating the operating cycle of a typical firm. The operating cycle is equal to the length of the inventory and receivables conversion periods.

Operating cycle = Inventory conversion period + Receivables conversion period.

The inventory conversion period is the length of time required to produce and sell the product. It is defined as follows:

Inventory conversion period = Average inventory/ Cost of sales/ 365

The receivables conversion period, or average collection period, represents the length of time required to collect the sales receipts. It is calculated as follows:

Receivables conversion period = Accounts Receivables/ Annual credit sales/365

The payables deferral period is the length of time the firm is able to defer payment on its various resource purchases (for example, wages, and taxes) Equation 4 is used to calculate the payables deferral period:

Account payable + Salaries, benefits, and payroll taxes payable/ (Cost of sales + selling, general and administrative expenses)/365

The cash conversion cycle represents the net time interval between the collection of cash receipts from product sales and the cash payments for the company's various resource purchases. It is calculated as follows: Cash conversion cycle = Operating cycle – payables deferral period.

Optimum Level of Working Capital Investment

The optimal level of working capital investment is the level expected to maximize shareholder wealth. It is a function of several factors, including the variability of sales and cash flows and the degree of operating and financial leverage employed by the firm. No single working capital investment policy is necessarily optimal for all firms.

It has to determine the proportions of short and long-term debt to use in financing these assets. This decision also involves tradeoffs between profitability and risk. Sources of debt financing are classified according to their maturities. They can be categorized as being either short-term or long-term, with short-term sources having maturities of 1 year or less and long-term sources having maturities of greater than 1 year.

Long term interest rates normally exceeds short-term rates because of the reduced flexibility of long-term borrowing relative to short-term debt, even when short-term interest rates are equal to or greater than long-term rates. With long-term debt, a firm incurs the interest expense even during times when it has no immediate need for the funds, such as during seasonal or cyclical downturns. With short-term debt, in contrast, the firm can avoid the interest costs on unnecessary funds by paying off (or not renewing) the debt.

Therefore, the cost of long-term debt generally is higher than the cost of short-term debt.

Significance of Working Capital

Firms should keep no unproductive assets and should finance with the cheapest available sources of funds. Working capital policy is the determination of the level and composition of current assets which should be maintained by the company and the proportion of current liabilities and permanent capital which should finance the investment in current assets. This is a policy of aggressive or tight liquidity if management puts more weight to the more liquid assets are non-earning, like cash. The reverse is true if the working capital policy is conservative or slack liquidity.

While the firm has many strategies available to address these circumstances, strategies that utilize investment or financing with working capital accounts often offer a substantial advantage over other techniques. Assume that the firm is faced with uncertainty regarding the level of its future cash flows will incur substantial costs if it has insufficient cash to meet expenses. Strategies may be formulated to address this uncertainty and the cost , that if may engender. Some of these working capital investment are holding additional cash balances beyond expected needs, holding a reserve of short-term marketable securities, or arranging for the availability of additional short term borrowing capacity. One of these strategies (or a combination of them) may well be the least costly approach to the problem. The existence of fixed set-up costs in the production of goods may be addressed in several ways, but one possible alternative is to hold inventory.

Fundamentals of Net Working Capital

The balance sheet of the firm provides information about the structure of a firm's investments on the one hand and the structure of its financing sources on the other. The structures chosen should consistently lead to the maximization of the value of the owner's investment in the firm. Important components of the firm's structure include the level of investment in current assets and the extent of current liability financing. It should not be surprising to know that short-term financial management – managing current assets and current liabilities – is one of the financial manager's most important and time-consuming activities.

Current assets, also known as working capital, represent the portion of investment that circulars from one form to another in the ordinary conduct of business. This embraces the recurring transition from cash to inventories to receivables and back to cash that forms the operating cycle of the firm. Marketable securities are considered part of working capital, as cash securities. Prepaid expenses are included as working capital because they represent services owed to the company, thereby eliminating the need for later cash outlays.

Current liabilities represent the firm's short-term financing, because they include all debts of the firm that come due (must be paid) in 1 year or less. These debts usually include amounts owed to suppliers (accounts payable), banks (notes payable), and employees and governments (accruals) among others.

Commonly, net working capital is the difference between the firm's current assets and its current liabilities. When the current assets exceed the current liabilities, the firm has positive net working capital. It is also the firm's portion of the firm's current assets financed with long-term funds (the sum of long-term debt and stockholders' equity) Because current liabilities represent the firm's sources of short-term funds, the amount by which current assets exceed current liabilities must be financed with long-term funds. When current assets are less than current liabilities, the firm has negative net working capital. Therefore, net working capital is the portion of the firm's fixed assets financed with current liabilities.

The conversion of current assets from inventory to receivable to cash provides the source of cash used to pay the current liabilities. The cash outlays for current liabilities are relatively predictable. When an obligation is incurred, the firm generally knows when the corresponding payment will be due. Cash inflows is difficult to predict as the conversion of the current assets to more liquid forms. The more predictable its cash inflows, the less net working capital a firm need Most firms are unable to match cash inflows to outflows with certainty, current assets that more than cover outflows for current liabilities are usually necessary.

One of the most important decisions that must be made with respect to current assets and liabilities is how current liabilities will be used to finance current assets. The amount of current liabilities that is available is limited by the dollar amount of purchases in the case of accounts payable, by the dollar amount of accrued liabilities in the case of accruals, and by the amount of seasonal borrowing considered acceptable by lenders in the case of notes payable and commercial paper. Lenders make short-term loans to allow a firm to finance seasonable buildups of accounts receivable or inventory. They generally do not lend short term money for long-term uses.

There are two basic strategies for determining an appropriate mix of short term (current liability) and long-term financing – the aggressive strategy and the conservative strategy.

Chapter 3

CASH MANAGEMENT & MARKETABLE SECURITIES

The Management Function

The company's management of cash constitutes cash position which should be maintained and this also includes marketable securities investment which enhances the ability of the company to meet its cash requirements while maximizing the income on idle funds. The function covers the activities related to the collection, receipt, control and disbursement of cash in the company. In most companies, these functions are vested in the finance officer or manager who usually holds a managerial or vice-president position. The subsidiary functions related to the cash management role include credit and collection, cashiering, internal auditing and accounting and purchasing.

Cash is the most liquid and least identifiable asset of the company. This is associated with a number of managerial problems and tasks which are particular to the treasury function. The forecasting and monitoring of cash flows and balances must be conducted for relatively short periods – monthly, weekly and even daily – if the finance officer were to respond effectively to day-to-day situations affecting cash. An effective control system for cash is needed to avoid misappropriation and handling losses in the normal course of business. The first usually accomplished through a cash planning system which is oriented to the very short-run operating cycle of the company. The cash planning activity may be carried out by a staff. The patterns of cash position is actually disclosed by the regular reports of actual receipts/disbursements, and balances, and by such statistics as average daily/weekly cash collections, average interest rates on marketable securities, and average days' accounts receivable and payables.

The control system for cash is built around the monitoring and verification of cash balances and movement as well as an authorization procedure for the handling of cash. The objective of this system is not so much to optimize the cash balance as to minimize the actual losses associated with misappropriation and improper handling of cash. In many instances, other physical safeguards are instituted to help ensure adequate control of cash, e.g., armored cars, safety deposit boxes, and other methods. Bonding arrangements may also be resorted to, especially for personnel who handle cash in normal daily transactions.

Cash is the lifeblood of a business firm. It is needed to acquire supplies, resources, equipment and other assets used in generating the products and services provided by the firm. It is needed to pay wages and salaries to workers and managers, taxes to governments, interest and principal to creditors, and dividends to shareholders. Cash is the medium of exchange which allows management to carry on the various activities of the business firm from day to day activities.

Marketable securities serve as a back up pool of liquidity that provide cash quickly when needed. It provides a short-term investment outlet for excess cash and are also useful for meeting planned outflows of funds. Cash and short-term, interest-bearing investments (marketable securities) are the firm's least productive assets. They are not required in producing goods or services, unlike the firm's fixed assets. They are not part of the process of selling as are inventory and accounts receivable. When firms hold cash in currency or in non-interest bearing accounts, they obtain no direct return on their investment. Even if the cash is temporarily invested in marketable securities, its return is much less than the return on other assets held by the firm.

There are several good reasons why firms hold cash and marketable securities, despite the seemingly low returns. One important reason for holding cash in the form of non-interest-bearing currency and deposits is transactions demand. Since debts are settled via the exchange of cash, the firm must hold some cash in the bank to pay suppliers and some currency to make change if it makes sales from it.

Cash Assets as Hedges

There is quite an uncertainty for the firm's future cash needs for transactions; urgencies may arise for which the firm needs immediate cold cash. The firm must hedge against the possibility of these unexpected needs. Several types of hedges are possible. For instance, the firm can arrange to be able to borrow from its bank on short notice should funds suddenly be needed. Another approach is to hold extra cash and near cash assets beyond what would be needed for transactions purposes. By this, we mean interest-earning marketable assets that have very short maturities, and can be liquidated to provide funds on short notice with very little risk of loss.

The more of the total hedging reserve held in near-cash assets and the less held in cash, the greater the interest earned. There is a trade-off between this interest revenue and the transactions costs comprised in purchasing and selling such near-cash assets. These transactions assets have a fixed cost components; the firm bears these fixed costs when it buys or sells these assets regardless of the size of investment. Whether it is economical to invest part of all of the hedging reserve in near-cash assets depends on the amount of reserve. Firms that keep smaller reserves(because their transactions needs are either smaller or more certain, more likely to hold these reserves in cash, while firms with larger reserves keep them in near-cash assets.

Many firms experience some seasonality in sales. Often, there will be times during the year when firms have excess cash , in this situation firm have several choices. One alternative is to pay out the excess cash to its security holders when this cash is available, and then issue new securities, later in the year when funding is required. The costs of issuing new securities make this a disadvantageous strategy. More commonly, firms will temporarily invest the cash in interest-earning marketable securities from the time the cash is available until the time it is needed. Proper planning and investment choices for this strategy can garner a reasonable return on such temporary investment.

Cash Collection Systems

The cash system of a firm is the mechanism that provides the linkage between cash flows. The Finance Manager, therefore, has to develop and maintain the policies and procedures required to achieve an efficient cash flow for the firm's operations. This includes collection system for getting cash into the firm and disbursement system for paying the suppliers and other receivers of cash. The internal portion of the cash system consists of a concentration system to move cash from the entry point in the firm to the concentration bank and a disbursement funding system to move funds from the concentration bank to the disbursement banks so that payments can be made. Since banks are the major institutions involved in the payment system, the financial manager is also responsible for maintaining adequate banking relations to ensure the smooth flow of cash into, through, and out of the firm

The financial manager must make certain that the investment in cash is efficiently used. In order to minimize cash leaks, the financial manager should establish some sort of control system over incoming cash. If the receipt of such funds can broker up into two ore three and responsibility for each assigned to different employees, the ability to embezzle is greatly reduced. Collusion between two or more people is usually difficult to achieve. Petty cash funds should also be under a tight control system. Cheques made in payment for bills should also be strictly controlled to assure that the materials were actually ordered and received. Aside from these consideration, cash management involves at least two special functions, namely; ways in which to speed cash in flows ; and ways in which to slow disbursement, both having the obvious purpose of keeping the cost of financing the stock of cash (and its attendant costs) to a minimum.

A collection system is a set of procedures and banking arrangement used to move value from customers or other payers to the payer's deposit bank account. Since the finance manager is concerned with value transfer, the analysis of collection system focuses on creating an available balance in the deposit account and not just receiving transfer information (e.g., a cheque) Collection systems must also be concerned with payment information that supports the payment. A payment received without sufficient documentation may incur high search cost for locating information that permits accounts receivable to credit the appropriate customer's account. An efficient collection system performs the functions of mobilizing cash, providing accurate cash flow information, timely information on sales and customers accounts, and an audit trail for goods control.

When a selling firm transfers value to a buyer through a provision of goods or services. There is an opportunity cost incurred if value is not promptly received in return. A primary objective of a collection system is to receive value from the buyer as quickly as possible. A second objective is to receive and process information associated with the payment. The third related factor to consider in designing a collection system is the relationship the firm has with those making payments. Collection procedures have the potential to harm payer-payee relationships. Collection system design must also consider costs associated with receiving payments and the accompanying information. These costs may be associated directly with transaction processing, such as bank costs, postage costs, etc. or may be more administrative in nature. An additional cost factor primarily relates to systems in which coin and currency is the predominant payment vehicle, costs of losses from theft and fraud.

Cost of Collection Float

One of the most important factors in the objective function is to minimize the cost of collection float. To illustrate, assume a company is losing approximately 6 calendar days of interest on P2,000,000 each week. The annual cost of this float at 12% opportunity cost is:

P 2,000,000 X 6 days X .12/365 X 52 = Php205,150 per annum

Collection Float

The term collection float refers to the total time lag between the mailing of the payment by the payor and the availability of cash in the bank. Mail float results from the time that elapse from the mailing until received. Processing float is due to the processing time before the cheque is deposited in the banking system. The last component of collection float is availability float, which is a result of the firm's not being granted immediate availability on all deposit items. These last two elements of collection float were referred as deposit float. They represent the difference between the cash that is recorded as a deposit on the company's books and the increase in the available balance at the bank.

The measurement of float is a function both of the time lag and of the amount involved. Float is usually measured in a given currency, amount days, which are calculated by multiplying the time lag in days by the Pesos, amount being delayed. Float can be measured either on each item that is processed or on an average daily basis.

The float on each item is found by multiplying the amount of the payment by the number of days of delay for that payment. It is the product of these two quantities, and not either one individually, that is important in measuring float. We can see from the calculation of collection float in this illustration that the float on a Peso currency. 10,000 item that is delayed for 6 days is identical to the float on Peso 20,000-item that is delayed for 3 days.

A Check for P10,000 is mailed from customer A on August 8, Friday, because of mail, processing and availability delays, it is not credited as available funds in the bank of Xylex Enterprises until the following Thursday, 6 days later the float for this check is :

Float = P 10,000 X 6 days = 60,000 –days.

A Check for P20,000 is mailed from customer, B on August 8, but it is available on Monday, 3 days later. The float for this check is

Float = 20,000 X 3 days = Php60,000 - days

Concentration & Cash management strategy

Sometimes a neglected past of cash management is concentration because firms tend to think that when the cash is in their banking system, the battle is over. There are significant managerial decisions, which nevertheless, must still be made to insure that cash is moved efficiently to accounts where it can benefit the firm. Once the remittance from the firm's customers have been received and cleared, the resulting cash balances are available in the firm's lockbox or depository banks. It is useful for the firm to gather these balances from the lockbox banks into a central bank account. The process of collecting funds is called cash concentration. There are two reasons why cash concentration is advantageous. First, the collection process results in a larger pool of funds. The larger pool makes any temporary interest-earning investments more economical because it reduces the transactions costs on investment. For instance, if the firm obtains, Php 10,000 from each of 10 accounts, the firm will have Php 100,000 to invest, resulting in one purchase of securities rather than 10. Te larger the amount of funds may enable the firm to take advantage of higher-interest investments that require a larger minimum purchase. Second, with all the cash in a central location, keeping track of the cash (controlling the cash) is considerably simplified.

Advantages of Concentration

Cash concentration costs arise from several sources: opportunity costs of holding excess balances in deposit banks; transaction costs of moving cash into the concentration bank; the value of dual balances (in which the same cash is counted in both the deposit bank and the concentration bank at the same time).; administrative costs of managing the concentration system; and control costs associated with the risks of cash losses encountered in some concentration systems. To intelligently design a concentration system and establish concentration polices it is necessary to deal with all five of these cost factors simultaneously.

Although each technique evolved seek to reduce one or more cost factors, we must keep in mind the other factors may be adversely affected at the same time. The goal is to realize an overall reduction in the objective function.

Delays often occur in receiving deposit information from field managers. Once the firms requires deposit information to be gathered along with sales and inventory information and processed through several administrative levels. The result is a delay of several days before the cash manager receives deposit information to pass along to the concentration bank. By removing deposit information at an early stage and routing directly to the cash manager, a significant reduction in excess balances is realized.

Disbursement Systems & the Value of Float

Disbursement systems include the banks and the delivery mechanisms and procedures firms use to facilitate the movements of cash from the firm's centralized cash pool to disbursement banks and then on to suppliers and other payers. Disbursement banks are the banks on which disbursement checks are drawn. A disbursement system may be more complex than a collection system in one sense; management must choose not only the disbursement banks but also the check-issuing points. A lockbox bank is the check-receiving point, in contrast, and management has no control over the drawee bank.

The objective of disbursement is to process the payment obligation to vendors, employees, and creditors. In attempting to maximize the present value of the firm, it is beneficial to delay the time at which value is transferred from the firm in a disbursement system. However, any potential gain in value must be balanced against the costs of delay.

The main elements of the cash outflow timeline, are payment initiation, mail, vendor processing, and clearing time. Prolonging one or more of these segments may be beneficial to the firm. Usually, the disbursement problem is concerned primarily with eh latter elements of this timeline. It is useful to consider the payment initiation time as part of the decision process.

Elements of Payment Float

Payment float is the entire outflow timeline, while disbursement float is measured from the time the payor mails the check to the time of presentment at the payor's bank. Disbursement float consists of ; mail float, measured as the time between the payor's mailing of the check and the payee's receipt of it; processing float, the time required by the payee to deposit the checks after it has been received; and presentation, or clearing float, the time required by the banking system to return the check and present it against the payor's disbursement account. There is an additional time segment that is not associated with the transfer of value, and it is not shown as part of the timeline. The segment has to do with reconciling check that have cleared and otherwise processing the information associated with value transfer. This takes place after the value transfer has been affected.

Investment in Marketable Securities

Investment in marketable securities is an important financial management function because of the intimate relationship between cash and marketable securities. Determining the amount of marketable securities is one important aspect to hold. The other major aspect of the problem of investment in marketing securities is deciding which securities should the firm invest in. A vast array of types and maturities is available, and the financial manager must among these alternatives.

An assessment of certain criteria can provide the financial manager with a useful framework for selecting a portfolio of marketable securities. The firm will be particularly interested in the safety of the securities, their marketability, and their maturity. Differences in these features are the primary determinants of the yield differences among securities and differences in these features also explain why firms select certain kinds of securities for short-term investments.

The firm would like to receive as high a yield on its investment in marketable securities as possible. However, seeking higher rates of return to accepting larger amounts of risk. Since the firm keeps marketable securities for the precautionary reasons and to know scheduled outflows of cash, the firm will tend to invest in very safe marketable securities. Firms tend to buy the highest yielding marketable securities they can find subject to the constraints that the securities have an acceptable risk level. Risk in this context refers to risk of default. The issuer fails to redeem the security as per the contract. In a less severe sense the price of the security could fall at a time when the firm needs to liquidate the security.

The lower the maturity of a security, the more possibility is for price fluctuations price to its maturity. Since downside price fluctuations are undesirable for safety reasons, the firm will prefer short-lived securities. Firms prefer marketable securities, at the long end of the maturity spectrum, whose remaining life is no longer than six to nine months. Firms, at the short-end, can and do invest funds overnight.

Marketability refers to the ability to transform a security into cash. The financial manager will want to cash quickly, and he will not want to accept a large price concession in order to convert the securities. Thus, in the formation of preferences for the inclusion of particular instruments in the portfolio, consideration will be given to the time period needed to sell the security and the likelihood that the security can be sold at or near its prevailing market place, or where trades are accomplished only with large price changes between transactions, will be avoided.

Kinds of Marketable Securities

Some marketable securities are held for a speculative motive are often long-term. The securities that are most commonly held as part of the marketable securities portfolio are divided into two groups: governmental issues; and non-governmental issues. The short-term obligations issued by the central government and available as marketable security are treasury bills. Government securities could have maturities of more or less than one year, at the time of issue. The securities with a maturity of between three to twelve months, at the time of issues, are called treasury bills.

The firm can deposit its excess cash with the commercial banks for some fixed maturity. Deposit scheme are tailored suiting to the needs of the depositors. By various combinations of demand, term and recurring deposits, banks have brought spectrum of deposit schemes.

Cash Conversion Model

The cash conversion quantity depends on a number of factors, including the fixed cost of transferring funds between cash and marketable securities, the rate of interest that can be earned on marketable securities, and the firm's demand for cash. Because of the number of factors, reasonably sophisticated models are required to determine the optimism cash conversion quantity. These cash conversion models balance the relevant costs and benefits of holding cash versus investing in marketable securities to determine the economically optimum quantity of each. Two of the best- known cash conversion models – the Baumol model and the Miller-Orr model.

Baumol Model

The *Baumol model* is a simple approach that provides for cost-efficient cash balances by determining the optimal cash conversion quantity. Much like the process of determining optimal order quantities of inventory. The Baumol model treats cash as an inventory item whose inflows and outflows can be predicted with certainty. A portfolio of marketable securities acts as a backup reservoir of funds, from which cash balances can be replenished or to which excess cash can be moved in order to earn a return.

The firm manages its cash inventory by calculating two costs: the cost of converting marketable securities to cash and vice versa and the cost of holding cash rather than marketable securities. The first of these is called the conversion cost; the second is the opportunity cost. The conversion cost includes the fixed cost of placing an order for cash or marketable securities. It includes the cost of communicating the need to transfer funds to or from the cash account, paperwork costs, brokerage fees, and the cost of any follow-up action. The conversion cost is stated as dollars per conversion. The opportunity cost is simply the rate of interest that can be earned on marketable securities. It can be viewed as the interest earnings per dollar given up as a result of holding funds in a non-interest-earning cash account.

Economic Conversion Quantity

The model calculates the economic conversion quantity using the conversion and the opportunity costs. This amount is the cost-minimizing quantity in which the firm should convert marketable securities to cash or cash to marketable securities. By using the inventory analogy, it is the optimum size, in dollar terms, of the firm's order for cash or marketable securities. The ECQ is calculated by the following formula:

$$ECQ = \sqrt{\frac{2 \text{ X conversion cost X demand for cash}}{\text{opportunity cost (in decimal form}}} \quad (16.3)$$

Total Cost

The sum of the total conversion and total opportunity costs of the firm is called the total cost of cash. Total conversion cost equals the cost per conversion times the number of conversion per period. The number of conversion per period can be found by dividing the period's cash demand by the economic conversion quantity (ECQ) The total opportunity cost equals the opportunity cost (in decimal (form) times the average cash balance; this cost is expressed as a dollar amount). The average cash balance is found by dividing ECQ by 2. The total cost equation is

Total cost = (cost per conversion X number of conversion) +

(opportunity cost (in decimal form) X average cash balance) (16.3)

The objective of the Baumol model is to determine the economic conversion quantity of cash that minimizes total cost. Cash transfers that are larger or smaller than ECQ result in higher total cost.

(We use the dollar ($) currency in this instance)

For instance: The *Thermex Company*, a distributor of a variety of beverages, anticipates $ 1,500,000 in cash outlays (demand) during the coming year. The firm has determined that it costs $ 30 to convert marketable securities to cash and vice versa. The marketable securities portfolio currently earns an 8% annual rate of return. Substituting into Equation 16.3 results in the economic conversion quantity of cash:

$$ECQ = \sqrt{\frac{2 X \$ 30 X \$ 1{,}600{,}000}{.08}} = \$33{,}541$$

Jemex Company $ 33,541 each time it replenishes the cash discount. During the year the firm will make 45 conversions to replenish the cash account - $ 1,500,000/ $ 33.541 = 44.7. The average cash balance is $ 16,770.50 ($ 33,541/12). The total of managing the cash is found by substituting the appropriate values into Equation 16.4

Total cost = ($ 30 X 45)+(.08 X $ 16,770.50) = $ 2,692

Cash transfers that are either larger or smaller than $ 33,541 will result in higher total cost of managing *Jemex Company's* cash holdings.

Miller-Orr Model

The *Miller-Orr Model* is generally more realistic and appropriate than the Baumol model. The *Baumol model* is based on the assumption of certain cash flows. The Miller-Orr model provides for cost-efficient cash balances by determining an upper limit (maximum amount) and a return point for them. The return point represents the target cash balance level. Cash balances are allowed to fluctuate between the upper limit and a lower limit, which we assume to be a zero balance.

Bermek Model

Bermek hypothesized firms where the cash inflows were steady, but the outflows were periodic. This is the mirror image of the time pattern of cash flows within the Baumol model, where inflows were periodic and outflows were steady. In this model, cash would be collected continuously at a uniform rate, but would be disbursed over a short time as a group of the firm's checks reached its bank and were paid. The challenge is to profitably invest the funds between the time of their receipt and the time when a group of checks are presented to the bank for payment. The trade-off between interest income and transactions expense and the strategies employed are parallel to those of the *Baumol model.* For example, the firm could wait until one-half of the incoming cash has been accumulated, then invest this cash until the end of the period when it is needed. The formula for the optimum number of transactions is the same as that of the *Baumol model.* In this model, the cash is accumulated gradually (rather than disbursed gradually), so the transactions pattern would involve a series of investments followed by one disinvestment at the end of the period.

(in this instance, we use the peso currency)

For illustrations, say a firm receives P 100,000 per day, which it will eventually needs to make disbursements, and follows a policy of writing checks every two weeks. Over a two-week period, it accumulates P 1,400,000. It can invest at an interest of 6.825 percent per year (0.2625 per cent for two weeks),. The transaction cost of investment or disinvestment is P37.50. What investment strategy should the firm follow and how much will this strategy earn?

The optimal number of transaction is:

$N^* = (iY/2a)^{½}$

= [0.002625)(1,400,000)= P 1,200,000

In the *Bermek model,* these seven transaction consist of six deposits and one withdrawal. The amount of the final withdrawal is:

[n* - 1)/n]Y = 6/7(1,400,000) =P 1,200,000

The amount of the periodic investments will ((1.n)Y, or (P 200,000) The initial investment will require two days to accumulate, and will be made at the end of the second day. The other investment, in the same amount, will be made at the end of the fourth, sixth, eight, tenth, and twelfth days. The accumulated balances of P1,200,000 will be withdrawn on the fourteenth day. And with the cash accumulated during days 13 and 14 , will constitute the P 1,400,000 needed to cover the checks presented to the bank at that time. The profit from this strategy will be :

Profit = [(n-1)(/2n]iY-na
={(7-1)/2(7)]0.002625(1,400,000)-7(37.50)
=1575-262.5= P 1,312.50

Which they addressed time patterns of cash flow, neither the Baumol nor the Bermek models deal with risk; they both assume that the amounts of cash inflows and outflows are known with certainty. In using these models, the firm must use a hedging strategy. A firm facing the cash flow pattern in the Bermek model might keep a reserve of cash. If cash inflows then turned out to be less than expected for a particular part of the period, the firm could temporarily draw from the cash reserve to make deposits of economical size.

The Return Point and Upper Limit

The value the firm selects for the return point depends on ; conversion costs; the daily opportunity cost of funds, and the variance of daily net cash flows. The variance is estimated by using daily net cash flows (inflows minus outflows for the day). The equation for determining the return point is :

Return point = √ 2 X conversion cost X variance of daily net cash flows (16.5)

4 X daily opportunity cost (in decimal form)

3 _ _

Where \/ means to take the cube root of the solution under \/ sign.

In the Miller-Orr model, the upper limit for the cash balance is always set at three times the return point.

When cash balance reaches the upper limit, an amount equal to the supper limit minus the return point is converted to marketable securities:

Cash converted to marketable securities = upper limit – return point (16.6)

When cash balance falls to zero (the lower limit), the amount converted from marketable securities to cash is the amount represented by the return point:

Marketable securities converted to cash = return point – zero balance (16.&)

Illustration

(we use the dollar ($) in this instance)

Jamex Company costs it $ 30 to convert marketable securities to cash and vice versa, the firm's marketable securities portfolio earns an 8% annual return, which is 0.0222% daily (8%/360 days). The variance of Jamex Company's daily net cash flows is estimated to be $ 27,000. Substituting into Equation 16.5 yields the return point:

$$\text{Return point} = \sqrt{\frac{2 \text{ X } \$ 30 \text{ X } \$ 27{,}000}{4 \text{ X } 0.000222}} = \$ 1{,}399$$

The upper limit is 3 X return point:

Upper limit = 3 X $ 1,399 = $ 4,197

The firm's cash balance will be allowed to vary between $ 0 and $ 4,197. When the upper limit is reached, $ 2,798 ($ 4,197 - $ 1,399) is converted from cash to marketable securities . When the cash balance falls to zero (the lower limit), $ 1,399($ 1,399-$ 0) is converted from marketable securities to cash.

Problems:

1.

The following checks were received by *Azenith Company* during January. Calculate the amount of opportunity costs for the company if the opportunity cost rate is 12% per annum.

Face Amount	Days delay
100,000.00	4
150,000.00	5
50,000.00	3
75,000.00	6

2.

A disbursement is currently made by *JJ Enterprises* from its concentration bank at a cost of P 100 per month for account maintenance and P10 per check processed. The controlled disbursement bank will charge P120 per month for account maintenance and P20 per check processed. The controlled disbursement account will add ½-day float to the disbursements. The company issues 100 checks of average face amount of P30,000 per day. The treasurer maintains an overnight portfolio of about P 500,000, on which she currently earns about 6% per annum. She estimates that she could earn an additional 25 basis points on the investments if she could invest earlier in the day. Transfers to the controlled disbursement account could be done at a cost of P20 per transfer. Determine the annual net benefit, or cost, of using the controlled disbursement account instead of the current system.

3.

Nero Company maintains a centralized billing system at its home office to handle average daily collections of P450,000. The total time for mailing, processing, and clearing has been estimated at 4 days.

a. if the company's opportunity cost on short-term funds is 15%, how much this time lag of 4 days costing the company?

b. If management has designed a system of lock-boxes with regional that would have reduced the float by 1 ½ days and home office credit department expense by P 52,000 annually, what is the largest total amount of required compensating balance that the firm should he willing to accept with the lock-box arrangement?

4.

JO is a manufacturer of Id cards and invitation cards. They sell to retail shops and stores in multistate area in the western part of the Philippines. Mr. Santos, the treasurer, is considering the use of a lockbox for the collection of their customer's remittance. Their customers fall into two categories: single outlets and regional chains. During a typical month they receive an average of 5,000 checks with an average face amount of P 300 from a customer and 2,000 checks with an average face amount of P2,500 from the regional-chain customers. It takes a total of 7 days for JO to receive the payments, process the deposit, and receive available funds. Bank X has offered a lockbox service that would reduce the total to 3 days. The cost for the lockbox would be a fixed charge of P 500 per month and P 50 per processed. *JO* currently pays P .05 per item deposited at its bank. Santos does not believe there will be any additional savings to be achieved if the company eliminates the internal processing of the customers' remittances. *JO* has an opportunity cost rate of 10% per annum.

a. If *JO* uses the lockbox, should they have both classes of customers send their remittances to the lockbox.

b. Should *JO* use the lockbox?

5.

The Greenmax Company makes payments by checks. The Bluemax Company, a supplier has requested that Greenmax allow Bluemax to debit their account 10 days after the invoice date. Greenmax pays Bluemax with a check mailed 30 days after the invoice date. It takes an average of 5 days for the check to the cleared through Greenmax account. The average payment to Bluemax is P 500. It costs Greenmax an average of P 10 to process the invoice through their accounts payable department and to issue a check. These costs would be eliminated by the proposed procedure. The opportunity costs of funds to Greenmax is 10%.

a. Should Greenmax accept Bluemax offer?
b. Greenmax has received a similar offer from Redmax Company. Payments to Redmax company average P 5,000. All other information is unchanged from the Bluemax., Should Greenmax accept Redmax's offer?

6.

Cash Conversion cycle.

Helix Company pays account pays accounts payable on the tenth day after purchase. The average collection period is 30 days, and the average age of inventory is 40 days. The firm currently spends about P 15 million on operating cycle investments. The firm is considering a plan that would stretch its accounts payable by 20 days. If the firm pays 12% for its financing, what annual savings can it realize by this plan? Assume no discount for early payment of trade credit and a 360-day year.

7.

Lockbox decision

Hyperion Corp., a firm that has an annual opportunity cost of 9% is contemplating installation of a lockbox system at an annual cost of P 90,000. The system is expected to reduce mailing time by 1 ½ days, reduce processing time by 1 ½ days, and reduce check clearing time by 1 day. If the firm collects P 300,000 per day, would you recommend the system? Explain.

8.

Malayan Industries, Inc.

The Malayan Industries,Inc. maintain an account with Bank of Malaya for collection in the southeastern marketing area. The bank handles collection of P 750,000 per day in return for a compensating balance of P 500,000.

The company is considering an alternative of opening two separate accounts in the southeastern area. It has been projected that total processing time could be reduced by 2 days if accounts are maintained in a Colony Bank and in an Freedom Bank, each requiring a P 500,000 compensating balance. Would you recommend two bank system to Malayan Industries, Inc.?

If Bank of Malaya offers to drop the required compensating balance in favor of flat fee, what is the maximum fee Malayan Industries should be willing to pay to leave its business with that bank?

9.

Union Enterprises currently has a centralized billing system . On an average 5 days are required for customer's mailed payments to reach the central location. An additional 2-days are required for processing payments before a deposit can be made. The firm has a daily average collection of P800,000. The company has recently investigated the possibility of initiating a lockbox system. Such a system would reduce the mailed payments period from five to three days. Further, processing time would be reduced by one day, because each lockbox bank would pick up mailed deposits twice a day.

a. Determine the reduction in cash balance that can be achieved through the use of a lockbox system.

b. Determine the opportunity cost of the present system, assuming a 7.5% return on short term instruments.

c. If the annual cost of the lockbox system will be P120,000, should such a system be initiated?

10.

Exant Technologies,Inc. expects to have P 2,500,000 in cash outlays for next year. The firm believes that it will have an opportunity interest rate of 12.5% and will incur a cost of P 150 each time it borrows (or withdraws). Cash outlays are expected to be steady over the year. Using the inventory model:

a. Determine the optimal borrowing or withdrawal lot size for the Exant Technologies, Inc.

b. What is the total cost for the use of cash needed for transactions demanded?

c. What will be the cash cycle for the firm (velocity)?

d. What will be the average cash balance for the firm?

11.

Refer to the same problem (10) assume that the Exant Technologies,Inc. began the year with P 2,500,000 in cash.

a. How much would initially be invested in securities?
b. How much would be invested in securities after 113 days?

12

The *Grander Company* is setting up a new account with Independent Bank. Grander Company plans to issue checks in the amount of P 1,000,000 each day and to deduct them from its own records at the close of business on the day they are written. On average, the bank will receive and clear the check at 5 P.M., the third day they are written; for example, a check written on Monday will be cleared on Thursday afternoon. The firm's agreement with the bank required it to maintain a P 500,000 average compensating balance; this is P 250,000 greater than the cash balance the firm would otherwise have on deposit. It makes a P 500,000 deposit at the time it opens the account.

a. Assuming that the firm makes deposits at 4 PM each day (and the bank includes them in that day's transactions) how much must it deposit daily in order to maintain a sufficient balance once it reaches a steady state? Indicate the required deposit on Day 1, day 2, day 3, if any, and each day thereafter, assuming that the company will write checks for P1,000,000 on day 1 and each day thereafter.

b. How many days of float does Grander have?

c. What ending daily balance should the firm try to maintain (1) on the bank's records and (2) on its own records?

Chapter 4

SHORT-TERM FINANCING & ACCOUNTS RECEIVABLE MANAGEMENT

Financial requirements of Company

The financing requirements of the firms can be separated into a permanent and a seasonal need. The permanent need, which consists of fixed assets plus the permanent portion of the firm's current assets, remains unchanged over the year. The seasonal need, which consists of the temporary portion of current assets, varies over the year.

An Illustrative example is Jade Company's estimate of current, fixed, and total asset requirements on a monthly basis for the coming year which is given in columns 1,2, and 3 of Table 1.1

Table 1.1 Estimated Funds Requirements for Jade Company

Month	Current Assets	Fixed Assets	Total Assets	Permanent funds requirement	Seasonal funds requirement
	(1)	(2)	[(1) +(2)] (3)	(4)	[(3)-(4)] (5)
January	4,000.00	13,000.00	17,000.00	13,800.00	3,200.00
February	3,000.00	13,000.00	16,000.00	13,800.00	2,200.00
March	2,000.00	13,000.00	15,000.00	13,800.00	1,200.00
April	1,000.00	13,000.00	14,000.00	13,800.00	200.00
May	800.00	13,000.00	13,800.00	13,800.00	
June	1,500.00	13,000.00	14,500.00	13,800.00	700.00
July	3,000.00	13,000.00	16,000.00	13,800.00	2,200.00
August	3,700.00	13,000.00	16,700.00	13,800.00	2,900.00
September	4,000.00	13,000.00	17,000.00	13,800.00	3,200.00
October	5,000.00	13,000.00	18,000.00	13,800.00	4,200.00
November	3,000.00	13,000.00	16,000.00	13,800.00	2,200.00
December	2,000.00	13,000.00	15,000.00	13,800.00	1,200.00
Monthly average				13,800.00	1,950.00

* This represents the firm's funds requirements

Take note of the stable level of total assets over the year reflects, for convenience, an absence of growth by the firm. Columns 4 and 5 break down the total requirement into permanent and seasonal components. The permanent (column 4) is the lowest level of total assets during the period; the seasonal portion is the difference between the total funds requirement for each month and the permanent funds requirement.

By comparing the firm's fixed assets (column 2) to its permanent funds requirement (column 4), we see that the permanent funds requirement exceeds the firm's level of fixed assets. A portion of the firm's current assets is permanent, because they are apparently always being replaced. This value represents the base level of current assets that remains on the firm's books throughout the entire year. This value can also be found by subtracting the level of fixed assets from the permanent funds requirement (P 13,800 – P 13,000 = P 800.

Considerations of Cost

Under the aggressive strategy, Jade Company's average short term borrowing (seasonal funds requirement) is P 1,950, and average long-term borrowing (permanent funds requirement) is P 13,800 (columns 4 & 5 of Table 1.1) If the annual cost of short -term funds needed by Jade is 3 % and the annual cost of long-term financing is 11 percent, the total cost of the financing strategy is estimated as follows:

Cost of short-term financing = 3% X P 1,950 = P 58.50
Cost of long-term financing = 11% X 13,800 = 1,518.00
Total cost P 1,576.50

Risk Considerations

The aggressive strategy operates with minimum net working capital, because only the permanent portion of the firm's current assets is shown financed with long-term funds. For Jade Company, in table.1.1, the level of net working capital is P 800, which is the amount of permanent current assets (P 13,800 permanent funds requirement – P 13,000 fixed assets = P 800.)

The aggressive financing strategy is risky not only from the standpoint of low net working capital but also because it forces the firm to draw as heavily as possible on its short –term sources of funds to meet seasonal fluctuations in its requirements. If the total requirement turns out to be, say, the level represented by dashed line B in table 1.1, the firm may find it difficult to obtain longer-term funds quickly enough to satisfy short-term needs. This risk associated with the aggressive strategy results because a firm has only a limited amount of short-term borrowing capacity. If it draws too heavily on this capacity, unexpected needs for funds may become difficult to satisfy.

Credit Terms

Credit terms that suppliers offer to a firm allow the latter to delay payment for its purchases. Probably, because the supplier's cost of having its money tied up in merchandise after it is sold is reflected in the purchase p[rice, the purchaser is already indirectly paying for this benefit. The purchaser should therefore carefully analyze credit terms that include a cash discount, it has two options – to take the cash discount or to give it up.

If a firm intends to take a cash discount, it should pay on the last day of the discount period. There is no cost associated with taking a cash discount.

Jamex Industries, Inc, operator of a small chain of food condiments, purchased P 1,000 worth of merchandise on February 27 from a supplier extending terms of 2/10 net 30 EOM. If the firm takes the cash discount, it must pay P 980 [P 1,000-.(02 X P 1,000)] by March 10, thereby saving P 20.

Giving up Cash Discount

If the firm opts to give up the cash discount, it should pay on the final day of the credit period. There is an implicit cost associated with giving up a cash discount. The cost of giving up a cash discount is the implied rate of interest paid to delay payment of an account payable for an additional number of days. The amount is the interest being paid by the firm to keep its money for a number of days. This cost can illustrated by a simple example. The example assumes that payment will be made on the last possible day (either the final day of the cash discount period or the final day of the credit period).

Jamex Industries could take the cash discount on its February 27 purchase by paying P 980 on March 10. If Jamex gives up the cash discount, payment can be made on March 30. To keep its money for an extra 20 days, the firm must give up an opportunity to pay P980 for its P 1,000 purchase. It will cost the firm P 20 to delay payment for 20 days.

To calculate the cost of giving up the cash discount, the true purchase price must be viewed as the discounted cost of the merchandise, which is P 980 for Jamex Industries. The annual percentage cost of giving up the cash discount can be calculated using equation 15.1:

Cost of giving up cash discount = CD X 360 (15.1)

100% - CD N

Where

CD = stated cash discount in percentage terms

N = number of days payment can be delayed by giving up the cash discount

Substituting the values for CD (2%) and N (20days) into Equation 15.1 results in an annualized cost of giving up the cash discount of 36.73% [(2%/98%) X (360 / 20)] A 360-day year is assumed.

A simple way to approximate the cost of giving up a cash discount is to use the stated cash discount percentage. CD, in place of the first term of Equation 15.1:

Approximate cost of giving up cash discount = CD X 360/ N (15.2)

The smaller the cash discount, the closer the approximation to the actual cost of giving it up. Using this approximation, the cost of giving up the cash discount for Jamex Industries is 36% [2% X (360 / 20)]

The Finance Manager must determine whether it is advisable to take a cash discount. It is important to recognize that taking cash discounts may represent an important source of additional profitability.

Cost of Trade Credit

Trade credit is considered a spontaneous source of financing because it normally expands as the volume of a company's purchase increases. For example, a company experiences increased demand for its products. The company increases purchases from suppliers by 20 percent from an average of P 10,000 per day to an average of P12,000 per day. Assuming that these purchases are made on credit terms of "net 30" and that the company waits until the last day of the credit period to make payment, its average accounts payable outstanding (trade credit) automatically will increase by 20 percent from P300,000(P10,000 X30) to P 360,000 (P 12,000 X 30).

If the terms of sale include a cash discount, the firm must decide whether or not to take it. If the firm takes the cash, it forgoes the credit offered by the supplier beyond the end of the discount period. Assuming that the firm does not take the cash discount and wants to make maximum of the credit offered by suppliers, it should pay its bills on the last day of the discount period.

The annual financing cost (AFC) forgoing a cash discount is equal to the fractional interest cost per period times the number of borrowing periods per year:

AFC = Percentage discount X 365

100- Percentage discount Credit period = Discount period

Suppose Heimill Company has extended P 15,000 of trade credit on terms of "2/10, net 30. The company can either pay the discounted amount P 14,700 by the end of the discount period (day 10) or the full amount of the invoice (P 15,000 by the end of the credit period (day 30). By not paying on the tenth day- that is, that is, by foregoing the cash discount – the company has the use of P 14,700 (98 percent of the invoice amount) for an additional 20 days and effectively pays P 300 in interest. Substituting this information into Equation – 1 yields the following :

$$AFC = \frac{2}{100-2} \times \frac{365}{30-10} = 37.2\%$$

The annual cost of forgoing cash discount can be quite high. Therefore, when making financing decisions, a company should compare this cost to the costs of other sources of credit.

The company that offers credit terms of "2/10, net 30" should consider the annual financing cost of having the use of funds for an additional 20 days.

Factors Affecting Credit Terms

Credit terms vary by industry and even within industries. Differences are linked to product characteristics as well as market structure and market condition. Credit terms of companies are often set based on competitive condition and rarely changed. Analysis of the optimal cash discount has led to the following conclusions:

1. The optimal cash discount depends on a product's variable cost: the lower a product's variable set the higher the possible discount. Companies with lower gross margins are the most likely to reduce or eliminate their cash discount.

2. Logically, the cash discount offered should be based on the offering company's cost of funds when the opportunity cost of funds changes, so should the cash discount.

3. Both the timing effect of the payments for discount takers and the effect for those not taking the discount must be considered when setting or changing the discount.

4. The size of the cash discount should be based on the product's price elasticity of demand, or in this context, how responsive sales are to changes in the cash discount.

5. The higher the rate of bad debt losses being experienced, the higher the optimal cash discount per cent.

In determining the appropriate accounts receivable policy, these variables will now be analyzed in a decision making context, which is termed marginal analysis.

Marginal Analysis

Marginal Analysis involves a systematic comparison between the marginal returns and the marginal costs from a change in the discount period, the risk class of the customer, or the collection process. The change should be accepted if the marginal return from a proposed change in the management of accounts receivable is greater than the marginal costs on additional investment.

To illustrate the use of marginal analysis, let us assume that the Max Steel has annual sales , all credit, of P 5,000,000 and a receivable turnover ratio of six times per year. The current level of bad debt losses is P 156,250 and the firm's required rate of return on any new investment in receivables is 14%. Further assume that this firm produces only one product, the variable costs equating 80% of the selling price. The company is contemplating a relaxation of its credit policy and the expected effects of two proposed policies. A and B are compared below:

	Present Policy	Policy A	Policy B
Annual sales (all credit)	5,000,000.00	5,468,750.00	5,781,250.00
Average collection period	2 months	3 months	4 months
Bad debt losses	156,250.00	187,500.00	334,375.00

To determine the marginal profitability from relaxing the credit policy first from the policy to policy A and then from policy A to policy B and compare the marginal profitability to the required return on the additional investment in receivable yields, let's apply marginal analysis approach.

The results of the marginal analysis of relaxing credit standards are presented in table 2.

	Present Policy	Policy A	Policy B
Annual sales	5,000,000.00	5,468,750.00	5,781,250.00
Average collection period	2 months	3months	4months
Accounts receivable turnover ratio	6 times	4 times	3 times
Average level of receivables	833,333.00	1,367,187.50	1,927,083.30
Step 1: Determine the marginal benefits			
Marginal increase in sales (above previous policy)		468,750.00	312,500.00
Profit on marginal increase in sales (20%)		93,750.00	62,500.00
Marginal increase in bad debt loses		31,250.00	46,875.00
Profit on marginal increase in sales (less marginal increase in bad debt loss)		62,500.00	15,625.00
Step 2: Determine the required rate of return on the Marginal Investment			
Marginal increase in receivables (above previous policy)		533,854.50	559,895.80
Marginal increase in investment in receivables (above previous policy)		427,083.60	447,916.60

Required return (14%) on marginal increase in investment in receivables	59,791.74	62,708.53

Step 3: Compare the Marginal Benefits with the required return

Profit on marginal increase in sales (less marginal increase in bad debt loss) less: required return (20%) on marginal investment in receivables.	2,708.26	47,083.33

Table 2 shows that the marginal benefits by shifting from the present policy to policy A is P 62,500. In addition, the required return on the increased investment in accounts receivable, which can be thought of as the marginal cost associated with this change, is P 59,791.74. Thus, since the marginal benefit is P 2,708.26 greater than the required return (or marginal cost) a change in the credit policy should be made from the current policy to policy A.

With respect to the change from policy A to policy B, the associated marginal benefit is P 15,625. The required rate of return on the increase in accounts receivable or marginal cost associated with this change is P 62,708.38. Thus, since the marginal benefit is P 47,083.33 less than the required return or marginal cost, the credit policy should not be changed from policy A to policy B.

The logic behind this approach to credit policy is to examine the incremental or marginal benefits, and costs or required returns associated with any change in the credit policy. If the change promises more benefits than costs, the change should be made, if, however, the incremental costs are greater than the benefits, the proposed change should be dropped.

Accruals

Accruals are the second source of short-term business financing. Accruals are liabilities for services received for which payment has yet to be made. The most common items accrued by a firm are wages and taxes. Because taxes are payments to the government, their accrual cannot be manipulated by the firm. However, the accrual of wages can be manipulated to some extent. This is accomplished by delaying payment of wages, thereby receiving an interest-free loan from employees who are paid sometime after they have performed the work. The pay period for employees who earn an hourly rate is often governed by union regulations or by state or federal law. In other cases, the frequency of payment is at the discretion of the company's management.

Accrued Expenses and Deferred Income

These expenses and income are additional spontaneous sources of unsecured short term credit.

Accrued Expenses

Accrued expenses – such as accrued wages, taxes, and interest – represent liabilities for services rendered to the firm that have not yet been paid for by the firm. As such, they constitute an interest-free source of financing.

Accrued wages represent the money a business owes to its employees. A company can increase the average amount of accrued wages by lengthening the period between paydays. A company can increase accrued expenses by delaying the payment of sales commissions and bonuses. The amounts of accrued taxes and interest that a firm may accumulate also is determined by the frequency with which these expenses must be paid.

Deferred Income

Deferred income consists of payments received for goods and services that the firm has agreed to deliver at some future date. Because these payments increase the firm's liquidity and assets namely, cash – they constitute a source of funds.

Advance payments made by customers are the primary sources of deferred income. These payments are common on large, expensive products, such as aircraft. Because theses payments are not earned by the firm until delivery of the goods or services to the customers, they are recognized on the balance sheet as a liability called deferred income.

Bank loans

Short-term, self-liquidating loan is a major type of loan made by banks to businesses . They are intended merely to carry the firm through seasonal peaks in financing needs that are due primarily to buildups of accounts receivable and inventory. As receivables and inventories are converted into cash , the funs needed to retire these loans are generated. The use to which borrowed money is put provides the mechanism through which the loan is repaid – hence the term self-liquidating. Banks lend unsecured, short-term funds in three basic ways: through single-payment notes, lines of credit, and revolving credit agreements.

Evaluating the Credit Applicant

The risks of granting credit are of two kinds; the chance that this will be a "slow policy", trying up unwarranted sums in accounts receivable. The magnitude of these risks depends ultimately on the customer's financial strength and willingness to pay. The credit evaluation procedure involves three related steps obtaining information on the applicant, analyzing this information to determine the applicant's credit-worthiness, and monitoring the accounts receivable policy.

Sources of Credit Information

Though a number of sources supply credit information but for some accounts, especially small ones, the cost of collecting it may out weight the potential profitability of the account. Therefore, a firm extending credit may have to be satisfied with a limited amount of information of which to base a decision. In addition to the cost, the firm must consider the time it takes to investigate credit applicant. The amount of information collected needs to be considered in relation to the time and expenses required. Depending upon these consideration, the credit analyst may use one or more of the following sources of information.

By requiring the credit applicant to provide financial statements for the past few years the firm can analyze the applicant's financial stability, liquidity, debt capacity, and profitability. Insight into the firm's financial position may indicate the nature of its overall financial management, although no specific information with respect to past payment patterns is shown on a balance sheet or on an income statement. The willingness of the applicant firm to provide these statements may be indicative of its financial position. Audited financial statements are a must for the analysis of credit applicants desiring to make large credit purchases or to be extended lines of credit.

Trade checking & Bank reference

Credit information frequently is exchanged among companies selling to the same customer. Through various credit organizations, credit people in particular area become a closely knit group. A company can ask other suppliers about their experiences with an account. Information includes the length of time they have had the account, the maximum credit is extended, the amount of the line of credit, and whether payment are prompt of slow.

It may be possible for the firm's bank to obtain credit information from the applicant's bank. However, the type of information obtained is most likely to be vague unless the applicant aids the firm in obtaining it. This is true since the credit applicant' bank cannot disclose specific information such as account balances, loan balances, and so forth, without the consent of the applicant. Typically, an estimate of the firms cash balance is provided. For example, it may be found that a firm maintains a high five-figure balance.

Credit Bureaus

The services of credit bureaus are required in the advanced countries to get a comprehensive and correct information about the applicant. These credit bureaus specialize in consolidating the experiences of other firms with the applicant. These credit bureaus specialize in consolidating the experiences of other firms with the applicant. Credit bureaus compile a history of the applicant's credit payment performance as reported by the credit granting firms. A firm may try to compile, its own information or when a firm is approached by a customer desiring credit terms, the firm's credit department typically begins the credit evaluation process by requiring the credit applicant to fill up various forms involving financial and credit information and credit references. Working from the credit application, the firm then obtains additional credit information from other sources. It will have its own historical information on the applicant's payment patterns, if the firm has previously extended credit to the applicant. If the credit request is large enough, it may send a credit department employees to visit personally with the credit applicant and gives as much financial information as possible.

Credit Analysis and Decision

The firm must make a credit analysis of the applicant and determine if the company falls above or below the minimum quality standard, having gathered credit information. How does evaluation of the risk of extending credit to any applicant transpire? What are the standards or criteria applied in extending credit?

The credit analyst tries to assess the credit worthiness of the applicant in the traditional approach to the credit-granting decision on marginal accounts. These aspects include the business history of the applicant, the manner in which the applicant makes payments to other trade suppliers, the profitability of the products that the applicant wants to purchase, the applicant's financial position, and so forth. Critical evaluation of the borrower's projected cash budget and most recent statement of cash flows are instrumental here. The general economy and industry environment, as well as reason for loan request, comprise the conditions. The traditional way of organizing this information is to characterize the applicant along the five C's of Credit – *capital, character, collateral, capacity, and conditions.*

Capital - The evaluation of the applicant' capital refers to an analysis of the applicant firm's financial position. Questions may arise on the applicant firm's financial strength, weaknesses which will make his application creditworthiness. The credit analyst considers the data obtained from the applicant's financial statements. It involves procedure using ratio analysis, comparing the applicant's financial ratios to ratios for the applicant's industry and performing trend analysis of the applicant's ratios over time. This ratio analysis can be quite sophisticated using graphical presentation of ratio trends and statistical comparison of the applicant's ratios with industry standards.

Some credit analysts choose to emphasize a few of the financial aspects of the applicant and deemphasize other. They will focus on the applicant firm's aggregate liquidity position and its total debt position. The first is measured by ratios such as the current ratio and the quick ratio, while the latter is measured by the total debt to total equity and total debt to total asset ratios. They use it because the seller wishes to know the likelihood of payment from the applicant, how long it will take to receive the payment, and what is likely to happen if the applicant defaults. Ratios assess the relative amounts of current assets and current debt, and thus the funds received and disbursed as part of the applicant's working capital cycle. As problem within the working capital cycle are a major cause of default, measures of aggregate liquidity are related to the applicant's ability to pay.

Total debt position tells the relationship between the applicant's assets, equity, and debt. Debt position is also related to the possibility of default, since more debt means a greater probability of default. however, in relation to the analysis of collateral ratios measuring debt position tell something about the likely recovery of trade creditors, If the applicant default and is forced to liquidate. The more debt and the fewer assets, the lower will be the recoveries of individual creditors in such liquidations.

*Characte*r - The applicant must have both the funds to pay the debts and the willingness to pay the debts, in order to make payments to trade suppliers. The capital dimension involves the former, while the character dimension involves the latter. The credit analyst considers all the information that relates to willingness to pay be the applicant's management.

*Collatera*l - The applicant may be compelled to liquidate if he experiences financial crisis. Recoveries to trade creditors will depend on: the recoveries on assets sold; the amount of debt owed by the firm; and the extent to which these debts are secured. If the firm liquidates, the recoveries on assets that are security for debt will go to the holders of that secured debt. The secured creditors get paid first from the revenues of selling the assets that obtain secured position, this means that the recoveries to trade creditors are significantly lower when the applicant has financed by using secured borrowings. Information on secured borrowings is gleaned from the applicant's financial statements, from the applicant's bank, from credit reports on the applicant, or directly from conversations with the applicant. More existing secured financing means lower creditworthiness from the trade creditor's standpoint.

Capacity. - The two aspects of this dimension are: management's capacity to run the business and the applicant firm's plant capacity.

Management's capacity to run the business relates to the competency (ability) of the management personnel in the applicant's operations. Any information relevant to this capacity is assessed, including personal impressions, the history of success or failure by the managers running the applicant business, the number of years that the applicant has been in business and so forth.

Physical capacity refers to the value and technology of the applicant's production or service facilities. The unrealistic picture of the value of assets in which accounting convention can paint, particularly if the technology of the applicant's industry is subject to rapid change. The more up-to-date and well-maintained are the applicant's facilities, the more likely that the applicant will be able to stay in business and to take advantage of business upturns.

Conditions - The possibility of failure and default to trade creditors is larger, if there is a good deal of foreign and domestic competition in the applicant's industry, since profit margins are likely to be lower. If the economy in general is undergoing a contraction, failures are more likely to occur than during an expansionary period. Once the credit analyst has gathered information on these of the marginal credit applicant and information on the profitability of the product to be purchased, the traditional approach requires that all this information by analyzed and synthesized. By this process, the analyst is to make an informed judgment on the overall credit worthiness of the applicant. Unfortunately, there are some problems endemic to this traditional analysis methodology which call its usefulness into substantial question.

Constraints with the Traditional Approach

The traditional judgmental approach to credit-granting decisions on marginal accounts is very flexible. The analyst, in the process of synthesis, can take into account any and all of the special features that may affect the desirability of the applicant as a customer. Set against this flexibility are several substantial disadvantages inherent in this decision methodology.

No Analytic Framework . Most financial decision methods start with a basic analysis technique, such as net present value. It is then up to the financial analyst to make the necessary estimations to execute the technique. There is no such analytic framework in the traditional credit analysis methodology. The analyst is asked to make a judgment, with few guidelines on what the appropriate criteria for that judgment should be. Given the large amount of information encompassed in the five C's and the lack of specific evaluation criteria, this judgment is not easy to make.

No link to shareholder Wealth Maximization. The analyst, in most decision methods, starts with a technique that is theoretically and empirically linked to shareholder wealth maximization. It is known, for instance, that shareholders value cash flows, so techniques such as net present value concentrate on the evaluation of these flows. The traditional credit-granting decision technique does not contain such an explicit link to the creation of shareholder wealth, so there is no necessity that decisions based on this technique will be consistent with that goal.

No Consistency of Analysis The results it produces can be inconsistent because the synthesis process is almost totally judgmental. The analyst considers the same applicant on different days can reach different decisions, as can two different analyst considering the same applicant. This inconsistency gives the impression to those outside of the credit department that decision are being made in an arbitrary fashion. This seeming arbitrariness can cause friction between the credit and other departments of the firm.

Difficulty for Inexperienced Analyst . A credit analyst, over time, through trial and error, will become experienced at assessing the strengths and weaknesses of applicants, but any judgments will be biased by the analyst's experience. If the analyst grants credit to several applicants who are below-average with respect to a particular ratio and these applicants then default, the analyst will tend to be biased against applicants with such ratios in the future even if the default of these applicants was aberration, and the particular ratio involved was not truly related to the default. The longer an analyst continues with the traditional method, the larger will be the sample of applicants analyzed, and the less will be the likelihood of such bias.

Bank Credit Arrangements

Bank borrowing constitutes several types of credit arrangements, including lines of credit, term loans, letters of credit, banker's acceptance, etc. Each has a unique combination of maturity, interest rate, free, indentures (such as the collateral required), and the conditions under which the credit can be called or revoked.

Letter of Credit

A letter of credit is a guarantee from a bank stating that a loan will be made to the client if specified conditions are met. It is commonly used to finance international trade. Because an exporter does not know an importer or because information, language, and cultural differences make it difficult to perform an adequate credit analysis, the exporter is not willing to sell to the importer on open credit. The importer presents a letter of credit from its bank, stating that the amount necessary for payment of the shipment will be paid on a specified date if conditions are met. This allows the importer to substitute the bank's credit rating for its own credit rating, thereby reducing the risk to the exporter.

Revocability: A letter of credit can be either revocable, in which case the bank has the right to cancel the letter, or irrevocable, in which case the bank is bound to honor the terms if the specified conditions are met.

Pricing and Maturity: The maturity of the loan connected to the letter is dictated by the event that evoked the need for the letter. In most instances, it is of relatively short duration, for example, 30 to 90 days. The loan usually has a fixed rate based on the prevailing rte at the time the loan is issued. A commitment fee is usually charged for issuing a letter of credit, whether the loan is issued or not.

Banker's acceptance:

A banker's acceptance is generated by a time draft for which a bank is committed to making the payment to the holder at maturity. Banker's acceptance most frequently arise from international transactions when the conditions for a letter of credit have been met. Financing is provided when the bank makes an advance on the time draft issued. Some banks use the term banker's acceptance to refer to a loan issued to finance the purchase of specific good, whether for an international or a domestic transaction.

Factors to be Considered in Granting Credit to Applicant

In granting credit, the following factors are to be considered:

Credit requirements (C) of the applicant is the number one factor to be considered. This factor measures the applicant's dependency on the creditor. He or she will get 0% to the credit line if he plans to buy less than to 25% of his requirements from the creditor. A 5% allowance will be provided if the applicant plans to buy between 25 and 50%. Applicant gets a 10% allowance in case his plan is to buy over 50% .

Pay habits (P) of the applicant is the second factor. It is a measure of the willingness and ability to pay. Payments during the discount period rate are 10%. Payments during the credit period are worth 5%. Habitually late payments rate is minus 5%.

Year of business(Y) a third factor, is a measure of the ability of the firm to pay. Less than three years in business has not effect on increasing the limits. The limit is increase by 5% if Y is between 3 and 10 years. For more than 10 years existence in business, the rate is 10%.

Profit margin(M) is the fourth factor. Zero percent is contributed to the credit limit if margins are less than 5% . In case the margin is more than 14%, 10% to be contributed to the credit limit.

Current ratio is (*C*)the fifth measure. A current ratio of 2.2 to 1 is considered to be a good indication of ability to pay and helps in contributing 10% towards the credit limit. A current ratio of less than 1.5: 1 is considered to be relatively weak and does not help in increasing the credit limit.

Total debt to asset ratio(T) is the sixth measure. It represents the ability to pay. The applicant is conservative if Total debt is less than 30% and adds to the credit limit. On the other hand a T of over 50% implies higher financial leverage and rates a minus 5% towards the credit limit.

Investor turnover (I) is the seventh factor. A lower inventory turnover implies low efficiency and vice versa. Inventory turnover can help contribute anywhere between 0% to 10% towards the credit limit.

Qualitative factor (Q) is the last factor and it lets the credit manager to use his discretion in subjective evaluation of the credit applicant's willingness and ability to pay.

These factors and their contributions are based on a particular firm's actual experience. However, the factors and their contributions to the credit limit may vary from firm to firm. Other factors such as accounts payable and the economic environment should also be considered in developing a credit evaluation decision model called *heuristic model.*

Types of Retail Credit

Retail Credit is a form of consumer credit which has taken two forms historically, namely: open account and installment.

Additional forms such as revolving credit, option terms credit, and other variations of the two basic types have become important during the past 35 years or so.

Open account Credit

Under an open account credit or regular charge account, the customer: receives the goods without any down payment and without pledging either the goods or any other asset as specific collateral for the debt; is billed for the full amount of the credit purchase at the end of the billing period (usually one month); and has the obligations to pay in full within a stipulated period (usually 30 days) from the bill's mailing date. Most of the stores offer open-accounts credit consider the cost involved as an operating expense to be covered by the profits on the goods sold. Charge to customers is not separately made. But some retailers, charge service fee when payments are delayed beyond the due date both to encourage prompt payment and to cover part of the extra costs associated with slow payment.

Retailers have minimum formal security for open-account credit, since they receive no down payment and cannot repossess the merchandise if the customer fails to pay the bill. They basically depend on the customer's financial capacity and personal integrity, although expensive and complicated legal procedures can be used as a last resort in case of non-payment. Open account credit is the traditional form extended by department stores and at one time was offered only to high net worth customers. Many credit managers believe that more conservative and stricter standards should be followed in approving open account credit than for other types of accounts.

Installment Credit

Installment credit differs from open-account credit where the customer is normally expected to make a single, full payment. It is usually divided into parts, or installments, which come due at set intervals in the future.

General Credit Contracts

Another type of installment agreement is the general credit contracts which does not give the seller the right to repossess. If the buyer defaults on payments, the seller's only recourse is to sue for the amount due.

Revolving Credit

Under the revolving credit plan the customer agrees to pay a fixed amount, for example P350 per month, during any month when he has an unpaid balance. The retailer then agrees to provide a "line of credit" or credit limit, which in this case might be P4,000. Whenever the debt to the store drops below the P4,000 limit, the customer is entitled to charge additional merchandise up to that amount. A service charge, oftentimes at the rate of 1.5 percent per month on the unpaid balance, is imposed and will be included in the regular monthly payment.

The customer is able to purchase without having to sign a separate contract for each purchase as would normally be required under installment credit. At the same time, payments can be spread out over a number of months. The fixed maximum credit line provides relatively tight control over the credit limit (although some stores will relax the limit for approved customers during peak buying periods such as Christmas and Easter) in contrast to the vague and indefinite limits usually associated with open-account credit.

Option Terms

The option-terms plan allows the customer to choose between paying the bill in full during the option period (generally 25 to 30 days after the billing date) or, if preferred, only paying some minimum portion (usually one tenth or one twelfth) of the amount at that time. No service charge is imposed if the bill is completely paid during the option period, but a charge (often 1.5 per cent of the unpaid balance per month) automatically goes into effect if the customer chooses the deferred payment arrangement.

This plan is sometimes called ," option-terms revolving credit", which is more flexible than the basic revolving credit plan. The peso amount of the monthly payment is fixed under the basic plan while it varies under option –terms in proportion to the size of the customer's unpaid balance. The automatic service charge is easier to collect and probably provokes less customer resentment than would an equivalent penalty fee for late payment of open-account bills. The retailers consider the option-term plan as an "ideal" credit arrangement which will ultimately be the most widely used for all credit plans.

Loan Interest Rates

The Prime rate of interest (Prime rate) is the lowest rate of interest charged by the nation's leading banks on business loans to their most important and reliable business borrowers. The prime rate fluctuates with changing supply-and-demand relationships for short-term funds. Banks generally determine the rate to be charged on loans to various borrowers by adding a premium to the prime rate to adjust it for the borrower's riskiness. The premium may amount to 4 percent or more, although most unsecured short-term loans carry premiums of less than 2 percent.

Fixed-and Floating-Rate Loans

Loans can have either fixed or floating interest rates. On a fixed-rate loan, the rate of interest is determined at a set increment above the prime rate on the date of the loan and remains unvarying at that fixed rate until maturity. On a floating-rate loan, the increment above the prime rate is initially established, and the rate of interest is allowed to float, or vary, above prime as the prime rate varies until maturity. The increment above the prime rate on a floating-rate loan will be lower than on a fixed-rate loan of equivalent risk because the lender bears less risk with a floating-rate loan. The sometimes volatile nature of the prime rate, coupled with the widespread use of computers by banks to monitor and calculate loan interest, has been responsible for popularity of floating-rate loans.

Methods of Computing Interest

Once the nominal (or stated) annual rate is established, the method of computing interest is determined. Interest can be paid either when a loan matures or in advance. If interest is paid at maturity, the effective (or true) annual rate – the actual rate of interest paid-for an assumed 1-year period is equal to:

$$\frac{\text{Interest}}{\text{Amount borrowed}} \quad (15.3)$$

Most bank loans to businesses require the interest payment at maturity. When interest is paid in advance, it is deducted from the loan so that the borrower actually receives less money than is requested. Loans on which interest is paid in advance are called discount loans. The effective annual rate for a discount loan assuming a 1-year period is calculated as

$$\frac{\text{Interest}}{\text{Amount borrowed} - \text{interest}} \quad (15.4)$$

Paying interest in advance raises the effective annual rate above the stated annual rate.

Example:

Western Company, a manufacturer of footwear, wants to borrow P 10,000 at a stated annual rate of 10% interest for 1 year. If the interest on the loan is paid at maturity, the firm will pay P 1,000 (.10 X P10,000) for the use of the P10,000 for the year. Substitution for the Equation 15.3 on the effective annual rate follows:

$$\frac{\text{P}1{,}000}{\text{P }10{,}000} = 10.0\%$$

If the money is borrowed at the same stated annual rate for 1 year but interest is paid in advance, the firm still pays P 1,000 in interest, but it receives only P 9,000 (P 10,000- P 1,000). Thus, the effective annual rate in this case is

$$\frac{P\ 1{,}000}{P\ 10{,}000 - P\ 1{,}000} = \frac{P\ 1{,}000}{P\ 9{,}000} = 11.1\%$$

Paying interest in advance thus makes the effective annual rate (11.1%) greater than the stated annual rate (10.0%).

Single Payment of Notes

A single-payment note can be obtained from a commercial bank by a creditworthy business borrower. It is usually a "one-shot" deal made when a borrower needs additional funds for a short period. The resulting instrument is a note, which must be signed by the borrower. The note states the terms of the loan, which include the length of the loan and the interest rate. This type of short-term note generally has a maturity of 30 days to 9 months or more. The interest charged is generally tied in some way to the prime rate of interest and may have either a fixed or a floating rate.

Example:

Glader Company, a producer of shaver, recently borrowed P 100,000 for each of two banks, bank A and bank B. The loans were incurred on the same day, when the prime rate of interest was 9%. Each loan involved a 90-day note with interest to be paid at the end of 90 days. The interest rate was set at 1 ½% above the prime rate on bank. A's fixed-rate note. Over the 90-day period, the rate of interest on this note will remain at 10 ½% (9% prime rate + 1 ½% increment) regardless of fluctuations in the prime rate. The total interest cost on this loan is P 2,625 (P100,000 X (101/2% X 90/360)]. The effective 90-day rate on this loan is 2.625% (P2,625/P100,000).

Assuming that the loan from bank A is rolled over each 90 days throughout the year under the same terms and circumstances, its effective annual interest rate is found by using Equation 5.10. Because the loan costs 2.625% for 90 days, it is necessary to compound (1+ 0.02625) for four periods in the year (i.e. 360/90 and then subtract 1:

Effective annual rate = (1+ 0.02625)4 -1

= 1.1092-1 = 0.1092 = 10.92 %

The effective annual rate of interest on the fixed rate, 90-day note is 10.92%. Bank B set the interest rate at 1% above the prime rate on its floating-rate note. The rate charged over the 90 days will vary directly with the prime rate. Initially, the rate will be 10% (9% + 1%), but when the prime rate changes, so will the rate of interest on the note. For instance, if after 30 days, the prime rate rises to 9.5 %, and after another 30 days, it drops to 9.25%, the firm would be paying .833% for the first 30 days (' 10% X 30/360), and .854 percent for the last 30 days (10.25% X 30/360). Its total interest cost would be P 2,562 [P 100,000 X (.833% + .854%)]

Resulting in an effective 90-day rate of 2.562% (P2,562/ P100,000).

Assuming the loan is rolled over each 90 days throughout the year under the same terms and circumstances, its effective annual rate is 10.65%:

Effective annual rate = (1+ 0.02562)4-1

= 1.1065 -1= 0.1065 =10.65%

The floating rate loan would have been less expensive than the fixed-rate loan due to its generally lower effective annual rate.

Calculating the Compounded Effective Annual Interest Rate

The next question is the cost of financing, after the firm has known the amount of financing source will yield. We call it the compounded effective annual interest rate or compounded (EAI) of the funding source. The compounded EAI is calculated the same way for any source of funding. It is the yearly compounded internal rate of return for the cash flows from the funding source. To compute this cost statistic, the analyst obtains the cash flows fro the funding source and their timing, calculates the internal rate of return (IRR), and compounds this IRR to a yearly basis. This gives a comparative cost statistic for the various available sources of funding which is based on net cash flows and is properly adjusted for the different manurities of the various funding sources.

Illustration

Strax Arts maintained an excellent working relationship with its commercial bank . It has an average monthly balance of about 135,000 and the company typically arranges a revolving credit agreements with a limit of P1,000,000. The Chairman, Hugo White, has made changes that caused him to question whether the credit arrangement is in the company's best interest. He has initiated cash management techniques that could allow the cash account to be reduced to P 60,000,if possible. The requirement is 20% of actual amounts borrowed. Another concern to Hugo is the commitment fee, which is 0.005 on the average portion of the credit limit.

For the upcoming year, the Company's borrowing needs will be P 600,000 not including the borrowing needed to maintain the compensating balance. Hugo believes that the bank will charge 8% interest on the average borrowing. He is considering not renewing the agreement and, instead, arranging a series of term loans that will average P 600,000. He expects the interest on these loans will average 9%.

Should the company continue its current arrangement with the bank, or should it select the new credit source?

Solution:

Determine the required loan amount (RLA) as
follows:
RLA = P600,000+(0.20RLA-P60,000
0.8 RLA = P 540,000
RLA = P 675,000

Next, determine the interest on this average balance: P 675,000 X 0.08 = P54,000
The average unused portion of the line= P 325,000(P1,000,000-P675,000),which has
a cost of P1,675(P325,000 X 0.005)
Adding these two and dividing by the usable funds of P600,000 gives the annual
percentage cost of 0.09271 (P 55,625/P600,000)
Evaluate the proposal. Since this exceeds the annual cost of 0.090 on the alternative
credit arrangement, the alternative is the better choice. However, there are intangibles
Hugo should consider. First, the credit limit guarantees available credit up to
P 1,000,000. Does the alternative have any guarantee? Second, will the company
relationship with the bank weaken if the agreement is not renewed?

Interest Rates

The interest rate on a line of credit is normally stated as a floating rate – the prime rate plus a percentage. If the prime rate changes, the interest rate charged on new as well as outstanding borrowing automatically changes. The amount a borrower is charged in excess of the prime rate depends on its creditworthiness. The more creditworthiness the borrower, the lower the interest increment above prime, and vice versa.

Compensating Balances

To ensure that the borrower will be a good customer, many short-term unsecured bank loans- single-payment notes and lines of credit- often require the borrower to maintain a compensating balance in a checking account equal to a certain percentage of the amount borrowed. Compensating balances of 10 to 20 percent are frequently required. A compensating balance not only compels the borrower to be a good customer of the bank but may also raise the interest cost to the borrower.

Revolving Credit Agreement

A line credit and *revolving credit agreement* are similar but is usually established for more than 1 year. Common maturities extend for 2 or 3 years, during which time the customer may borrow and repay loans several times. Many revolving credit agreements contain a clause that allows the borrower to convert to a term loan. The revolving credit agreement, frequently, is sometimes referred to as an *evergreen loan*. The pricing on a revolving credit agreement is similar to that of a credit line. There is a commitment fee, met either by balances or by cash fees. The commitment fee is usually charged only on the unused portion of the credit agreement. The interest rate is almost always variable, based either on the prime rate or on money market rates.

The loan made under a banker's acceptance is usually a discount loan. The discount from face value advanced to the borrower includes an amount for the interest at prevailing money market rates, plus a fee, or a commission, of approximately 1.5%. Because of the commission, the cost to the borrower is usually above the commercial paper rate, but because it is based on money market rates, it may be below the prime rate.

A reverse repurchase agreement, or reverse repo, is simply the other side of the transaction in a repurchase agreement. The owner of a security needs funds for a shorter period than the maturity on a security held in its marketable securities portfolio. Rather than sell the security and have an investment decision to make when the funds are no longer needed, the firm sells the security with an agreement to repurchase it. This transaction is very similar to a loan with the security used as collateral. Since this is a very secure loan, the rate is usually below that on the other types of loans. The sale and repurchase prices are usually sufficiently below the face value of the security used to ensure that the market value will not drop below the repurchase price during the term of the agreement.

Unsecured Borrowing

Many lending agreements with commercial banks are unsecured. Lines of credit and revolving credit agreements are usually unsecured loans, made on the basis of the general financial strength of the borrower. This type of lending is sometimes referred to as financial statement lending because the loan is based on the strength of the income statement and the balance sheet of the organization. The bank looks at both the cash flow generating capability of the organization and the liquid resources as repayment sources.

If the borrower defaults, the bank is a general creditor and has no specific claim on any assets of the firm. Although every company desires a loan with the fewest number of restrictions, banks make unsecured loans only to those customers for which they perceive little, if any, repayment problem. Unsecured loans are usually granted only to firms that have a long, stable history of solid financial performance.

Secured Borrowing

A secured loan is any loan that, as part of the loan agreement, gives the lender a claim on a specific set of assets in case of default. There are two different approaches to secured lending; a collateralized loan and an asset-based loan.

Collateralized loan

The bank, in a collateralized loan, still views the credit from a financial statement perspective. However, the customer represents too much risk for the bank to grant credit on an unsecured basis. Just as fire requlations require that there be two exits to any building, the bank wants a second way out of a loan in case the primary "exit" in unavailable. Collateral pledged as security for the loan provides this second exit. If the borrower defaults on one of the conditions of the loan and the loan cannot be paid when it is called, the collateral can be seized, after the appropriate legal steps are taken, and disposed of to generate (hopefully), the funds to retire the loan. Although the collateral is sometimes called a secondary repayment source, the bank does not view it as a means of repaying the loan but rather as a way of minimizing any potential loss if the loan is not repaid.

Loans secured by accounts receivables.

In this arrangement, the borrower-company sells to its customers on credit in the normal course of business, generating accounts receivables. The lender then advances the funds to the borrower in exchange for the receivables as security for the loan. Because the lender's advance is a proportion of the face amount of the receivables, the first phase of the transaction is called discounting of receivables. The transfer of the legal claim to the receivables in favor of the lender is called an assignment.

The borrower's customer may or may not be notified by the lender about the assignment transaction. Finally, the transaction cycle is completed with the payment by the customer of his receivables. Once the loan and interest charges are fully satisfied, any residual payment by the lender against shrinkage in uncollectibles, a third party may be required to guaranty the borrower's loan.

Loans secured by inventories

When the inventories are of relatively stable resale value, (i.e., consumer durables) financing through pledge of inventories is especially attractive. The financing institution advances only a proportion of the total resale value of the inventory to guard against any possible decline in market value. This form of financing is commonly called a floor plan and usually applies to all forms of consumer durables.

In spite of the pledge, the borrower retains physical control of the inventories but it usually executes a legally-binding trust receipt agreement in favor of the lender. Under this security agreement, the borrower agrees to hold the inventory, and the proceeds from its sale in trust for the lender, who retains the legal ownership of the inventory. The borrower must immediately remit the proceeds from sale to the lender in order to cover the amount of the loan.

The lender further protects its interest in the inventory (and any proceeds from its sale) by filing a financing agreement with the appropriate public office. This act puts the borrower's other creditors on notice that title to the borrower's inventory probably rests with the lender. Other required safeguards include an insurance of the inventory with the lender as beneficiary and unannounced and irregular audits of the borrower's inventory to determine actual sales and consequent liabilities of the borrower.

Bank's Indicators of high credit risk

Certain rules-of-thumb of experienced bankers have evolved in identifying potentially high credit risk accounts. The following list of indicators has been referred to as the profile of a high-risk borrower:

1. Lack of adequate experience of principals;
2. Heavy personal obligations of principals;
3. Relatively new business;
4. Financing proceeds are going out of the business;
5. Business debt is disproportionate to business equity;
6. Inventory is excessive, old, slow-moving or "high-style";
7. Sales and earnings trends are down;
8. Equity is centered in questionable assets;
9. Reluctance of principals to sign in their personal capacity;

10. Poor paying record and spotty credit history of the principal;
11. Excessive competition;
12. Vague or evasive respond or answers to banker's questions;
13. Apparently aging principals;
14. Prevalent fire history;
15. Business location in a changing environment;
16. High degree of failure for the type of business;
17. Business is engaged in fad or luxury market;
18. Customer needs of money yesterday;
19. Principal's history of business bankruptcy;
20. Inadequacy of future business plans.

Policies of Bank in Credit Facilities

No lines of Credit: Specific deals only

Some banks are tend to be conservative and avoid any form of continuing commitment or grant loans to a customer. Every loan is extended on a special transactions, or case-to-case basis only, with the amount and terms of the loan decided upon in the light of the current application and conditions of the customer. In crisis situation, bank, for example, have similar conditions in the country in mid-1984, banks may freeze all credit lines to conserve loan funds and protect themselves against the prevailing abnormally high risks.

Credit line restrictions to large corporations

It is common for some Filipino commercial banks to arrange their credit facilities to specific client sectors. Large companies, e.g., defined facilities to specific client sector. Large companies, e.g. defined in the top corporations , may be allowed to draw against pre-contracted lines of credit because these are considered as acceptable risk. The rest of the customers of the bank, in contrast, may be considered on a special transactions basis.

As a rule, grant line of credit to acceptable customers but actual loan releases are subject to approval. This is the more common policy of banks. The advantage of this policy is that it gives the customer a definite understanding of its borrowing prospects with the bank. At the same time, the bank still holds the exit door open by exercising approval of loan releases. If situation deteriorates, the bank suspends the line. A bank pursuing this policy uses various labels – credit line, stand-by commitment and revolving credit – in its credit facility transaction in order to differentiate among its customers commitments.

Specific policies of banks vary depending on the bank's tolerance for risk and its intention to become competitive in the market. A large universal bank has the following particular policies for lines of credit granted to finance general working capital requirements of client-firms. Minimum requirements of the applicants must satisfy the minimum qualifications.

Annual Sales	500,000.00
Total Assets	250,000.00
Net Worth	100,000.00
Current Ratio	1:1
Leverage	2.5:1
Profit to Sales ratio	3 percent
Business experience	3 years

Credit limit

The maximum amount of loan should not exceed 60 per cent of the average annual sales of the past three years.

Availments

Each availment against the credit line should be paid in 120 days.

Special transactions

Any special loan transaction to finance working capital should be for a maximum term of 360 days. Where the term is 360 days, the loan must be amortized at least quarterly.

Factoring

Factoring is the sale of accounts receivable, usually without recourse, to another party, called the factor. Once the account has been purchased, it is the property and responsibility of the factor. There are three major types of factoring arrangements: 1) maturity factoring; 2) conventional factoring; and 3) maturity factoring with an assignment of equity.

Maturity Factoring

Maturity factoring consists of the sale of accounts receivable to a factor with no advance of funds at the time of sale. When the seller notifies the factor. The factor conducts a credit analysis of the potential customer and, if the risk is acceptable approves the sale and assumes all responsibility for collection and bad debts. The seller notifies the customer to remit directly to the factor. The factor forwards cash to the seller in the amount of the receivable less the commission on an agreed upon average maturity date.

The factor performs all of the credit and collection functions, while many companies do not have a credit department and yet use a factor. The cost of using the factor may be less than the cost of establishing a credit department. It may establish to achieve the economies of scale in credit analysis, administration, and collection of receivables. The factor deals with a broader group of customers than the seller and may have the opportunity to reduce risks through diversification. In industries with many small competitors, the factor may serve several competing manufacturers and have more leverage in collection than would any one company. Due to the nature of the credit function performed, most arrangements with a factor are of long duration, not an emergency sale of accounts receivable.

Cost of Factoring

The cost of using a factor has two distinct elements : 1) the factor's commission and 2) the interest cost of cash advances. Whether the factor's commission is included in the cost of financing for retail sales. It performs the credit function of the parent company. The receivables appear on the subsidiary's books and not on those of the parent.

Since the consolidated position is the same with or without a subsidiary, the rationale for finance subsidiaries must be something other than the effect on the financial statements. The reasons given for the use of a finance subsidiary are as follows: 1) a captive finance company may stimulate sales by providing easier access to credit for distributors or retail customers; 2) it may be cheaper to operate the financing function separately from the other operations of the company and view the credit arm as a separate profit center; 3) the concentration of accounts receivable in a captive finance company may increase the total debt capacity of the firm or may lower the short-term borrowing costs by clearly defining the assets being financed.

Commercial Papers

Some of the larger and more stable corporations can issue their own securities or commercial papers in order to access financing from money-market sources. This is conducted through money-market dealers on a "wholesale" arrangement. The dealers can turn around and retail the papers to a broad-based group of investors in that market. The universal banks which handle such transactions in effect bear the risk of not being able to sell the commercial papers to the investors, in which case an automatic credit line is offered, supported by the promissory note.

The default risk and the responsibility for repayment of investors who purchased the paper are taken up by the bank. To avoid such risks, the financial institution can act as a broker for the commercial paper in its sale to investors. It evaluates the commercial paper as a money-market credit line application by the borrower.

Commercial Finance

Commercial finance includes all loans secured by accounts receivable or inventory. This is used by companies as a source of working capital funds since the availability of the credit varies in proportion to the amount of the collateral itself. The loan is determined by applying a formula to eligible assets, e.g., 80 percent of accounts receivable or 50 percent of finished goods inventory. The residual percentage is intended to insure the bank against any risk of bad debt on receivables or shrinkage of inventories. The basic transaction flow varies depending on the asset financed.

Commercial finance companies are private companies that make commercial loans. A substantial difference between commercial banks and commercial finance companies is the source of funds. Commercial banks raise much of their funds from the public in the form of deposits, either demand or time. Commercial finance companies raise their funds through direct issuance of securities, such as commercial paper or longer-term notes, equity shares, and bank loans. Commercial finance companies restrict their loans to business firms and do not take deposits.

The loan customers of commercial finance companies are frequently businesses that are considered too risky to be granted credit by a commercial bank. Consequently, commercial finance companies generally charge higher interest rates than banks and concentrate on asset based- lending.

The asset-based loans of commercial finance companies are similar to those of banks. They are based primarily on the underlying value of the assets rather than on the financial strength of the company. The asset most frequently used as collateral is accounts receivable. The loan base is a percentage of the acceptable receivable. Acceptable accounts are those from customer with an acceptable credit risk and a maturity shorter than a designated maturity, often three times normal credit terms. Accounts receivable are usually pledged as collateral on a non-notification, full-recourse basis; receivables customers are not notified of the arrangement, and the borrower has full responsibility for collection. When a receivable is either collected or the maturity exceeds the agreed maturity, it is no longer part of the borrowing base and the funds advanced against the collateral are repaid.

If the amount of acceptable accounts receivable is insufficient to meet the desired financing requirements, inventory and possible machinery and equipment may be used as collateral. The percentage of borrowing against the collateral is adjusted for the expected liquidation value.

Availability problems in Financing

Two problems occur in determining the net availability from a potential source of financing. The first of these is up-front expenses that may make the amount of cash financing different from the face value of the debt. To see this, assume that one option in a firm's short-term financing package is 180-day discounted not with a P1,000 principal amount. The interest for the 180-day period will be 5 percent. Such a note will not provide P1,000 in financing. Since the interest is discounted, the P 1,000 note will net the firm only P950 in cash (equal to P1,000 minus interest of 0.05 (1000). Similar up-front expenses occur for several other types of current debts, including skipping the discount on accounts payable. Assume that the firm has the option of skipping the discount on invoices with a face value of P50,000 that have terms of 2 percent 10 days, net 90 days., If the firm pays in 10 days, the cash outflow will be P49,000; if it skips the discount, only this amount of cash outflow is delayed.

The maximum financing from this source is P49,000, not P50,000. Any time that interest or other expenses are paid when financing is undertaken, and not at maturity, the net availability will be less than the face value of the liability.

A second problem in calculating the net availability from a liability occurs when the financing from the liability changes over time. There are several types of short-term financing with this characteristics, including short maturity term loans and accruals. For example, if the firm takes out a 180-day term loan with monthly amortization payments, the financing will not be the principal amount of the term loan, Since the principal decreases over time (in a nonlinear fashion), the average financing will be some lesser amount.

Term loan : Average Financing

Month	Beginning Principal	Interest Payment	Principal Payment	Ending Payment
1	10,000.00	100.00	1,625.48	8,374.52
2	8,374.52	53.75	1,641.74	6,732.78
3	6,732.78	67.33	1,658.16	5,074.62
4	5,074.62	50.74	1,674.74	3,399.88
5	3,399.88	34.00	1,691.48	1,708.40
6	1,708.40	17.08	1,708.40	
Average	35,290.20			

Assume that the principal amount on such a loan was P10,000, the interest is 1 percent per month, and equal monthly amortization payments are required. An analysis of the net availability from a such a loan is given in the said table. The monthly payment is P 1,725.48. Assuming that the payments on the loans are made at the end of the month, the beginning principal amounts constitute the financing for the month. The financing provided by the loan for the second month if P 8,374.52. The average financing over the term of the loan is P 5,881.70

Interest on Commercial Paper

Commercial paper is sold at a discount from its par, or face, value. The interest paid by the issuer of commercial paper is determined by the size of the discount and the length of time to maturity. The actual interest earned by the purchaser is determined by certain calculations, calculations, illustrated by the following example:

Janux Corporation, a large food manufacturer, has just issued P1 million worth of commercial paper that has a 90-day maturity and sells for P980,000. At the end of 90 days, the purchaser of this paper will receive P1million for its P980,000 investment. The interest paid on the financing is therefore, P20,000 on a principal of P980,000. The effective 90-day rate on the paper is 2.04% (P20,000/ P980,000). Assuming the paper is rolled over each 90 days throughout the year, the effective annual rate for *Janux Corporation's* commercial paper, found by using Equation 5.10, is 8.41% [(1+ 0.0204)4 -1].

One interesting characteristic of commercial paper is that it normally has a yield of 2 to 4 percent below the prime rate. In other words, firms are able to raise funds more cheaply through the sale of commercial paper than by borrowing from a commercial bank. The reason is that many suppliers of short-term funds do not have the option, as banks do, of making low risk business loans at the prime rate. They can invest only in marketable securities such as Treasury bills and commercial paper. The yields on these marketable securities on January 22, 1999, when the prime rate of interest was

7.75 percent, were about 4.3 percent for 3-month Treasury bills and about 4.9 percent for 3-month commercial paper.

Although the stated interest cost of borrowing through the sale of commercial paper is normally lower than a bank loan, Additional costs include the fees paid by most issuers to obtain the bank line of credit used to back the paper, fees paid to obtain third-party ratings used to make the paper more salable, and flotation costs. In addition, even if it is slightly more expensive to borrow from a commercial bank, it may at times be advisable to do so to establish a good working relationship with a bank.

Common Sources of Short-Term Financing

Short- term Financing

Accounts Payable

Accruals

Unsecured Sources of Short-Term Financing

Bank Sources

Single-payment notes

Lines of credit

Revolving credit agreements

Commercial paper

Secured Sources of Short-term Financing

Pledging

Factoring

Inventory collateral

-Floating liens

-Trust receipts

-Warehouse receipts

Source
Suppliers of merchandise

Employees and government

Commercial banks

Commercial banks

Commercial banks

Other business, banks, life insurance companies, pension funds, and money market.

Commercial banks and commercial finance companies

Factors, commercial banks, and commercial finance companies

Commercial banks and commercial finance companies

Commercial banks and commercial finance companies	Cost or Condition No stated cost except when a cash discount is offered for early payment.
Commercial banks and finance companies	Free

Prime plus 0% to 4% risk premium-fixed or floating rate.

Prime plus 0% to 4% risk premium –fixed or floating rate. Often must maintain 10% to 20% compensating balance and clean up the line.

Prime plus 0% to 4% risk premium – fixed or floating rate. Often must maintain 10% to 20% compensating balance and pay a commitment fee of approximately .5% of the average unused balance.

Generally 2% to 4% below the prime rate of interest.

2% to 5% above prime plus up to 3% in fees. Advance 50% to 90% of collateral value.

1% to 3% discount from face value of factored accounts. Interest levied on advances of 2% to 4% above prime. Interest earned on surplus balances left with factor of about -5% per month

1% to 5% above prime. Advance less than 50% of collateral value.

3% to 5% above prime. Advance less than 50% of collateral value.

Characteristics

Credit extended on open account for 0 to 120 days.

3% to 5% above prime plus a 1% to 3% warehouse fee. Advance 75% to 90% of collateral value.

Wages of employees and taxes are paid at discrete points in time after the service has been rendered. This source of financing is difficult to manipulate.

A single-payment loan used to meet a funds shortage expected to last only a short period of time.

A prearranged borrowing limit under which funds, if available, will be lent to allow the borrower to meet seasonal needs.

A line of credit agreement under which the availability of funds is guaranteed. Often for a period greater than 1 year.

An unsecured short-term promissory note issued by the most financially sound firms.

Selected accounts receivable are used as collateral. The borrower is trusted to remit to the lender on collection of pledged accounts. Done in non-notification basis.

Selected accounts are sold-generally without recourse – at a discount. All credit risks go with the accounts. Factor will loan (make advance) against uncollected accounts that are not yet due. Factor will also pay interest on surplus balances.

A loan against inventory in general. Made when firm has stable inventory of a variety of inexpensive items.

A loan against inventory in general. Made when firm has stable inventory of a variety of cheap items.
Inventory used as collateral is placed under control of the lender by putting it in a terminal warehouse or through a field warehouse. Third party- a warehousing company- guards the inventory for the lender. Inventory is released only on written approval of the lender.

Problems:

Aggressive vs. Conservative financing strategy

Jade Company has forecast its total funds requirements for the coming year as shown in the following items:

Month	Amount	Month	Amount
January	8,400,000.00	July	6,800,000.00
February	6,500,000.00	August	5,500,000.00
March	5,000,000.00	September	5,000,000.00
April	5,500,000.00	October	6,300,000.00
May	6,900,000.00	November	6,400,000.00
June	7,000,000.00	December	7,800,000.00

a. Divide the firm's monthly funds requirement into a permanent and a seasonal component, and find the monthly average for each of these components.

b. Describe the amount of long-term and short-term financing that is used to meet the total funds requirement under: 1) an aggressive strategy; and 2) a conservative strategy. Assume that under the aggressive strategy, long-term funds finance permanent needs and short-term funds are used to finance seasonal needs.

c. Assuming short-term funds cost 10% annually and long-term funds cost 16% annually, use the averages in a to calculate the total cost of each of the strategies described in b.

d. Discuss the profitability-risk trade-offs associated with the aggressive strategy and the conservative strategy.

Problem 2.

Cash Discount decision

The credit terms for each of four suppliers of ***Majal Enterprises*** are shown as follows:

Supplier	Credit Terms
X	1/10 net 55 EOM
Y	2/10 net 30 EOM
Z	2/20 net 60 EOM

Majal Enterprises requirements:

a. Determine the approximate cost of giving up the cash discount from each supplier

b. Assuming that the firm needs short –term financing recommend whether it would be better to give up the cash discount or take the discount and borrow from a bank at 15% annual interest. Evaluate each supplier separately using your findings in a.

c. What would be the fact and impact to the firm that could stretch its accounts payable (net period) by 20 days from supplier Z have on your answer in b relative to this supplier?

1. *Permanent vs. Seasonal funds requirements*

Manheim International Corp.s current fixed, and total assets for each month of the coming year are summarized as follows:

Month	Current Assets Assets a	Fixed Assets b
January	15,000.00	25,000.00
February	22,000.00	25,000.00
March	25,000.00	25,000.00
April	19,000.00	25,000.00
May	6,500.00	25,000.00
June	6,500.00	25,000.00
July	9,500.00	25,000.00
August	9,000.00	25,000.00
September	16,500.00	25,000.00
October	21,000.00	25,000.00
November	23,000.00	25,000.00
December	21,000.00	25,000.00

a. Divide the firm's monthly total funds requirement (total assets) into a permanent and a seasonal component.
b. Find the monthly average: permanent ;and seasonal funds requirements using your findings in a.

Aging Accounts Receivable

Collection of receivables is detailed by means of aging schedule , according to the length of time they have been outstanding. A simple aging receivables is as follows:

Age	% Accounts Receivable
0- 30 days	52
31-60 days	31
61-90 days	12
91-120 days	5
bad debts	
	100%

The schedule above states that 52% of the company's receivables on the date of analysis have been outstanding for 30 days or less. Similarly, 5% have been outstanding for 91-120 days; and any accounts older than 120 days are written off as bad debt.

Comparing aging receivable schedules for different period, the credit officer can get some idea of any changes in collection experience, additionally, he can determine those individual accounts requiring attention. Like the collection period, however, a weakness of the aging schedule is that it is influenced by changes in sales. For example, if in the month prior to the analysis sales were usually high, it is probable that an inordinately high percentage of accounts will be in the 0-30 days category –even though collection experience may not have improved at all.

Aging is a technique that indicates the proportion of the accounts receivable balance that has been outstanding for a specified period of time. It requires that the firm's accounts receivable be broken down into groups based on the time of origin. The breakdown is made typically every month basis going back 3 to 4 months.

Example

Maxim Corp extends 30-day EOM credit terms to its customers. The firm's December 31, 2000, balance sheet shows P 200,000 of accounts receivable. An evaluation of those accounts receivable results in the following:

Days	Current	0-30	31-60	61-90	Over 90	
Month	December	November	October	September	August	Total
Accounts Receivable	60,000.00	40,000.00	66,000.00	26,000.00	8,000.00	200,000.
Percentage of total	30	20	33	13	4	100

It is assumed that *Maxim Corp* gives its customers 30 days after the end of the month in which the sale is made to pay off their accounts, any December receivables that are still on the firm's books are considered current. November receivables are between zero and 30 days overdue, October receivables still unpaid are 31 to 60 days overdue, and so on.

Its shows that 30% of the firm's receivables are current, 20% are 1 month late, 33% are 2 months late, 13 % are 3 months late, and 4% are more than 3 months late. There is an irregularity in these data, although payment seems generally slow, that is, the high percentage represented by October receivables. This indicates that some can be attributed to the hiring of a new credit manager, the acceptance of a new account that has made a large credit purchase it has not yet paid for, or ineffective collection policy. Thus, the financial analyst should determine its cause when such discrepancy occurs.

Factors affecting collection of receivables are the collection period and an aging of accounts receivable.

Collection Period or Day's Sales Outstanding

To determine the efficiency of credit and collections in the collection period, or number of days' sales outstanding in receivables. It is computed as follows:

Receivables

Collection Period = Credit Sales per day

If, for instance, a company's year-end accounts receivable were P 1,500,000 and its credit sales for the year were P 12,000,0000, its collection period would be:

= P 1,500,000 = 45 days

P 12,000,000/ 360 days

The figure can be interpreted as either the average time lag between a credit sale and payment for the sale or as the average day's worth of credit sales tied up in accounts receivables. Since the collection period measures account receivables per unit sales, a change in the collection period is a rough measure of changing collection experience. However, a major weakness of the ratio for this purpose is that it is quite sensitive to seasonal variations in sales. Consequently, unless sales are quite stable overtime, the collection period can mask fundamental changes in collection experience.

Date:	November	December	January	February	March	April	May	June
Sales (000)	50	200	300	500	100	300	100	100

An examination of the company's receivables ledgers for each of these months allows us to determine the amount of each month's sales which remain uncollected in subsequent months. This information is summarized as follows:

Sales (000) Month of Sales Subsequent Months	Nov.	Dec	Jan	Feb	Mar	Apr	May	June
November	40							
December	25	160						
January	15	100	240					
February	5	60	150	400				
March	2.5	20	90	250	80			
April	0	10	30	150	50	240		
May	0	0	15	50	30	150	80	
June	0	0	0	25	10	90	50	80

The matrix above shows that P 50,000 in November sales, P 40,000 remained uncollected at the end of the month, P 25,000 was uncollected at the end of December, P 15,000 at the end of January, and so on. The remaining columns are interpreted similarly. Of the P 200,000 in sales in December, P 160,000 remained uncollected at month end, P 100,000 at the end of January and so on.

To construct the collection-experience matrix, we represent the amount uncollected in each month as a percent of sales in the month account originated. To illustrate sales in November were P 50,000 of this amount, P 40,000 or 80%, remaining uncollected of month's end. Eighty per cent is, therefore, the first, entry in the table below.

At the end of December, P 25,000 or 50% of the original total, was still outstanding, 50% is, therefore, the second entry in column 1.

Sales
(000)

Subsequent Months	Month of Sales Nov.	Dec	Jan	Feb	Mar	Apr	May	June
November	80							
December	50	80						
January	30	50	80					
February	10	30	50	80				
March	5	10	30	50	80			
April	0	5	10	30	50	80		
May	0	0	5	10	30	50	80	
June	0	0	0	5	10	30	50	80

To use the collection-experience matrix, we compare entries along a diagonal. Apparently, the company's collection experience has remained absolutely stable throughout the entire eight month of observation. In every instance, 80% of the month's sales remain uncollected at month end, 50% remain uncollected at the end of second month, 30% after three months, and so on. An increase in these percentages over time would indicate a worsening collection experience, and vice versa.

We compute a collection period for the most recent four months, based on the preceding months' sales. Beginning with March, note from the collection experience matrix in the above table.

Receivable = 0% March sales + 50% Feb. sales + 30%Jan. sales + 10% Dec sales + 5% Nov. sales

= P 442,500

Sales per day, based on the previous five month's sales, are:

Sales per day in March = (Mar. sales + Feb. sales + Jan. sales + Dec Sales + Nov. sales)

= P 7,670.

The collection period for March, assuming all the sales are on credit, is:

Collection period for March = P 442,500/ P 7,670 = 58 days.

A tabulation based on analogous computed for the three months appears below:

Month	Collection Period
March	58
April	51
May	37
June	35

The collection period wrongfully shows a steady improving collection experience, a distortion caused by the high sales in January and February. Examination of aging schedules over the period would also evidence this same false trend.

Suppose in the above examples, we wish to forecast account receivables for next month, July 31, assuming sales of P400,000. The collection experience matrix, accounts receivable on July 31 will be :

Receivables July = 80% July sales + 50% June sales + 30% May sales + 10% April sales + 5% March sales

= 80% (P 400,000) + 50% (P 100,000) + 30% (P 100,000)+

= P 438,000

Changes and Effects in Collection

Changes and effects on residual income that are anticipated to result from an increase in collection are as follows:

Variable	Direction of change	Effect on profits
Sales Volume	None or decrease	None or negative
Investment in accounts receivable	Decrease	Positive
Bad debt expenses	Decrease	Positive
Collection expenditures	Increase	Negative

Increased in collection efforts should reduce accounts receivable and bad debt expenses, increasing profits. It the level of collection effort is too intense, the cost of this strategy may include lost sales in addition to increased collection expenditures. In other words, if the firm pushes its customers too hard to pay their accounts, they may take their business elsewhere. The firm should therefore be careful not to be overly aggressive. The quantitative effects of changes in collection policy expenditures can be evaluated in a way similar to that used to evaluate changes in credit standards and cash discounts.

Collection Techniques

A number of collection techniques are used in collecting accounts as accounts become more and more overdue, the collection effort becomes more personal and more intense. Computers can monitor accounts receivable and send collection letters at certain predetermined points if payment has not been received. A special notice will be generated, after a prescribed number of letters have been sent without receipt of payment, probably as part of a report to the credit manager. The collection efforts become more directly personal at this point, while actions such telephone calls, personal visits, and use of a collection agency will then be taken into consideration. Thus, legal action is also a possible alternative course of action.

Problems

1. ***Ajax Technologies,Inc,.*** is considering a change in its credit policy from net 20 to 2/10 net 30. Its sales should increase from P 500,000 to P 700,000, its cost of goods sold will go from 55% to 50 % of sales. Miscellaneous administrative costs remain steady at P 40,000, but collection costs will increase from P 20,000 to P 30,000 and bad debt losses will go from 5 to 10% of its average accounts receivables. 40% of the customers are expected to take the discount. This company current has indebted for P200,000 at 5%, which include the financing costs for the funds currently tied up in receivables. If the balance in receivables increases or decreases with the new policy, the extra costs of funds tied up will be computed at the 10% estimated cost of the firm's new debt.

a. What is the likely receivables balance with each policy?

b. What will be the forecasted net income after taxes with each policy?

2. ***Fernex Canned Products,Inc.*** thought of tightening its credit policy. The credit manager proposed this change in credit policy to the Chairman asserting that the 90-day terms of their company with the 30-day terms of the industry. Fernex is selling P 1,600,000 a year and costs are 80% variable and P 10,000 fixed. On the basis of a survey of Fernex's customers, the credit manager expects the following relationships between germs and sales:

Policy	Terms	Annual Sales
A	90	1,600,000.00
B	75	1,500,000.00
C	60	1,450,000.00
D	45	1,425,000.00
E	30	1,350,000.00
F	15	1,300,000.00

If the opportunity cost of capital is 15%, which policy is to be adopted? Assume that the average collection period corresponds to the terms given.

3. ***Prexis Company*** has annual credit sales of P 2,400,000. Average collection period is of 2 months. Average selling price per unit is P 10 and the average cost per unit of P 8.60. Prexis can reduce the average collection period by one month by giving 2% cash discount as 50% of the customers will avail of this cash. The required return for Prexis is 20%. Should Prexis liberalize credit policy?

4. ***Meldex Enterprises*** had earnings per share of P 4 last year, and it paid a P 2 dividend. Total retained earnings increased by P 1.20 during the year, while book value per share at year-end was P 4 . Meldex has no preferred stock, and no new equity was issued during the year. Meldex Enterprises's year-end debt (which equals its total liabilities) was P 12 what was the company's year-end debt/ assets ratio?

5. ***Shellex Distribution Company*** has the following data:

Cash and marketable securities	100.00
Fixed Assets	283.50
Sales	1,000.00
Net Income	50.00
Quick ratio	2.0X
Current ratio	3.0X
DSO	40 days
ROE	12%

Shellex has no preferred stock – only equity, current liabilities, and long-term debt.

a. Find Shellex's accounts receivable; current liabilities; current assets; total assets; ROA; equity; and long-term debt.

b. You should have found Shellex's accounts receivable (A/R) = P 111.1. If Shellex could reduce its DSO from 40 days to 30 days while holding other things constant, how much cash would it generate? If this cash were used to buy back equity shares (at book value) thus reducing the amount of equity, how would this affect the ROE; ROA; and the total debt/total assets ratio?

Chapter 5

INVENTORY MANAGEMENT

The importance of the investment in inventory tends to be proportional to the company's need to protect itself against potential lost sales. It is a necessary current asset that permits the production-sale process to operate with a minimum of disturbance. Like accounts receivable, inventory represents a significant investment for more firms. For the average manufacturer, it accounts for about 42 percent of current assets and about 18 percent of total assets.

Inventory is a significant working capital component when the production or processing time is long, when raw materials require substantial purchasing lead time and when the finished goods require sufficient exposure to potential buyers at the point of sale. Inventory constitutes the link between purchasing or production and sales of a product. The concern of finance manager in a manufacturing firm is limited to controlling the total investment in that asset and the related flow of funds. The decisions in managing inventory are oftentimes vested on the production manager. The economics of production and the related production policies precede inventory level determination, for instance, the basic question of whether to produce to stock or to order will depend on the costs of shifting capacity, the effects of capacity changes on labor and on inventory quality, inventory carrying costs and be aware of the impact of alternative production policies on the level of investment and financial risks.

Economic Order Quantity

Assuming that for a given period of time, the company has determined the acquisition cost of inventory and its total requirements . The company has two basic options with regard to the amount of inventory. It could either be zero inventory (i.e. order as often as there are sales transactions) or purchase the entire requirement for the period at the outset. The extreme strategies do not appear realistically. If the company orders inventory upon sale, it will incur high order-processing costs which tend to be fixed per transaction (e.g. transportation, handling costs or delivery) Its inventory holding costs will be held to the minimum, (e.g. opportunity cost of capital, storage, insurance and spoilage) If the company decides to hold its entire requirement on inventory, the cost positions are reversed – holding costs are high while ordering costs are limited to a single purchase transaction. Total inventory-related cost is just the sum of the holding and the ordering costs.

The inventory problem appears to practically addressed by formulating an order quantity problem. What is the economic fixed lot size per order if we know the total requirements in inventory. We may see the ordering costs increase with the number of orders and decrease with the order quantity. Carrying costs must be increasing with lot size per order. The further assumption that either cost is high at the extreme inventory strategies gives rise to " u-shaped" total inventory cost hypothesis .

The average carrying cost is equal to the cost of capital, handling and transportation cost per unit times the average number of units held in stock.

Carrying Cost + C Q/2

Where:

C= fixed carrying cost per unit

Q = quantity per order

The average ordering cost is just the total cost of each transaction times the number of orders.

Ordering Cost = O S/ Q

Where:

O = fixed cost per order transaction

S = total inventory requirement per period

Total inventory cost, T, is the sum of the two costs.

T = CQ/ 2 + OS/ Q

The economic order quantity, Q is derived by differentiating the total cost function with respect to Q, setting this derivative equal to zero and solving for Q.

1/2

Q* = [2SO]

The optimal lot size increases with ordering cost and decreases with carrying cost, as can be expected. Economies of scale are evident from the "square root rule", e.g. an increase in total inventory requirement is associated with a smaller increase in optimal order quantity (Q*)

Illustration:

Assume that the total requirement for year is 5,000 units, ordering cost is P200 per order and carrying cost is P50 per unit per year. Then economic order quantity is:

1/2

Q* = [2X5XP200/P50] = 200 units

25 times should be ordered by the company (5,000 divided by 200 units per order) during the year. To show the economies of scale in inventory control , assuming that the requirements increased by 50 per cent, to 7,500 units . The Q* increase to only 245 units, or by only 22.5 per cent. A smaller percentage increase in stocks can handle a comparatively larger expansion in total inventory requirements.

There are many complex modifications in the basic EOQ formula.

Types of Inventory

There are three basic types of inventory: raw materials, work in process, and finished goods. *Raw materials inventory* consist of items purchased by the firms usually, basic materials such as screws, plastic, raw steel, or rivers – for use in the manufacture of a finished product. If a firm manufactures complex product with numerous parts, its raw materials inventory may consist of manufactured items that have been purchased from another company or from another division of the same firm. *Work-in-process inventory* consists of all items that are currently in production. These are normally partially finished goods at some intermediate stage of completion. *Finished goods inventory* consists of items that have been produced but not yet sold.

Inventory as Investment

Inventory is an investment in the sense that it requires that the firm tie up its money, thereby giving up certain other earning opportunities. The higher a firm's average inventories, the larger the dollar investment and cost required, the lower its average inventories, the smaller the dollar investments and cost required. When evaluating planned changes in inventory levels, the financial manager should consider such changes from a benefit-versus-cost standpoint.

Example

Truman Manufacturing is considering larger production runs to reduce the high setup costs associated with the production of its only product, industrial hoists. The total annual reduction in setup costs that can be obtained has been estimated to be P10,000. As a result of the larger production runs, the average inventory investment is expected to increase from P200,000 to P300,000. If the firm can earn 15% per year on equal-risk investments, the annual cost of the additional P100,000 inventory investment will be P 15,000 (.15XP100,000). Comparing the annual P 15,000 cost of the system with the annual savings of P10,000 shows that the proposal should be rejected because it results in a net annual loss of P 5,000.

Accounts Receivable vs. Inventory

The level of management of inventory and accounts receivable are closely related. When an item is sold, it moves form inventory to accounts receivable and ultimately to cash. Their management should not be viewed independently. The decision to extend, for example, credit to a customer can result in an increased level of sales, which can be supported only by higher levels of inventory and accounts receivable. The credit terms extended will also affect the investment in inventory and receivables, because longer credit terms may allow a firm to move items from inventory to accounts receivable. It is an advantageous strategy because the cost of carrying an item in inventory is greater than the cost of carrying an account receivable. The cost of carrying inventory includes, addition to the required return on the invested funds, the costs of storing, insuring, and otherwise maintaining the physical inventory.

Example:

AJ Industries, metal fabricator, estimates that the annual cost of carrying P1 of merchandise in inventory for a 1-year period is 25 cents, whereas the annual cost of carrying P1 of receivables is 15 cents. The firm currently maintains average inventories of P300,000 and an average investment in accounts receivable of P200,000. The firm believes that by altering its credit terms, it can cause its customers to purchase in larger quantities, reducing its average inventories to P150,000 and increasing the average investment in accounts receivable to P350,000. The altered credit terms are not expected to generate new business but to result in a shift in purchasing and payment patters. The costs of the present and proposed inventory-accounts receivable systems are as follows:

Variables	Cost/ returns	Present Average investment	Cost	Proposed Average investment	Cost
			1X 2		
	1	2	3	4	5
Average Inventory	25%	300,000.00	75,000.00	150,000.00	37,500.00
Average Receivable	15	200,000.00	30,000.00	350,000.00	52,500.00
Totals		500,000.00	105,000.00	500,000.00	90,000.00

The table above shows that by shifting P 150,000 of inventory to accounts receivable, AJ Industries is able to lower the cost of carrying inventory and accounts receivable from P 105,000 to P 90,000 – a P 15,000 addition to profits. This profit is obtained without changing the level of average inventory and accounts receivable investment from its P 500,000 total. Rather, the profit is attributed to a shift in the mix of these current assets so that a larger portion of them is held in the less costly form of accounts receivable.

The relationship between the two is affected by decisions made in all areas of the firm –finance, marketing, manufacturing, and purchasing. The financial manager should consider the interaction between the two when developing strategies and making decisions related to production-sale process.

The ABC System

The ABC System being used by the firm is divided into three groups: A, B and C. The A group includes those items that require the largest dollar/peso investment. In the typical distribution of inventory items, this group consists of the 20 percent of inventory items that account for 80 percent of the firm's dollar/peso investment. The B group consists of the items accounting for the next largest investment. The C group typically consists of a larger number of items accounting for a relatively small dollar/peso investment.

Dividing inventory into A, B., and C items allows the firm to determine the level and types of inventory control procedures needed. Control of the A items should be most intensive because of the high dollar investment involved. The use of perpetual inventory record keeping that allows daily monitoring of these inventory levels is appropriate. B items are frequently controlled through periodic checking – possibly weekly – of their levels, C items could be controlled by using unsophisticated procedures such as a red-line method, which a reorder is placed when enough inventory has been removed from a bin containing the inventory item to expose a red line drawn around the inside of the bin. The economic order quantity (EOQ) model is appropriate for use in monitoring A and B items.

Illustration of the ABC system . The various plants and divisions at St, Michael Corp classifies its raw materials based on value as well as usage level of materials. The high value and usage inventory items are the critical materials in production which are usually imported.

Re order Point

Once the firm has calculated its economic order quantity, it must determine when to place orders. A reorder point is required that considers the lead the time needed to place and receive orders. Assuming a constant usage rate for inventory, the reorder point can be determined by the following equation:

Reorder point = lead time in days X daily usage.

If a firm knows that it requires 10 days to place and receive an order, and if it uses five units of inventory daily, the reorder point would be 50 units;(10X5 units per day) Thus, when the firm's inventory level reaches 50 units, an order will be placed for an amount equal to the economic order quantity. If the estimates lf lead time and daily usage are correct, the order will be received exactly when the inventory level reaches zero. Because of the difficulty in precisely predicting lead times and daily usage rates. Because of the difficulty in precisely predicting lead times and daily usage rates, many firms typically maintain safety stocks, which are extra inventories that can be drawn down if needed.

Just-In-Time (JIT) System

The just-in-time (JIT) system is used to minimize investment. The norm is that materials should arrive at exactly the time they are needed for production. Ideally, the firm would have only work-in-process inventory. Because its objective is to minimize inventory management, a JIT system uses no, or little, safety stocks. Extensive coordination must exist between the firm, its suppliers, and shipping companies t ensure that material inputs arrive on time. Failure of materials to arrive on time results in a shutdown of the production line until the materials arrive. When quality problems arise, production must be stopped until the problems are resolved.

The objective of the JIT system is manufacturing efficiency. It uses inventory as a tool for attaining efficiency by emphasizing quality in terms of both the materials used and their timely delivery. When JIT is working properly, it forces process inefficiencies to surface and be resolved. A JIT system requires cooperation among all parties involved in the process – suppliers, shipping companies, and the firm's employees.

Materials Requirement Planning (MRP) System

MRP system is being by most manufacturing companies to determine what to order, when to order, and what priorities to assign to ordering materials. MRP uses EOQ concepts to determine how much to order. Using computer, it simulates each product's bill of materials structure, inventory status, and manufacturing process. The bill of materials structure simply refers to every part of material that goes into making the finished product. For a given production plan, the computer simulates needed materials requirements by comparing production needs to available inventory balances. On the basis of the time it takes for a product that is in process to move through the various production stages and the lead time required to get materials, the MRP system determines when orders should be placed for the various items on the bill of materials.

The advantage of the MRP system is that it forces the firm to more thoughtfully consider its inventory needs and plan accordingly. The objective is to lower the firm's inventory investment without impairing production. If the firm's opportunity cost of capital for investments of equal risk is 15 percent, every dollar of investment released from inventory increases before –tax profits by P 15.

Review Questions

1. Briefly describe each of the following techniques for managing inventory:
   a. EOQ, economic order quantity
   b. Reorder point
   c. JIT- just -in –time system
   d. MRP materials requirement system
   e. ABC system
2. What is the objective of the finance manager in cash management? What conditions must be satisfied in meeting this objective?
3. What are the objectives that a company may have for holding liquid assets. Explain the costs and benefits associated with holding liquid assets.
4. What action can the manager to reduce the company's cash requirements?

5. How do excess balances arise in a disbursement system? Why are ethical problems a greater issue in disbursement than in collection?

6. What are the potential conflicts among the objectives of a disbursement system?

7. Why do some firms neglect the importance of cash concentration systems in designing a cash management system?

8. What is meant by control in concentration system? Which types of systems would have more problems with control issue?

9. Consider the basic inventory model for cash management. If cash is ordered in lot sizes known as the Optimal Cash Conversion Size, what does the firm minimize by this action?

10. Discuss the merits of the following inventory models for cash management:

a. Baumol b. Miller- Orr model b. Bermek

Problems:

1. Collection Efforts

The *Regents Auto Supply* is attempting to evaluate whether it should ease collection efforts. The firm repairs 72,000 rugs per year at an average price of P32 each. Bad debt expenses are 1% of sales, and collection expenses are P 60,000. The average collection period is 40 days, and the variable cost per unit is P 28. By easing the collection efforts, Regents expects to save P 40,000 per year in collection expense. Bad debts will increase to 2% of sales, and the average collection period will increase to 58 days. Sales will increase by 1,000 repairs per year. If the firm has a required rate of return on equal-risk investments of 24% what recommendation would you give the firm? Use your analysis to justify your answer.

2. EOQ Analysis

The *Polybest Company* uses 60,000 gallons of emulsion per year. The cost of ordering emulsion is P200 per order, and the cost of carrying the emulsion in inventory is P1 per gallon per year. The firm uses emulsion at a constant rate every day throughout the year:

a. Calculate the EOQ;

b. Calculate the total cost of the plan suggested by the EOQ;

c. Determine the total number of orders suggested by this plan;

d. Assuming that it takes 20 days to receive an order once it has been placed, determine the reorder point in terms of gallons of emulsion.

3. Accounts Receivable

The *Crown Company* currently has an average collection period of 45 days and annual credit sales of P 1million. Assume a 360-day year.

a. What is the firm's average accounts receivable balance?
b. If the variable cost of each product is 60% of sales, what is the average investment in accounts receivable?
c. If the equal-risk opportunity cost of the investment in accounts receivable is 12%, what is the total opportunity cost of the investment in accounts receivable?

6

CASH FLOWS

Cash Flow Statement

A Cash Flow Statement is a basic component of the financial statements summarizing the operating, investing and financing activities of an enterprise. The cash flow statement provides information about the cash receipts and cash payments of an enterprise during a period. According to PAS 7, an entity shall prepare a cash flow statement and shall present it as an integral part of its financial statements for each period for which financial statements are presented

Net Cash Flow and Cash

Taking into account all cash inflow and outflows, cash receipts and cash disbursements schedules are then now combined to obtain the net cash inflow or outflow for each month. The net cash flow may be added to beginning cash in January, which is assumed to be P 100,000, and the projected cash position computed month by month for the period. The following final schedule is shown as follows:

Net Cash Flow & Cash Balance

(In thousands)

	January	February	March	April	May	June
Total Cash Receipts	335.5	294.0	209.5	250.5	300.5	348.5
Total Cash Disbursements	260.0	360.0	310.0	290.0	285.0	320.0
Net Cash Flow	75.5	(66.0)	(100.5)	(39.5)	15.5	28.5
Beginning Cash without Financing	100.0	175.5	109.5	9.0	(30.5)	(15.0)
Ending Cash without Financing	175.5	109.5	9.0	(30.5)	(15.0)	13.5

The cash budget shown signifies that the company is expected to have cash deficit in April and May. Its deficit is caused by a decline in collection through March, capital expenditures totaling P 200,000 in February and March, and a cash dividend of P 20,000 in March. May and June collections are increased, the cash balance without financing rises to P 13,500 in June. The cash budget indicates that peak cash requirements occur in April. If the firm has a policy of maintaining a minimum cash balance of P 75,000 and of borrowing from its bank to maintain this minimum, it will need to borrow an additional P 66,000 in March. Additional borrowings will peak at P 105,500 in April, after which they will decline to P 61,500 in June, if all goes according to prediction.

The firm may be able to delay its capital expenditures or its payment for purchases . One of the primary objectives of a cash budget is to determine the timing and magnitude of prospective financing needs, so that the most appropriate method of financing can be arranged. When financing is not needed, the cash budget enables one to plan for the efficient transfer of excess funds from cash to marketable securities.

Purposes of Cash Flows

The primary purpose of a cash flow statement is to provide relevant information about cash receipts and cash payments of an entity during a period. It provides information that enables users to evaluate the changes in net assets of an entity, its financial structure, liquidity and solvency.

Cash flow information is useful in assessing the ability of the entity to generate cash and cash equivalents. The cash flow statement also enhances the comparability of operating performance by different entities.

The Statement of cash flows lays out these transactions in a way that highlights where the cash comes from and goes to. The where from and which to are commonly called sources and uses of cash, respectively. The statement goes on to demonstrate that the beginning balance in the bank plus the net cash flow equals the ending balance in the bank. An example is as follows:

Cash income	50,000.00	
Cash used on living expenses	(40,000.00)	
Net source of cash from Income		10,000.00
Source of Cash from Loan		25,000.00
Use of Cash to buy car		(30,000.00)
Net inflow/(outflow) of cash		5,000.00
Beginning cash balance	10,000.00	
Net cash flow	5,000.00	
Ending cash balance	15,000.00	

In the above example, the net source of cash from income is analogous to a business income adjusted for non-cash items. This item is an important source of income, say for Jake. Jake used P30,000 to buy a car. In other words, he increased the assets by P30,000. In other words, assets may be increased anytime, cash is used while Jake also received P 25,000 from the bank when he took out the loan, which has incurred liability. He realized a source of cash by increasing also liabilities through the loan he received.

Assuming all his money is in the bank, the beginning balance plus the net cash flow has to equal the ending balance.

Assuming at the beginning of the year, Sandy got a brand new car with a market value of P500,000 and a P250,000 loan outstanding on it. At that time his bank balance was P50,000. During the year he had after tax income of P100,000, but spent P45,000 on living expenses. In an effort to reduce expenses, he sold his new car for P400,000 and bought a second hand model for P150,000(without any loan) When he sold the new car he paid off the loan. At the end of the year, his bank balance was P10,000. Sandy's cash flows looks something as follows:

Cash Income	100,000.00	
Cash used on living expenses	(45,000.00)	
Net source of cash from income		55,000.00
Source of cash from sale	400,000.00	
Use of cash to buy a used one	(150,000.00)	
Net source from car investments		250,000.00
Use of cash to pay off the first car		(250,000.00)
Net inflow/(outflow) of cash		55,000.00
Beginning cash balance	50,000.00	
Net cash flow	55,000.00	
Ending cash balance	105,000.00	

Sandy reduced his assets by selling the first car for P 450,000. The proceeds from sale as a source of cash . Notice that the sale of asset reduces it balance since that reduction is a source of cash. The purchase of the second car was apparently an increase in asset and a used of cash (meaning a reduction in asset) When sandy paid off his car loan, cash was used. Thus, asset was reduced while reducing his liability. Sandy's ending cash balance is still positive as shown in the above flow of transaction. This may prompt Sandy to still use or increase his cash or reduce it whenever necessary or depending upon his activity.

Cash Flow Rules

Four simple rules are illustrated which can be applied to any business financial statements. All we need to do is analyze cash in order to keep those rules in mind as there may or may not be changes in the transactions :

Asset increase = Use

Asset decrease = Source
Liability increase = Source
Liability decrease = Use

Cash Flows are inflows and outflows of cash and cash equivalents. The cash flow statement shall report cash flows during the period classified as follows:

a. Operating activities
b. Investing activities
c. Financing activities

Classification activity provides information that allows users to assess the impact of those activities on the financial position of the entity and the amount of its cash and cash equivalents.

Bank borrowings are generally considered as financing activities. Bank overdrafts which are repayable on demand form an integral part of an entity's cash management. In these circumstances, bank overdrafts are included as component of cash and cash equivalents. A characteristic of such banking arrangements is that the bank balance often fluctuates from being positive to overdrawn. Bank overdrafts generally are not permitted.

Constructing Cash Flows

Constructing a business cash flow statement requires balance sheets at the beginning and end of the period under consideration and an income statement for that period.

Consider the following statements for the *McG Company* where the balance sheet is presented vertically:

McG Company
Balance Sheet
For the period ended Dec 31, 2002
(In thousands)

	12/31/2001	12/31/2002
Assets		
Current Assets		
Cash	1,000.00	1,400.00
Accounts Receivable	3,000.00	2,900.00
Inventory	2,000.00	3,200.00
Total Current Assets	6,000.00	7,500.00
Fixed Assets		
Gross	4,000.00	6,000.00
Accumulated Depreciation-Net	(1,000.00)	(1,500.00)
Net	3,000.00	4,500.00
Total Assets	9,000.00	12,000.00
Liabilities & Equity		
Accounts Payable	1,500.00	2,100.00
Accruals	500.00	400.00
Current Liabilities	2,000.00	2,500.00
Long-term debt	5,000.00	6,200.00
Equity	2,000.00	3,300.00
Total Capital	7,000.00	9,500.00
Total Liabilities & Equity	9,000.00	12,000.00

McG Company
Income Statement
For the period ended Dec 31, 2002
(In thousands)

Sales	10,000.00
Cost of Goods Sold	6,000.00
Gross Margin	4,000.00
Expenses	1,600.00
Depreciation	500.00
EBIT	1,900.00
Interest	400.00
EBT	1,500.00
Tax	500.00
Net Income	1,000.00

Accounts receivable decreased from P3,000 to P 2,000, providing a P100 source of cash because according to the second rule an asset decrease is a source. Inventory increased from P2,000 to P3,200 for a use of P1,200 according to the first rule.

The third rule and fourth rules to the changes in accounts payable and accruals to get the following sources and uses.

Accounts	Source/use
Receivables	100.00
Inventory	(1,200.00)
Payables	600.00
Accruals	(100.00)
	(600.00)

The sum of the current account changes and operating income is cash from operating activities. The typical presentation is as follows:

Net Income	1,000.00
Depreciation	500.00
Net changes in current accounts	(600.00)
Cash from Operating activities	900.00

Operating activities

Operating activities are the cash flows derived primarily from the principal revenue producing activities of the entity. Operating activities generally result from transactions and other events that enter into the determination of net income or loss. Operating activities have to do with running the business on a day-to-day business. Typically, operating activities include buying inventory, producing and selling products and paying expenses and taxes, and collecting credit sales. The focus, in other words of this activity is the production of net income. Net income in this activity includes items that don't represent cash flows in the current period. In an illustrative example below on *McG Company*, the only adjustment necessary to calculate operating income is to add back depreciation which was subtracted in the calculation of net income. This is shown as follows:

Net Income	1,000.00
Depreciation	500.00
Operating Income	1,500.00

We recognize that the money from operating transactions runs through the current balance sheet accounts. Therefore, changes in those accounts are part of operating cash flow. We analyze the balances other than cash other than cash and classify the changes as sources or uses of cash according to the cash flow rules. The cash account is handled separately later.

Examples of cash flows from operating activities are:

a. Cash receipts from sale of goods and rendering of services;

b. Cash receipts from royalties, rentals, fees, commissions and other revenues;

c. Cash payments to suppliers for goods and services;

d. Cash payments for selling, administrative and other expenses;

e. Cash receipts and cash payments of an insurance enterprise for premiums and claims, annuities and other policy benefits;

f. Cash payments or refunds of income taxes unless they can be specifically identified with financing and investing activities;

g. Cash receipts and payments for securities held for dealing or trading purposes.

Trading securities

An entity may hold securities and loans for dealing or trading purposes, in which case they are similar to inventory acquired specifically for resale. Therefore, cash flows arising from the purchase and sale dealing or trading securities are classified as operating activities.

Cash advances and loans made by financial institutions are usually classified as operating activities since they relate to the main revenue producing activity of that entity.

Investing Activities

Investing activities are the cash flows derived from the acquisition and disposal of long-term assets and other investments not included in cash equivalent. As a simple guide, investing activities include cash flows from transactions involving non-operating assets. Investing activities occur when the firm buys (invests in) or sells things with the fixed assets that enable it to do business while it also includes purchases term and sales of financial assets.

Cash from investing activities is simple . Taking McG Company as an example, the only entry coming from an increase in this activity is the fixed assets of P2,000. This is reflected by the increase in gross fixed assets from P 4,000 to P 6,000, which is a use of cash according to the first rule. We use the gross fixed assets account for this calculation rather than the net because the net figure includes a reduction for accumulated depreciation. The change in which is the other side of the entry that put depreciation on the income statement. That depreciation is already included in the cash flow statement in the operating section, and we avoid repeating it. Cash from investing activities is Purchase of fixed assets (P 2,000)

Examples of cash flows from investing activities are:

a. Cash payments to acquire property, plant and equipment, intangibles and other long-term assets;

b. Cash receipts from sales of property, plant and equipment, intangibles, and other long-term assets;

c. Cash payments to acquire equity or debt instruments of other entities and interests in joint ventures (current and long-term investments).

d. Cash receipts from sales of equity or debt instruments of other entities and interests in joint ventures;

e. Cash advances and loans to other parties (other than advances and loans made financial institution);

f. Cash receipts from repayment of advances and loans made to other parties;

g. Cash payments for future contract, forward contract, option contract and swap contract;

h. Cash receipts from future contracts, forward contract, option contract and swap contract.

h. Cash receipts from future contract, forward contract, option contract and swap contract.

Financing Activities

Financing activities are the cash flows derived from the equity capital and borrowings of the entity. In other words, financing activities are the cash flows that result from transactions between the entity and its owners (equity financing) and between the entity and its creditors (debt financing)

As a simple guide, financing activities include the cash flows from transactions involving "non-trade liabilities" and " equity" of an entity. Financing activities occur when the company borrows money, pays off loans, sells stock, or pays dividends. They have to do with raising money securing the obligations that come along with it.

In Mc G Company, there are three financing activities being depicted here. The first is an increase in long-term debt, a source according to the third rule. The company appeared to have taken out another loan. The second is a sale of stock and the third is the dividend payment. The sale of stock results in an increase in equity, a liability, or a loan, which is a source according to third rule. The dividend payment is clearly a use of money. It reduces equity and is therefore, a use according to the fourth rule.

Cash from financing activities is calculated as follows:

Increase in long-term debt	1,200.00
Sale of stock	800.00
Dividend paid	(500.00)
Cash from financing activities	1,500.00

Examples of cash flows from financing activities are:

a. Cash receipts from issuing shares or other equity instruments (for example, issuance of common and preferred stock).;

b. Cash payments to owners to acquire or redeem the enterprise's shares (for example, payment for treasury stock);

c. Cash receipts from issuing debentures, loans, notes, bonds, mortgages, and other short for long-term borrowings;

d. Cash payments for amounts borrowed;

e. Cash payments by a lessee for the reduction of the outstanding liability relating to a finance lease;

The cash payments to settle such obligations as trade accounts and notes payable, income tax payable, accrued expenses; and similar items are operating activities, not financing activities.

Investing and financing transactions that do not require use of cash or cash equivalents shall be excluded from the cash flow statement.

Such transactions shall be disclosed elsewhere in the financial statements either in the notes to financial statements or in a separate schedule.

The cash flow statement is strictly a cash concept. Accordingly, the following non-cash transactions are disclosed separately:

a. Acquisition of asset either by assuming directly related liability or by means of a finance lease;

b. Acquisition of asset by means of issuing capital stock or bonds payable;

c. Conversion of debt to equity, for example conversion of bonds payable to common stock;

d. Conversion of preferred stock to common stock.

Interest paid and interest received may be classified as operating cash flows because they enter into the determination of net income or loss, according to PAS 7, alternatively, interest paid may be classified as financing cash flow because it is a cost of obtaining financial resources. Interest received may be classified as investing cash flow because it is a return on investment. Interest paid, for financial institution, and interest received are usually classified as operating cash flows. Cash Flows from interest paid and interest received should be classified in a consistent manner from period to period as either operating, investing or financing activities.

Equity and Cash Accounts

In *McG Company*, we did not calculate the change in equity and classified it as source or a use of cash because the procedure breaks that change into three parts and includes them individually. The change in equity is the sum of net income and the sale of new stock less the dividend. These are as follows:

Net Income	1,000.00
Sale of stock	800.00
Dividend	(500.00)
Total change in equity	1,300.00

The stock sale and the dividend are included under financing activities, the addition of net income to equity shows up under operating activities. The cash account is apparently omitted because the cash flow total of the three activities that have been presented must equal the change in the cash account. That is shown as a reconciliation at the end of the statement.

In Mc G Company, the sum of operating, investing, and financing activities is a positive P 400, so we have the following reconciliation:

Beginning cash balance	1,000.00
Net cash flow	400.00
Ending cash balance	1,400.00

The statement of cash flows takes information from the income statement and balance sheet and displays it in a manner that highlights the movement of cash. No new information is created;

what is already there is simply re-arranged in a way that is more usable in the day-to-day running of the business.

The entire statement of cash flows for Mc G Company is shown as follows:

Mc G Company
Statement of Cash Flows
For the period ended 12/31/2002

CASH FROM OPERATING ACTIVITIES	
Net Income	1,000.00
Depreciation	500.00
Net changes in current accounts	(600.00)
Cash from operating activities	900.00
CASH FROM INVESTING ACTIVITIES	
Purchase of fixed assets	(2,000.00)
CASH FROM FINANCING ACTIVITIES	
Increase in long-term debt	1,200.00
Sale of stock	800.00
Dividend paid	(500.00)
Cash from financing activities	1,500.00
NET CASH FLOW	
Beginning cash balance	1,000.00
Net cash flow	400.00
Ending cash balance	1,400.00

The thing is, the bank might have been reluctant to advance more money to this company. The company's long-term debt plus equity is in the neighborhood of 70% debt. Yet Mc G Company is earning great profits in terms of net income, 10% of sales. Consequently, the firm can go broke profitably.

Free Cash Flows

Free cash flow refers to whether a firm generates cash beyond its own needs. Under normal conditions, most firms generate positive cash flows from operating activities, but some of those funds have to be used to maintain a long-run competitive position. Non-operating cash requirements typically include replacement worn-out fixed assets and paying dividends on preferred stock.

Free cash flow is defined as net cash flow less these requirements. It is essentially the cash available for distribution to common stockholders. If free cash flow is negative, the firm must either borrow or raise more equity capital to viable in the long run. The free cash flow concept is especially important when one company requires another. The acquiring firm needs to know whether or not its new business will need cash infusions after the acquisition or will generate funds that may be used elsewhere.

Uses of Free Cash Flow

Free cash flow is the amount of cash that is available for distribution to all investors, including both shareholders and debt holders. There are five good uses for Free Cash Flow:

a. Pay interest to debt holders, keeping in mind that the net cost to the company is the after-tax interest expense.

b. Repay debt holders, that is, pay off some of the debt;

c. Pay dividends to share holders.

Accounting in Free Cash Flow

If a company reports a large net income during the year, the amount of income reported on its year-end balance sheet may be the same or even lower than its beginning cash. The reason is that its net income can be used in a variety of ways, or it may be kept as cash in the bank. The firm may use its net income to pay dividends to increase inventories, to finance accounts receivable, to invest in assets, to reduce debt, or to buy back common stock. In fact, the company's cash position as reported on its balance sheet is affected by a great many factors in the following:

1. *Net income before preferred dividends.* Other things held constant, a net income will lead to more cash in the bank. Other things generally are not held constant;

2. *Non-cash adjustments to net income.* To calculate cash flow, it is necessary to adjust net income to reflect non-cash revenues and expenses, such as depreciation and deferred taxes, as shown in the calculation of net cash flow;

3. *Changes in working capital.* Increases in current assets other than cash as inventories and accounts receivable, decrease cash, whereas decrease in these accounts increase cash. For example, if inventories are to increase the assets, the firm must use some of its cash to acquire the additional inventory, inversely, if inventories decrease, this generally means the firm is selling inventories and not replacing all of them, hence generating cash. On the other hand, if payables increase, the firm has received additional credit from suppliers, which saves cash, but if payables decrease, this means it has cash to pay off its suppliers. Therefore, increases in current liabilities such as accounts payable increase cash, whereas decreases in current liabilities decrease cash.;

4. *Fixed assets* . If a company invests in fixed assets, this will reduce its cash, if the company uses cash to buy back outstanding stock or to pay off debt, or if it pays dividends to its shareholders, this will reduce cash.

Each of the above factors is reflected in the statement of cash flows, which summarizes the changes in a company's cash position. The statement separates activities into three categories, plus a summary section:

Operating activities, which includes net income, depreciation, changes in current assets and liabilities other than cash, short-term investments, and short term debt; ***Investing activities***, which includes investments in or sales of fixed assets; ***Financing activities***, which includes raising cash by selling short-term investments or by issuing short-term debt, long-term debt, or stock. Also, because both dividends paid and cash used to buy back outstanding stock or bonds reduce the company's cash, such transactions are included.

Accounting theory explains how to prepare the statement of cash flows, but the statement is used to help answer questions such as these: Is the company generating enough cash to purchase the additional assets required for growth? Is the firm generating any extra cash that can be used to repay debt or to invest in new products? Such information is useful both for managers and investors, so the statement of cash flows is an important part of the annual report.

Below is Artuz Company statement of cash flows as it appears in the company's annual report. The top section shows cash generated by and used in operations – for Artuz Company, operations provided net cash flows of minus P 2.5millions, This subtotal, the minus P 2.5 million net cash flow provided by operating activities is in many respects the most important figure in any of the financial statements. Profit as reported on the income statement can be manipulated by such tactics as depreciating assets too slowly, not recognizing bad debts promptly, and the like. However, it is more difficult to simultaneously manipulated profits and the working capital accounts. It is common for a company to report positive net income right up to the day it declares bankruptcy. In such cases, the net cash flows from operations almost always began to deteriorate much earlier, and analysts who kept an eye on cash flow could have predicted problem. If you are ever analyzing a company and are pressed for time, look first at the trend in net cash flow provided by operating activities, because it will tell you more than any other number.

The second section shows long-term fixed-asset investing activities. Artuz Company purchased fixed assets totaling P 230 millions; this was the only long-term investment it made during 2004.

In the third section, financing activities, includes borrowing from banks (notes payable) selling new bonds, and paying dividends on common and preferred stocks investments, but it paid P 61.5 millions in preferred and common dividends. Therefore, the net inflow of funds from financing activities was P 227.5 million.

In summary, where all of these sources and uses of cash are totaled, Artuz's statement of cash flows should be worrisome to its managers to outside analysts. The company had a P 2.5million cash shortfall from operations it spent an additional P 230 million on new fixed assets, and it paid out another P 61.5 million in dividends. It covered these cash outlays by borrowing heavily by liquidating P 65 million of short-term investments.

Artuz Company

Statement of Cash Flows for 2005

(in millions)

	C ash Provided or Used
Operating Activities	117.50
Net Income before preferred dividends	
Adjustments:	
Non-cash adjustments	
Depreciation	100.00
Due to changes in working capital	
Increase in accounts receivable	(60.00)
Increase in inventories	(200.00)
Increase in accounts payable	30.00
Increase in accruals	10.00
Net cash provided by operating activities	(2.50)
Long-term investing activities	
Cash used to acquire fixed assets	(230.00)
Financing Activities	
Sale of short-term investments	65.00
Increase in notes payable	50.00
Increase in bonds outstanding	174.00
Payment of preferred and common dividends	(61.50)
Net cash provided by financing activities	227.50
Summary	
Net change in cash	(5.00)
Cash at beginning of year	15.00
Cash at end of year	10.00

Depreciation is a non-cash expense that was deducted when calculating net income. It must be added back to show the correct cash flow from operations.

An increase in a current asset decreases cash. An increase in a current liability increases cash. For example, inventories increased by P 200 million, so that reduced cash by a like amount.

The net increase in fixed assets is P 130 million; however, this net amount is after a deduction for the year's depreciation expense. Depreciation expense would have to be added back to find the increase in gross fixed assets. From the company's income statement, we see that the 2005 depreciation expense is P 100 million, thus, expenditures on fixed assets were actually P 230 million.

Calculations

Artuz Company had P 1,455 million of total net operating capital at the end of 2004, but P 1,800 million at the end of 2005. Therefore, during 2005, it made a net investment in operating capital of :

Net investment in operating capital = P 1,800 – P 1,455 = P 345 million.

Artuz Company's free cash flow in 2005 was

1

FCP = NOPAT – Net investment in operating capital

= P 170.3 – P 345

= P 174.7 million.

Net fixed assets rose from P 870 to P 1,000 million, or by P 130 million. However, Artuz Company reported P 100 million of depreciation, so its gross investment in fixed assets was P 130 + P 100 = P 230 million for the year. With this background, the gross investment in operating capital is as follows:

2

Gross investment = Net investment + Depreciation

= P 345 + P 100 = P 445 million.

An algebraically equivalent for free cash flow is:

3

FCF = (NOPAT + Depreciation) – Gross investment in operating capital

= (P 170.3 + P 100) – P 445

= - P 174.7 million.

The two equations are equivalent because depreciation is added to both NOPAT and net investment in equation 1 to arrive at equation 1a. we usually use equation 1 because it saves us this step.

Operating Assets and Total Net Operating Capital

Most companies differ in financial structures, tax situations and different amounts of non-operating assets. These differences affect traditional accounting measures such as the rate of return on equity. This will cause two firms, or two divisions within a single firm, that actually have similar operations to appear to be operated with different efficiency. This is crucial because if managerial compensation systems are to function properly, operating managers must be judged and compensated for those things that are under their control, not on the basis of things outside their control. Therefore, to judge managerial performance, we need to compare managers' ability to generate operating income (EBIT) with the operating assets under their control.

The first step in modifying the traditional accounting framework is to divide total asset into two categories, operating assets, which consist of the assets necessary to operate the business, and non-operating asset, which would include cash and short-term investments above the level required for normal operations, investments in subsidiaries, land held for future use, and the like. Operating assets are moreover, divided into operating current assets, such as inventory, and long-term operating assets, such as plant and equipment. Apparently, if a manager can generate a given amount of profit and cash flow with a relatively small investment in operating assets, then the amount of capital investors must put up is reduced and the rate of return on that capital increases.

Most capital used in business is supplied by investors-stockholders, bond holders, and lenders such as banks. Investors must be paid for the use of their money, with payment coming as interest in the case of debt, and as dividends plus capital gains in the case of stock. If a company buys more assets than it actually needs, and thus raises too much capital, then its capital costs will be unnecessarily high.

Must all of the capital used to acquire assets be obtained from investors? The answer is no, because some of the funds will come from supplies and be reported as accounts payable, while other funds will come as accrued wages and accrued taxes, which amount to short-term loans from workers and tax authorities. Such funds are called operating current liabilities. Therefore, if a firm needs P 100 million of assets, but it has P 10 million of accounts payable and another P 10million of accrued wages and taxes, then its investors-supplied capital would be only P 80 million.

Those current assets used in operations are called operating working capital, and operating working capital less operating current liabilities is called net operating working capital. Therefore, net operating working capital is the working capital acquired with investor-supplied funds. This can be shown in equation as follows:

Net Operating working capital = Operating current assets –Operating current liabilities

In other words, some cash is required to conduct core operations on receivable, which is required for normal operations. Any short-tem securities the firm holds generally result from investment decisions made by the treasurer, and they are not sued in the core operations. However, any short-term securities the firm holds generally result from investment decisions made by the treasurer, and they are not used in the core operations. Therefore, short-term investments are normally excluded when calculating net operating working capital.

Some current liabilities-especially accounts payable and accruals – arise in the normal course of operations. Moreover, each peso of such current liabilities is a peso that the company does not have to raise from investors to acquire current assets. Therefore, to calculate net operating working capital, we deduct these operating current liabilities from the operating current assets. Other current liabilities that charge interest, such as notes payable to banks are treated as investor-supplied capital and thus are not deducted when calculating net working capital.

If you are ever uncertain about an item, ask yourself whether it is a natural consequence of operations or if its is a discretionary choice, such as a particular method of financing, or an investment in a financial asset. If it is discretionary, it is not an operating asset or liability.

We can apply these definitions to *Artuz Company*, using the balance sheet data given in the previous example. Here is the net operating working capital for 2005:

Net operating working capital = (Cash+ Accounts Receivable-Inventories) – (Accounts Payable-Accrual)

= (P 10+P375 + P 615) – (P60 + P 140)

= P 800million.

Artuz Company's total net operating capital at year-end 2005 was the sun of its net operating working capital and its operating long-term assets (which consist only of net plant and equipment):

Total net operating capital = (Net operating working capital)+(Operating long-term assets)

= P 800 + P 1,000

= P 1,800 million.

For the previous year, net operating working capital was:

Net operating working capital = (P 15 + P 345 + P 415) – (P 30 + P130)

= P 585 million.

Adding the P 870 million of fixed assets, its total operating capital at year-end 2004 was:

Total net operating capital = P 585 + 870

= P 1,455 million.

Note that we have defined total net operating capital as the sum of net operating working capital and operating long-term assets. In other words, our definition is in terms of operating assets and liabilities. However, we can calculate total net operating capital by adding up the funds provided by investors, such as notes payable, long-term bonds, preferred stock, and common stock. For Artuz Company, the total capital provided by investors at year-end 2004 was P 60 + P 580 + P 40 + P 840 = P 1,520 million. Of this amount, P 65 million was tied up in short-term investments, which are not directly related to Artuz Company's operations. Only P 1,520-P 65 = P 1,455 million of investor-supplied capital was used in operations. It is exactly the same value as calculated above. This shows that we can calculate total net operating capital either from net operating working capital and operating long-term assets or from the investor-supplied funds. We usually have our calculations upon the first definition since it is possible to perform this calculation for a division, whereas it is not possible to do so using the definition based on investor-supplied capital.

We use the terms total net operating capital, operating capital, net operating assets, and capital to mean the same thing. Unless we specifically say investor-supplied capital, we are referring to total net operating capital.

Artuz Company increased its operating capital to P 1,800 from P 1,455 million, or by P 345 million, during 2005. Furthermore, most of this increase went into working capital, which rose from P 585 to

P 800 million, or by P 215 million. This 37 percent increase in net operating working capital versus a sales increase of only 5 percent (from P 2,850 to P 3,000 million) should set off warning bells in your head: Why did *Artuz Company* tie up so much additional cash in working capital? Is the company gearing up for a big increase in sales, or are inventories not moving and receivables not being collected?

Net Operating Profit After Taxes (NOPAT)

When two companies have different amounts of interest charges, hence, they have different amounts of debt, they could have identical operating performances but different net incomes – the one with more debt would have a lower net income. Net income is certainly important, but it does not always reflect the true performance of a company's operations or the effectiveness of its operating managers. A better measurement for comparing managers' performance is net operating profit after taxes, or NOPAT, which is the amount of profit a company would generate if it had not debt and held no financial assets. NOPAT is defined as follows :

NOPAT = P 283.8 (1-0.4) = P 283.8 (0.6) = P 170.3 million.

This means Artuz Company generated an after-tax operating profit of P 170.3 million, a little better than its previous NOPAT of P 263 (0.6) = P 157.8 million. However, the income statements in the example show that Artuz Company earnings per share actually declined. This decrease in EPS was caused by an increase in interest expense, and not by a decrease in operating profit,. The balance sheets as shown in the example show an increase in debt. But why did it increase its debt? Its investment in operating capital increased dramatically during 2005 and that increase was financed with debt.

Market Value Added

The primary objective of most companies is to maximize shareholders' wealth which obviously benefits shareholders, but it also helps to ensure that scarce resources are allocated efficiently, which benefits the economy. Shareholder wealth is maximized by the difference between the market value of the firm's stock and the amount of equity capital that was supplied by shareholders. This difference is called the *Market Value Added (MVA)*

MVA = Market value added – Equity capital supplied byte shareholders

= (Share outstanding) (Stock price) – Total common equity.

To illustrate, Avenue Cola, in April 2004, its total market equity value was P 98.5 billion, while its balance sheet showed that stockholders had put up only P 11.6 billion. Thus, Avenue Cola's MVA was P 98.5, P 11.6, P 86.9 billion. Thus P 86.9 billion represents the difference between the money that Avenue Cola's stockholders have invested in the corporation since its founding – including retained earnings versus the cash they could get if they sold the business. The higher its MVA, the better the job management is doing for the firm's shareholders.

Sometimes MVA is defined as the total market value of the company minus the total amount of investor-supplied capital:

MVA = Total market value – Total capital

= (Market value of stock + Market value of debt))

- Total capital.

For most companies, the total amount of investor-supplied capital is the sum of equity debt, and preferred stock. We calculate the total amount of investor supplied capital directly from their reported values in the financial statements. The total market value of a company is the sum of the market values of common equity, debt, and preferred stock. It is easy to find the market value of debt. Hence, many analysts use the value of debt that is reported in the financial statements, or the debt's book value, as an estimate of its market value.

For Avenue Cola, the total amount of reported debt was about P 5.6 billion, and Avenue Cola had no preferred stock. Using this as an estimate of the market value of debt, Avenue's total market value was P 98.5+P 5.6 = P 104.1 billion. The total amount of investor-supplied funds was P 11.6 + P 5.6 = P 17.2 billion. Using these total values, the MVA was P 104.1 – P 17.2 = P 86.9 billion. This is the same answer that we got using the previous definition of MVA. Both methods give the same results if the market value of debt is approximately equal to its book value.

Economic Value Added (EVA)

Economic Value Added (EVA) focuses on managerial effectiveness in a given year. MVA measures the effects of managerial actions since the very inception of a company. The basic EVA formula is as follows:

EVA = Net operating profit after taxes (NOPAT)

- After tax dollar cost of capital used to support operations
- EBIT (1- Tax rate) – (Total net operating capital)-(WACC)

EVA can also be calculated in terms of ROIC:

EVA = (Operating capital)(ROIC – WACC)

This equation shows, a firm adds value, that is, a positive EVA – if its ROIC is greater than its WACC. If WACC exceeds ROIC, their new investments in operating capital will reduce the firm's value. For the year, EVA is an estimate of a business's true economic profit, and it differs sharply from accounting profit. EVA represents the residual income that remains after the cost of all capital, including equity capital, has been deducted, whereas accounting profit is determined without imposing a charge for equity capital. Equity capital has a cost, because funds provided by shareholders could have been invested elsewhere, where they would have earned a return. Shareholders give up the opportunity to invest elsewhere when they provide capital to the firm. The return they could earn elsewhere in investments of equal risk represents the cost of equity capital. This cost is an opportunity cost rather than an accounting cost, but it is quite real nevertheless.

In calculating EVA, depreciation is not added back. It is a cost since worn-out assets must be replaced, and it is deducted when determining both net income and EVA. Calculating EVA assumes that the true economic depreciation of the company's fixed assets exactly equals the depreciation used for accounting and tax purposes. If this were not the case, adjustments would have to be made to obtain a more accurate measure of EVA.

Artuz Company' s MVA & EVA (millions of Pesos)

	2005	2004
EVA Calculation		
EBIT	283.8	263.0
Tax rate	40%	40%
NOPAT = EBIT (1-T)	170.3	157.8
Total investor supplied operating capital	1800.0	1455.0
Weighted average cost of capital WACC (%)	0.1	10.8%
Peso cost of capital = Operating capital (WACC)	198.0	157.1
EVA= NOPAT-Capital cost	(27.70)	.'0.70
ROIC = NOPAT/Operating capital	9.46%	10.85%
ROIC-Cost of Capital = ROIC - WACC	(1.54%)	0.05%
EVA = (Operating capital)ROIC-WACC)	(27.70)	0.7

Artuz Company's MVA and EVA are calculated. The stock price was P 23 per share at year end 2005. down from P 26 per share the previous year. Its WACC, which is the percentage after-tax cost of capital was 10.8 percent in 2004 and 11.0 percent in 2005, and its tax rate was 40 percent. Other data in the table were given in the basic financial statements provided earlier. The 2005 MVA is still positive, but P 460 – P 254= P 206 million of stockholders value was lost during the year.

EVA for 2004 was just barely positive, and in 2005 it was negative. Operating income (NOPAT) rose, but EVA still declined, primarily because the amount of capital rose more sharply than NOPAT –by about 26 percent versus 8 percent – and the cost of this additional capital pulled EVA down.

Dividends & Interest

Dividend received may be classified as operating cash flow because it enters into the determination of net income, as provided by PAS 7, alternatively, dividend received may be classified as investing cash flow because it is a return on investment; Dividend paid, as provided by PAS 7, may be classified as financing cash flow because it is a cost of obtaining financial resources, alternatively, dividend paid may be classified as operating cash flow in order to assist users to determine the ability of the entity to pay dividends out of operating cash flows.

Classification of dividend received and dividend paid as either operating, investing or financing activity should also be made on consistent basis from period to period.

Interest income received by a corporation is taxed as ordinary income at regular corporate tax rates. However, 70 percent of the individuals received by one corporation from another is excluded from taxable income, while the remaining 30 percent is taxed at the ordinary tax rate. Thus, a corporation earning more than P 18,333,333 and paying a 35 percent marginal tax rate would pay only (0.30)(0.35) = 0.105 = 10.5% of its dividend income as taxes, so its effective tax rate on dividends received would be 10.5 percent. If this firm had P 10,000 in pre-tax dividend income, its after-tax dividend income would be P 8,950:

After-tax income = Before – tax income – Taxes

= Before – tax income – (Before – tax income)(Effective tax rate)

= Before – tax income (1- Effective tax rate)

= P 10,000 [- (0.30)(0.35)]

= P 10,000 (1-0.105) = P 10,000 (0.895) = P 8,950.

The income is ultimately subjected to triple taxation if the corporation pays its own after-tax income out to its stockholders as dividends : the original corporation is first taxed; second, corporation is then taxed on the dividends it received; and the individuals who receive the final dividends are taxed again. This is the reason for the 70 percent exclusion on inter corporate dividends.

The tax factor favors investment in stocks, which pay dividends, rather than in bonds, which pay interest, if a corporation has surplus funds that can be invested in marketable securities.

For example, suppose the *P & D Enterprises* had P 200,000 to invest, and it could buy either bonds that paid interest of P 16,000 per year or preferred stock that paid dividends of P 14,000, P & D is in the 35 percent tax bracket; therefore, its tax on the interest, if it bought bonds, would be 0.35(16,000) = P 5,600, and its after-tax income would be P 10,400. If it bought preferred (or common) stock, its tax would be 0.35 [(0.35)(0.30) (14,000) = P 1,470, and its after-tax income would be P 12,540. Other factors might lead P & D Enterprises to invest in bonds, but the tax factor certainly favors stock investments when the investor is a corporation.

Interest & Dividends as Payment by a Corporation

A corporation may either be financed with debt or equity capital, in which case, interest is paid if it uses debt, whereas if it uses equity, it is expected to pay dividends to the equity investors (stockholders). The interest paid by a corporation is deducted from its operating income to obtain its taxable income, but dividends paid are not deductible. Therefore, a firm needs P 1 of pre-tax income to pay P 1 of interest, but if it is in the 35 percent bracket, it must earn P 1.54 of pre-tax income to pay P 1 of dividends.

P 1 = P 1 = P 1.54

Pre-tax income needed to pay P 1 of dividends = 1- Tax rate 0.65

If a company has P 1.54 in pre-tax income, it must pay P 0.54 in taxes [(0.35)(P 1.54) = P 0.54] when it is worked backward. This leaves it with after-tax income of P 1.00.

	Use Bonds (1)	Use Stock (2)
Sales	5,000,000.00	5,000,000.00
Operating costs	3,500,000.00	3,500,000.00
Earnings before interest and taxes (EBIT)	1,500,000.00	1,500,000.00
Interest	1,500,000.00	0
Taxable Income	0	1,500,000.00
Income taxes (35%)	0	600,000.00
After-tax income	0	900,000.00
Income to investors	1,500,000.00	900,000.00
Rate of return on P10 million of assets	15.0%	9.0%

The table above shows a situation for a firm with P 10 million of assets, sale of P5 million, and P 1.5 million of earnings before interest and taxes (EBIT). If it is entirely financed by bonds, and if it made interest payments of P 1.5 million, its taxable income would be zero, taxes would be zero, and its investors would receive the entire P 1.5 million. (The term investors includes both stockholders and bondholders). However, in column 2, if the it had no debt and was financed by stock, all of the P 1.5 million of EBIT would be taxable income to the corporation, the tax would be P 1,500,000 (0.35) = P 600,000, and investors would receive only P 0.9 million versus P 1.5

million under debt financing. The rate of return to investors on their P 10million investment is much higher if debt is used.

Income Taxes in Cash Flows

Cash flows arising from income taxes should be separately disclosed and should be classified as cash flows from operating activities unless they can be specifically identified with investing and financing activities.

Illustration:

Cefagem X Corporation shows its comparative balance sheet and income statement for the year 2006 as follows:

Balance Sheet

As of December 31, 2006

Assets	2006	2005
Cash	3,220,000.00	2,225,000.00
Accounts Receivable	550,000.00	325,000.00
Inventory	225,000.00	155,000.00
Prepaid Insurance	25,000.00	35,000.00
Property, Plant & Equipment	2,575,000.00	2,575,000.00
Accumulated Depreciation	(650,000.00)	(550,000.00)
Patent	65,000.00	75,000.00
Total Assets	6,010,000.00	4,840,000.00
Liabilities & Equity		
Accounts Payable	250,000.00	225,000.00
Accrued Salaries Payable	550,000.00	466,300.00
Accrued Interest Payable	12,500.00	13,500.00
Income Tax Payable	295,000.00	195,000.00
Unearned Rent Income	12,500.00	35,200.00
Mortgage Payable	550,000.00	550,000.00
Common Stock	1,575,000.00	1,575,000.00
Retained Earnings	2,765,000.00	1,780,000.00
Total Liabilities & Equity	6,010,000.00	4,840,000.00

Income Statement

Year Ended December 31, 2006

Sales		8,500,000.00
Cost of Sales:		
Inventory - January 1	155,000.00	
Purchases	3,200,000.00	
Goods available for sale	3,355,000.00	
Less: Inventory - Dec.31	225,000.00	3,130,000.00
Gross Income		5,370,000.00
Rent Income		75,000.00
Total Income		5,445,000.00
Expenses :		
Salaries	750,000.00	
Insurance	40,000.00	
Other Expenses	425,000.00	
Depreciation	50,000.00	
Amortization of Patent	10,000.00	
Interest Expense	55,000.00	1,330,000.00
Income Before tax		4,115,000.00
Income tax		295,000.00
Net Income		3,820,000.00

FORECASTING CASH FLOWS

Cash forecast is an estimation of the flows in and out of the firm's cash account over a particular period of time, usually a quarter, month, week, or day. Cash forecasting is extremely important to most firms. It enables them to anticipate periods of surplus cash and periods where financing will be necessary. This anticipation is the reason that cash forecasts are generated. Anticipation enables the firm to plan much more effectively for investment and financing, and via this planning, produce superior returns.

Objectives of Cash Forecasting

1. Interest costs and Income. One major purpose of forecasting is to increase the firm's yield on its investment portfolio or depending on the firm's financial position, to decrease interest costs on its borrowing. Lack of an accurate forecast may force management either to invest in very short-term securities (thereby often earning the lowest yields) or to borrow unexpectedly at higher than usual interest rates.

2. Excess Balances. Accurate daily cash forecasts enable management to reduce balances in disbursement and/or deposit accounts and thereby move otherwise non-interest cash into other areas of the firm.

3. Administrative Costs Benefits. Forecasting may require extensive administrative efforts to collect and digest data. On the other hand, forecasting may provide administrative benefits in the form of better planning and more timely management reports.

4. Control. Daily cash budgets often provide a standard against which deposit reports from the field can be compared. It actual deposit vary from project deposits, inquiries may be warranted.

5. Forecast System Costs. These costs are associated directly with developing, maintaining and running the forecasting model and associated data bases. Some forecast systems require extensive computer time and information. Others are simple and inexpensive.

Forecasting Systems

Designing forecasting systems requires that management make trade off among these five cost factors. Depending on the horizon, the forecaster wishes to consider the cash forecasting may be divided into three horizons. Different techniques and purposes are associated with each horizon.

Long Range Forecasts

Cash forecasts of one or more years into the future are needed primarily to assess the viability of the firm's long-range financing and operating policies. Long-range forecasts give planners an idea of how much cash the firm needs to raise through debt or equity issues, internally generated cash, or other cash sources. These forecasts also assist managers in establishing dividend policies, determining capital investments, and planning mergers and acquisitions (or divestitures) program. It is typical for a firm to have a 5 or 10-year forecast that is updated annually.

Long-range forecasts are generally based on accounting projections and typically involved the generation of various scenarios for future economic and technological environments. Such forecasts are considered strategic in the sense that possible major changes are examined.

Medium-Range Forecasts

A forecast of quarterly cash flows over the next 4 quarters, with monthly detail over the next 3 months may be considered as medium-range forecasts to be those that cover cash flows during the next 12 months. Medium-range cash forecasting usually takes the firm's existing technology and long-range financing as given. Hence, this kind of forecast is considered tactical rather than strategic. Although it can be accounting based, adjustments are made to focus on cash flows rather than earnings. It is sometimes called cash budgeting.

The purpose of medium range forecasting is to determine the firms needs for short-term cash from credit lines, commercial paper sales, or credit and payables policies. It also helps firms to determining the makeup of their short-term investment portfolio. When a firm performs the task called budgeting, it generally designates the most likely (or most desirable) scenario of the medium-range forecasts as the budget. The budget is used to compare actual performance during the course of the year.

Daily Cash Forecast

Daily cash forecasts attempt to project cash inflows and outflows on a daily basis one (1) or more days into the future. That is, in order to perform accurately, Even though a firm may know precisely its revenues for the month, it may have difficulty determining specific cash inflows for given days of the month. For some firms, A daily forecast several months into the future is possible. For most, however, a forecast even 2 days into the future is difficult. The purposes of daily forecasting are to assist management in scheduling transfer in cash concentration, funding disbursement accounts, controlling field deposits, and making short-term investing and borrowing decisions.

Components of Major Cash Flows

The conventional pattern of cash flows include three basic components : an initial investment; operating cash inflows; terminal cash flow. All projects – whether for expansion, replacement, renewal, or some other purpose – have the first two components. Some, however, lack the final component, terminal cash flow.

The figure below portrays a time line cash flow for a project. Each of the cash flow components is labeled. The initial investment is P 50,000 for the proposed project. This is the relevant cash outflow at time zero. The operating cash inflows, which are the incremental after-tax cash inflows resulting from use of the project during its life, gradually increase from P 4,000 in the first year to P 10,000 in its tenth and final year. The terminal cash flow of P 25,000, received at the end of the project's 10-year life, is the after-tax non operating cash flow occurring in the final year of the project. It is usually attributable to liquidation of the project. Note that the terminal cash flow does not include the P10,000 operating cash inflow for the year 10.

Operating Cash Inflows

______________________________/|__________

5,000.00 7,000.00 8,0

4,000.00 6,000.00 7,000.00

^ ^ ^ ^ ^ ^

0 1 2 3 4 5 6

|/

50,000.00

initial

investment

Sunk Costs and Opportunity Costs

The firm must recognize any sunk costs and opportunity costs, when estimating the relevant cash flows associated with a proposed capital expenditure. These costs are easy to mishandle or ignore, particularly when determining a project's incremental cash flows. Sunk costs are cash outlays that have already been made (i.e., past outlays) and therefore have no effect on the cash flows relevant to the current decision. Sunk costs should not be included in a project's incremental cash flows. Opportunity costs are cash flows that could be realized from the best alternative use of an owned asset. They therefore represent cash flows that will not be realized as a result of employing that asset in the proposed project. Any opportunity costs should be included as cash outflows when determining a project's incremental cash flows.

Example:

Thermex Construction is considering renewing its auto cad softwares, for a new software introduced in the market today, which it purchased 7 years earlier for a total of P 237,000. The obsolete auto cad could be sold for a high bid of P 142,000 . *Thermex Construction* is in the process of estimating costs of using its cad features in its operation and the benefit of its softwares in other projects. The cost of P237,000 of auto cad is a sunk cost because of its earlier cash outlay. It would not be included as a cash outflow when determining the cash flows relevant to its use and benefits. Although it owns obsolete softwares, the proposed use of its special features in place of obsolete softwares represents an opportunity costs of P142,000 – the highest price at which it could be sold today. This opportunity cost would be included as a cash outflow associated with using the special feature of the auto cad softwares.

Disregarding Sunk Costs

Sunk costs must be ignored. One is concerned with incremental costs and benefits. The recovery of past costs is irrelevant. These are by gones and should not enter into the decision process. Also, we should take note that certain costs do not necessarily involve a peso outlay. If we have allowed a located plant space to a project and this space can be used for something else, the opportunity cost must be included in the project's evaluation. If the presently unused building can be sold of P 3 million, that amount should be treated as a cash outlay at the outset of the project. Thus, in deriving cash flows we must consider appropriate opportunity costs.

Uncertainty in Cash Forecasting

Sales uncertainty refers to the risk regarding the firm's future levels of sales. Most firms try to forecast accurately enough to hold errors in short-run sales forecasts to less than 10 percent but are often unsuccessful in these efforts. Sales-projections are a product of two other projections, units to be sold and price per unit. Both are often quite uncertain and depend on economic and competitive conditions. Note that any errors in sales forecasts have multiple impacts on the firm's cash flows, they impact on receivable levels (and therefore collections) and also on production expenses .(on disbursements)

Collection rate uncertainty is the uncertainty regarding the firm's actual future collection patters of receivables. The firm may historically have collected an average of a certain percent of its outstanding receivables from a particular period in another particular period, but this average contains considerable variability. Changing market and economic conditions may make for chancy extrapolation of post historic data into future period. Because of this and the uncertainties in forecasting sales, forecasts of the collection of future receivables contain at least three sources of uncertainty; uncertainty regarding the number of units that will be sold, uncertainty regarding the price at which these units will be sold, and uncertainty regarding the patterns with which the receivables generated by these sales will be collected.

Capital outflow uncertainty is one of the biggest sources of surprises in cash flow forecasting. This is the uncertainty regarding the timing of cash disbursements related to the firm's major capital expenditure and construction programs. The uncertainty arises from the nature of payments made for new construction. When the firm undertakes to build a new plant or other project of this sort. The total price (subject to specified revisions) is agreed upon in advance. Assuming that the firm has contracted to have built P 10 million buildings with a 10 percent retainage. Once the construction firm completes the first 20 percent of the project, a payment of P 1.8 million will be (P 10 million times 20 percent times 90 percent) Such payments are subject to at least two uncertainties. First, the weather, a very risky variable, plays a significant part in the rate of construction completion. Second, construction firms are notorious for filing late progress reports and then expecting immediate payment. While only a small percent of the firm's progress reports and then expecting immediate payment. While only a small percent of the firm's total bills are from capital construction programs, the amounts involved are usually very large. One unexpected item of this sort can destroy, carefully planned cash flow management strategy.

Review Questions:

1 Define the following terms:

a. Annual report; balance sheet, income statement

b. Depreciation; amortization; EBIT; EBITDA

c. Common stockholders' equity, or net worth; retained earnings

d. Operating current assets; operating current liabilities; net operating working capital;

total net operating capital

e. Accounting profit; net cash flow; NOPAT; free cash flow

g. Market value added; Economic value added

h. Statement of cash flows; Cash flows

2. What constitutes statement of cash flows?

3. Explain the difference between NOPAT and net income. Which is a better measure of the performance of a company's operations?

4. What is free cash flow? Why is the most important measure of cash flow?

5. What are the purposes of Cash Flows?

6. What are the rules in preparing cash flows?

7. What is cash forecasting? What are its objectives?

8. Explain cash flow from operations; investing; and financing. Give examples.

9. What are sunk costs and opportunity costs?

10. What are the components of major cash flows?

Problems:

1. *Ximex Corporation* had P 5,000,000 in operating income 9EBIT) The company had a net depreciation expense of P 1,000,000 and an interest expense of P 1,000,000; its corporate tax rate was 40 percent. The company has P 14,000,000 in non-interest-earning current assets and P 4,000,000 in non-interest-bearing current liabilities; it has P 15,000,000 in net plant and equipment. It estimates that it has an after-tax cost of capital of 10 percent. Assume that *Ximex Corporation's* only non cash item was depreciation.

a. What was the company's net income for the year?

b. What was the company's net cash flow?

c. What was the company's net operating profit after taxes (NOPAT)?

d. If capital in the previous year was P 24,000,000, what was the company's free cash flow (FCF) for the year?

e. What is the company's Economic Value Added (EVA)?

Chapter 7

FINANCIAL PLANNING & ANALYSIS

Financial planning involves analyzing the financial flows of a company; forecasting, the consequences of various investment, financing, and dividend decisions, and weighing the effects of various alternatives. The advantage of financial planning is that it compels management to take account of possible deviations from the company's anticipated path. The planning horizon depends on the company in which most is one year and the others are more than one to five years.

One of the valuable methods in analyzing financial statement is a funds-flow statement, with which a financial manager or a creditor may evaluate how a firm uses funds, and may determine how these uses are financed. The analyst in studying the past flows should evaluate flows by means of funds statement based on forecasts. Such a statement provides an efficient method for the financial manager to assess the growth of the company and its resulting financial needs as well as to determine the best way by which to finance those needs. Funds statement are very useful in planning short and long-term financing.

Cash budget and pro-forma are the subject of analysis of future funds flows where the cash budget is indispensable to the financial manage in determining the short-term cash needs of the firm and, accordingly, in planning its short-term financing. When cash budgeting is extended to include a range of possible outcomes, the financial manager can evaluate the business risk and liquidity of the company and plan a realistic margin of safety.

This margin of safety might come from adjusting the firm's liquidity cushion, rearranging the maturity structure of its debt, arranging a line of credit with a bank, or a combination of the three . Cash budgets prepared for a range of possible outcomes are valuable also in appraising the ability of the company to adjust to unexpected changes in cash flows. The preparation of pro forma balance sheets and income statements enables the financial manager to analyze the effect of various policy decisions on the future financial condition and performance of the firm.

Sustainable growth modeling is involved in the final method of analysis where we determine the sales growth objectives of the company are consistent with its operating efficiency and with its financial ratios. This allows us to simulate the likely effects of changes in target ratios when we move from a steady state environment. The integration of marketing, operational, and financial objectives permits better management of growth.

The Uses and Sources of Funds

The flow of funds is a visualized and continuous process. There must be an offsetting source for every use of funds; its liabilities and net worth represent net sources. For the going concern, there is no starting nor stopping point. A variety of finished product passes through a variety of inputs – such as, raw material, fixed assets, and labor – ultimately paid for in cash. The product then is sold either for cash or on credit. A credit sale involves a receivable, which when collected, becomes cash. If the selling price of the product exceeds all costs (including depreciation on assets) for a period of time, there is a profit for the period; if not, there is a loss.

The reservoir of cash, the focal point in the figure, fluctuates over time with the production schedule, sales, collection of receivables, capital expenditures, and financing. Take note that reservoirs of raw materials, work in process, finished goods inventory, accounts receivable, and trade payable fluctuate with sales, the production schedule, and policies on managing receivables, inventories, and trade payables.

The funds statement is a method by which the net funds flow between two points in time. These points conform to beginning and ending financial statement dates for whatever period of examination is relevant – a quarter, a year, or 5 years. We must emphasize that the funds statement portrays net rather than gross changes between two comparable financial statements at different dates. For example, gross changes might be thought to include all changes that occur between the two statement dates, rather than the sum of these changes – the net change as defined. An analysis of the gross funds flow of a firm over time would be much more revealing than an analysis of net funds flow, we are usually constrained by the financial information available, such as balance sheets and income statements that span particular periods of time.

Funds may be defined in several different ways, depending on the purpose of the analysis. They are often defined as cash, while many analysts treat funds as working capital, a somewhat broader definition. Other definitions are possible, although the two described are the most common by far.

In analyzing funds flows on a cash basis there are two similar but different approaches; first, a traditional way used by many financial analysts; and the second is an accounting statement of cash flows required in the presentation of audited financial results. This statement supplements the balance sheet and income statement.

Funds Statement on a Cash Basis

In preparing a funds statement on a cash basis it should be classified by its net balance sheet changes that occur between two points in time; changes that increase cash and changes that decrease cash; classifying, from the income statement and the shareholders' equity statement, the factors that increase cash and the factors that decrease cash; and consolidating this information in a source and use of funds statement form. We simply place one balance sheet beside the other and compute the changes in the various accounts, in the first.

Sources of Funds

The following are the sources of funds that increase cash:

1. A net decrease in any asset other than cash or fixed assets;
2. A gross decrease in fixed assets;
3. A net increase in any liability;
4. Proceeds from the sale of preferred or common stock;
5. Funds provided by operations

Funds provided by operations usually are not expressed directly on the income statement. To determine them, one must add back depreciation to net income after taxes.

Uses of Funds

The following are the uses of funds:

1. A net increase in any asset other than cash or fixed assets;
2. A gross increase in fixed assets;
3. A net decrease in any liability;
4. A retirement or purchase of stock;
5. Cash dividends

Gross changes in fixed assets are computed by adding depreciation for the period to net fixed assets at the ending financial statement date and subtract from this amount net fixed assets at the beginning financial statement date. The residual represents the gross change in fixed assets for the period, if the residual is positive, it represents a use of funds; if negative, it represents a source.

Table 1.1 below shows an illustration of sources and uses of funds for *Alexis Manufacturing Co.*

Alexis Manufacturing Company

Sources and Uses of Funds

March 31, 2003

Sources		Uses	
Funds provided by operations			
Net profit	201,242.00	Dividends	142,968.00
Depreciation	111,509.00	Addition to fixed assets	104,276.00
Decrease, accounts receivable	62,426.00	Increase, inventories	94,238.00
Decrease, other assets	467.00	Increase, prepaid expenses	3,559.00
Increase, bank loans	91,997.00	Increase, deferred income taxes	6,038.00
Increase, accounts payable	11,634.00	Increase, investments	65,376.00
Increase, accruals	26,653.00	Decrease, income taxes payable	91,252.00
Increase, long-term debt	4,323.00		
Increase, common stock and			
paid in capital	103.00	Increase in cash position	2,647.00
Total Sources	510,354.00	Total uses	510,354.00

Accounting statement of cash flows using indirect method employed by most firm is shown in the table 1.2 below . Again, this statement is derived from balance sheet and income statement information in Notice that changes that the increase in cash, all other things the same are shown as positive numbers, whereas changes that decrease cash are shown negative figures and appear in a single column.

Changes in table 1.2 are categorized into operating activities, investing activities, and financing activities A third difference is that accounting statement of cash flows records gross investment in not only property, plant, and equipment(fixed assets) but also dispositions. The two are combined. Repurchase of stock, not shown, is a separate item in the accounting statement of cash flows.

Alexis Manufacturing Company
Statement of Cash Flows
March 31, 2003

Cash flows from operating activities	
Net earnings	201,242.00
Adjustments to reconcile net earnings to cash provided by operating activities	
Depreciation	111,509.00
Changes in assets & liabilities	
Accounts receivables	62,426.00
Inventories	(94,238.00)
Prepaid expenses	(3,559.00)
Deferred income taxes	(6,038.00)
Accounts payable	11,634.00
Income taxes payable	(91,252.00)
Accruals	26,653.00
	218,377.00
Cash flows from investing activities	
Investment in prop.plant & eqpt.	(113,730.00)
Disposition of prop.plant & eqpt.	9,454.00
Purchase of long-term investments	(65,376.00)
Other	467.00
	(169,185.00)
Cash flows from financing activities	
Increase(decrease) short-term borrowing	91,997.00
increase (decrease) long-term debt	4,323.00
issuance of common stock	103.00
Dividends	(142,968.00)
	(46,545.00)
Increase(decrease) in cash and short-term inv	
Cash and short-term invest.at beg,.of year	2,647.00
Cash and short-term invest.at end.of year	175,042.00

177,689.00

Problems: Solutions in Appendix C

1. *Jones & James, Inc.* had the following financial statements for 20 X1 and 20 X 2.

a. Prepare a source and use of funds statement on a cash basis.

b. Prepare an accounting statement of cash flows.

c. Evaluate your findings

Assets		
Cash and cash equivalents	140,000.00	31,000.00
Accounts receivable	346,000.00	528,000.00
Inventories	432,000.00	683,000.00
Current assets	918,000.00	1,242,000.00
Net fixed assets	1,113,000.00	1,398,000.00
Total	2,031,000.00	2,640,000.00
Liabilities & Equity		
Accounts payable	413,000.00	627,000.00
Accruals	226,000.00	314,000.00
Bank borrowings	100,000.00	235,000.00
Current liabilities	739,000.00	1,176,000.00
Common stock	100,000.00	100,000.00
Retained earnings	1,192,000.00	1,364,000.00
Total	2,031,000.00	2,640,000.00

2. *S & S Milling Company* at December 31 shows its balance sheet in thousands. The company has received a large order and anticipates the need to go to its bank to increase its borrowings. As a result, it has to forecast the cash requirements for January, February, and

March. The company, typically collects 20 percent of its sales in the month of sale, 70 percent in the subsequent month, and 10 percent in the second month after the sale. All sales are credit sales.

Cash	50.00	Accounts payable	380.00
Accounts Receivable	530.00	Bank loan	400.00
Inventories	545.00	Accruals	212.00
Current assets	1,125.00	Current liabilities	972.00
Net fixed assets	1,836.00	Long-term debt	450.00
		Common stock	100.00
		Retained earnings	1,439.00
Total assets	2,961.00	Total liabilities & equity	2,961.00

Purchases of raw material to produce grain are made in the month prior to the sale and amount to 60 percent of sales in the subsequent month. Payments of these purchases occur in the month after the purchase. Labor costs, including overtime are expected to be P 150,000 in January, P 200,000 in February, at P 160,000 in March. Selling, administrative, taxes, and other cash expenses are expected to be P 100,000 per month for January through March. Actual sales in November and December and projected sales for January through April are as follows (in thousands)

November	500	January	600	March	650
December	600	February	1000	April	750

On the basis of this information:

a. prepare a cash budget for the months of January, February, and March

b. Determine the amount of additional bank borrowings

necessary to maintain a cash balance of P 50,000 at all times.

c. Prepare a pro forma balance sheet for March 31.

3. *Kingfisher Canning Company* reports the following changes from the preceding year end. Categorize each change as either a source of funds or a use of funds.

Item	Change
Cash	-100
Accounts receivable	700
Inventory	-300
Gross fixed assets	900
Depreciation	1000
Accounts payable	300
Accruals	-100
Long-0term debt	-200
Net profit	600
Dividends	400

4. *Kaiser Corporation* shows the following record of its balance sheets at December 31 (in millions)

Assets	20X1	20X2	Liabilities & Equity	20X1	20X2
Cash	5	3	Notes payable	20	0
Accounts Receivable	15	22	Accounts payable	5	8
Inventories	12	15	Accrued wages	2	2
Fixed Assets, net	50	55	Accrued taxes	3	5
Other assets	8	5	Long-term debt	0	15
			Common stock	20	26
			Retained earnings	40	44
Total assets	90	100	Total liabilities & equity	90	100

Kaiser's statement of income and retained earnings year ended December 31, 20X2:

Net sales		58,000,000.00
Expenses		
Cost of Goods Sold	35,000,000.00	
Selling, general & administrative	6,000,000.00	
Depreciation	4,000,000.00	
Interest	2,000,000.00	47,000,000.00
Net Income before taxes		11,000,000.00
Less : taxes		4,000,000.00
Net Income before taxes		7,000,000.00
Add: Retained earnings 12/31/x1		35,000,000.00
Subtotal		42,000,000.00
Less: Dividends		3,000,000.00
Retained earnings 12/31/x2		39,000,000.00

a. Prepare a source and use of funds statement on a cash basis for 20x2 for the Kaiser Company.

b. Prepare an accounting statement of cash flows.

c. Prepare a source and use of working capital statement for 20x2.

5. *Scheider Corporation* has the following financial statements:

	20x1	20x2		20x1
Cash	4.00	5.00	Accounts payable	8.00
Accounts receivable	7.00	10.00	Notes payable	5.00
Inventory	12.00	15.00	Accrued wages	2.00
Current assets	23.00	30.00	Accrued taxes	3.00
Net plant	40.00	40.00	Current liabilities	18.00
			Long-term debt	20.00
			Common stock	10.00
			Retained earnings	15.00
Total assets	63.00	70.00	Total liabilities & equity	63.00

Scheider Corporation Income Statement

20x2

(in millions)

Sales		95
Cost of Goods Sold	50	
Selling,general, & Administrative expenses	15	
Depreciation	3	
Interest	2	70
Net Income before taxes		25
Taxes		10
Net Income		15

a. Prepare a source and use funds statement for *Scheider Corporation.*
b. Prepare a source and use of working capital statement.

Uses and Limitations of Ratio Analysis

Ratio analysis is used by three main groups : managers, who employ ratios to help analyze, control, and thus improve their firm's operations; credit analysts, including bank loan officers and bond rating analysts who analyze ratios to help more closely at the basic factors that underlie each ratio, which will give you a better idea about how to interpret and use ratios. While ratio provide useful information concerning a company's operations and financial condition it does have limitations that necessitate care and judgment. Some potential problems are as follows:

1. Many large companies operate different divisions in different industries, and such will find it difficult to develop a meaningful set of industry averages. Ratio analysis is more useful for small, narrowly focused firms than for large, multidivisional ones.

2. Most firms want to be better than average, so merely attaining average performance is not necessarily good. As a target for high-level performance, it is best to focus on the industry distorted

firms' balance sheets – recorded value are often substantially different from true values.

3. Seasonal factors can also distort a ratio analysts. For example, the inventory turnover ratio for a food processor will be radically different if the balance sheet figure used for inventory is the one just before versus just after the closing of the canning season. The problem can be minimized by using monthly averages for inventory (and receivables) when calculating turnover ratios.

4. Different accounting practices can distort comparisons. Inventory valuation and depreciation methods can affect financial statements and thus distort comparisons among firms. At the same time, the liability associated with the leased obligation may not be shown as a debt. Leasing can artificially improve both the turnover and the debt ratios.

5. Effective use of financial ratios requires that the financial statements upon which they are based be accurate. Ratio analysis is useful but analysts should be aware of these problems and make adjustments as necessary.

The Basic Earning Power (BEP)

The basic earning power (BEP) ratio is calculated by dividing earnings before interest and taxes (EBIT) by total assets:

Basic earning power ration (BEP) = EBIT/ Total assets

This ratio shows the raw earning power of the firm's assets, before the influence of taxes and leverage, and it is useful for comparing firms with different tax situations and different degrees of financial leverage. Because of its low turnover ratios and low profit margin on sales a company can be getting as high a return on its assets as is the average company in its industry.

Analysis Of Financial Statements

The value of a company is determined by the size, timing, and risk of its expected future free cash flows (FCF). In here, the use of financial statements is shown as it evaluates a company's risk and its ability to generate free cash flows. If management is to maximize a firm's value, it must take advantage of the firm's strengths and correct its weaknesses. Financial statement analysis involves : comparing the company's performance with that of other firms in the same industry and evaluating trends in the firm's financial position over time. These studies help managers identify deficiencies and the n take actions to improve performance.

Financial statements report both on a firm's position at a point in time and on its operations over some past period. The real value of financial statements lies in the fact that they can be used to help predict future earnings, dividends, and free cash flow. From an investor's standpoint, predicting the future is what financial statement analysis is all about, while from management's standpoint, financial is useful both to help anticipate future conditions and, more important, as a starting point for planning actions that will improve the firm's future performance.

Financial ratios are designed to help evaluate financial statements. For example, firm A might have debt of P 5,248,760 and interest charges of P 419,900, while firm B might have debt of P 52,647,980 and interest charges of P 3,948,600 . Which company is stronger? The burden of these debts and the companies ability to repay them , can best be evaluated by comparing : each firm's debt to its assets and interest it must pay to the income it has available for payment of interest. Such comparisons are made by ratio analysis.

Financial Ratios

Financial ratio analysis involves methods of calculating and interpreting financial ratios to assess the firm's performance. The basic inputs to ratio analysis are the firm's income statement and balance sheet. Ratio analysis of a firm's financial statements is of interest to shareholders, creditors, and the firm's own management.

Both present and prospective shareholders are interested in the firm's current and future level of risk and return, which directly affect share price. The firm's creditors are primarily interested in the short-term liquidity of the company and its ability to make interest and principal payments.

A secondary concern of creditors is the firm's profitability; they want assurance that the business is healthy and will continue to be successful. Management, like stockholders, is concerned with all aspects of the firm's financial situation. Thus, it attempts to produce financial ratios that will be considered favorable by both owners and creditors. In addition, management uses ratios to monitor the firm's performance from period to period. Any changes are examined, to isolate developing problems.

Divisions of Financial Ratios

Financial ratios can be divided into four basic categories: liquidity ratios, activity ratios, debt ratio, and profitability ratios. Liquidity, activity, and debt ratios basically measure risk; profitability ratios, measure return. In the near term, the important categories are liquidity, activity, and profitability because these provide the information that is critical to the short-run operation of the firm. Debt ratios are useful primarily when the analyst is sure that the firm will successfully determine the short-run.

As a rule the necessary inputs to an effective financial analysis include, at minimum, the income statement and the balance sheet. Presented in the table 1 below is 2005 and 2004 income statements and balance sheets for ATS Company and table 2 demonstrate ratio calculations:

ATS Company Income Statement (P 000)
For the years ended
December 31

	2005	2004
Sales Revenue	3,074	2,567
Less: Cost of Goods Sold	2,088	1,711
Gross Profits	986	856
Less: Operating Expenses		
Selling Expense	100	108
General & Administrative Expenses	194	187
Lease Expense	35	35
Depreciation Expense	239	223
Total Operating Expense	568	553
Operating Profits	418	303
Less: Interest Expense	93	91
Net Profits before Taxes	325	212
Less: Taxes (rate = 32%)	104	68
Net Profits after Taxes	221	144
Less: Preferred Stock Dividends	10	10
Earnings available for common stockholders	211	134
Earnings per Share(EPS)	2.76	1.75

**Lease expense is shown as a separate item rather than being included as interest expense and amortization, as specified by the FASB for financial reporting purposes. The approach used is consistent with tax-reporting rather than financial procedures.*

**The 32 % tax rate for 2005 results since the company is operating as corporation.*

**Calculating the EPS, the common stock outstanding is 76,262 for 2005.;and 76,244 for 2004 which is obtained by dividing 2005* *earnings of P 211,000 by common stock outstanding of 76,262,EPS IS 2.76, while 2004 EPS of 1.75 is obtained by dividing earnings of 134,000 by 76,244.*

ATS Company

Balance Sheets

(P 000)

December 31

	2005	2004
Assets		
Current Assets		
Cash	363	288
Marketable securities	68	51
Accounts receivable	503	365
Inventories	289	300
Total current assets	1,223	1,004
Gross fixed assets (at cost)		
Land & Buildings	2,072	1,903
Machinery & Machinery	1,866	1,693
Furniture & Fixtures	358	316
Vehicles	275	314
Other (includes financial leaves)	98	96
Total gross fixed assets (at cost)	4,669	4,322
Less: Accumulated depreciation	2,295	2,056
Net fixed assets	2,374	2,266
Total assets	3,597	3,270
Liabilities & stockholders' equity		
Current Assets		
Accounts payable	382	270
Notes payable	79	99
Accruals	159	114
Total current liabilities	620	483
Long-term debt (includes financial leases)	1,023	967
Total liabilities	1,643	1,450
Stockholders' equity		
Preferred stock - cumulative 5%, P100 par, 2,000 shares authorized and issued	200	200

Common stock - P 2.50 par, 100,000 shares authorized, share issued and outstanding in 2005; 76,262; in 2004; 76,244	191	190
Paid-in capital in excess of par on common stock	428	418
Retained earnings	1,135	1,012
Total stockholders' equity	1,954	1,820
Total liabilities & stockholders' equity	3,597	3,270

**In 2005, the firm has a 6-year financial lease requiring annual beginning-of-year payments of P 35,000*

**Four years of the lease have yet to run.*

** Annual principal repayments on a portion of the firm's total outstanding debt amount to P 71,000.*

** The annual preferred stock dividend would be P 5 per share (5% X P 100 par) or a total of P 10,000 annually (P 5 per share X 2,000 shares)*

The Liquidity Ratios

The liquidity of a business firm is measured by its ability to satisfy its short-term obligations as they come due. Liquidity refers to the solvency of the firm's entire financial position – the ease with which it can pay its bills. A liquid asset is one that trades in an active market and can be quickly converted to cash at the going market price, and a firm's liquidity ratios deal this question : Will the firm be able to pay off its debts as they come due over next year or so? A full liquidity analysis requires the use of cash budgets relating the amount of cash and other current assets to current obligations as the analysis provides a quick, easy to use measure of liquidity. The three basic measures of liquidity are : net working capital; the current ratio, and the quick (acid-test) ratio.

Net Working Capital

Although not actually a ratio, is a common measure of a firm's overall liquidity. It is calculated as follows:

Net working capital = current assets – current liabilities

Often the contract under which a long-tem debt is incurred specifically states a minimum level of net working capital that the firm must maintain. This requirement protects creditors by forcing the firm to maintain sufficient operating liquidity. A time-series comparison of the firm's net working capital is often helpful in evaluating its operations.

Current Ratio

Current assets normally include cash, marketable securities, accounts receivable inventories. Current liabilities consist of accounts receivable, short-term notes payable for current maturities of long-term debt, accrued taxes, and other accrued expenses like wages.

One of the most commonly cited financial ratios, measures the firm's ability to meet its short-term obligations. It is shown as follows:

current assets

Current ratio = current liabilities

The current ratio for ATS Company in 2005 is = P 1,223,000/ 620,000 = 1.97

A current ratio of 2.0 is occasionally cited as acceptable, but a value's acceptability depends on the industry in which the firm operates. For example, a current ratio of 1.0 would be considered acceptable for a utility but might be unacceptable for a manufacturing firm. The more predictable a firm's cash flows, the lower the acceptable current ratio. The company is in a business with relatively predictable annual cash flow, its current ratio of 1.97 should be quite acceptable.

If the firm's current ratio is divided into 1.0 and the resulting quotient is subtracted from 1.0, the difference multiplied by 100 represents the percentage by which the firm's current assets can shrink without making it impossible for the firm to cove its current liabilities. For example, a current ratio of 2.0 means that the firm can still cover its current liabilities even if its current assets shrink by 50 percent ([1.0-(1.0/2.0)X]X100)

It is useful to note that a firm's ratio is 1.0, its net working capital is zero. If a firm has a current ratio of less than 1.0, it will have negative net working capital. Net working capital is useful only in comparing the liquidity of the same firm over time. It should not be used to compare the liquidity of different firms, the current ratio should be used instead.

Quick (Acid-test) Ratio

It is similar to the current ratio except that it excludes inventory, which is generally the least liquid current asset. The low liquidity of inventory results from two basic factors: many types of inventory cannot be easily sold because they are partially completed items, special purpose items, and the like; and inventory is typically sold on credit, which means that it becomes an account receivable before being converted into cash. In other words, the extent to which a firm can meet its short-term obligations without relying upon the sale of its inventories. It is computed as follows :

Current assets minus inventory

Quick Ratio = Current liabilities

The quick ratio for ATS Company in 2005 is :

P 1,223,000- P 289,000 = P934,000 = 1.51

P 620,000 P 620,000

A quick ratio of 1.0 or greater is occasionally recommended, but as with the current ratio, an acceptable value depends largely on the industry. The quick ratio provides a better measure of overall liquidity only when a firm's inventory cannot be easily converted into cash. If inventory is liquid, the current ratio is a preferred measure of overall liquidity.

Analyzing Activity

Activity ratios measure the speed with which accounts are converted into sales or cash. With regard to current accounts, measure of liquidity are generally inadequate, because differences in the composition of a firm's current accounts can significantly affect its true liquidity. For example, consider the current assets and liabilities on the balance sheets fro firms A and B . Both firms appear to be equally liquid, because their current ratios are both 2.0 (P 20,000 + P 10,000). However, a closer look at the differences in the composition of current assets and liabilities suggests that firm B is more liquid than firm A, This is true fro two reasons : Firm B has more liquid assets in the form of cash and marketable securities than firm A, which has only a single, relatively illiquid asset in the form of inventories, and firm B's current liabilities are in general more flexible than the single current liability – notes payable – of firm A,

Firm A

Cash	-	Accounts payable	-
Marketable securities	-	Notes payable	10,000
Accounts receivable	-	Accruals	-
Inventories	20,000		
Total current assets	20,000	Total current liabilities	10,000

Firm B

Cash	5,000	Accounts payable	5,000
Marketable securities	5,000	Notes payable	3,000
Accounts receivable	5,000	Accruals	2,000
Inventories	5,000		
Total current assets	20,000	Total current liabilities	10,000

Total current assets 20,000 Total current liabilities 10,000

Inventory Turnover

It is the most commonly measures the activity, or liquidity, of a firm's inventory. It is calculated as follows:

Inventory turnover = cost of goods sold / inventory

Applying ATS Company in 2005 yields: Inventory turnover = P 2,088,000/ P 289,000 = 7.2

The resulting turnover is meaningful only when it is compared with that of other firms in the same industry or to the firm's past inventory turnover. An inventory turnover of 20.0 would not be unusual for a grocery store, whereas a common inventory turnover for an aircraft manufacturer would be 4.0.

Inventory turnover can easily be converted into an average age of inventory by dividing it into 360 – the number of days in a year. For ATS Company, the average age of inventory would be 50.0 days (365 / 7.2). This value can also be viewed as the average number of days' sales in inventory.

Average Collection Period

The average collection period, or average age of accounts receivable, is useful in evaluating credit and collection policies. It is arrived at by dividing the average daily sales into the accounts receivable balance:

Average collection period = accounts receivable / average sales per day

= accounts receivable/ annual sales /360

The average collection period for ATS Company in 2005 is P 503,000/3,074,000/360 = P 503,000/P 8.539 = 58.9 days

The average collection period extends 30-dfay credit terms to customers, an average collection period of 58.9 days may indicate a poorly managed credit or collection department, or both. The prolonged collection period could be the result of an intentional relaxation of credit-term enforcement in response to competitive pressures. If the firm had extended 60-day credit terms, the 58.9-day average collection period would be quite acceptable. Additional information would be required to draw definitive conclusions about the effectiveness of the firm's credit and collection policies.

Average Payment Period

The average payment period, or a average of accounts payable is calculated in the same manner as the average collection period.

Average payment period = accounts payable/ average purchases per day

= accounts payable / annual purchases / 360

Ordinarily, purchases are estimated as a given percentage of cost of goods sold. If we assume that *ATS Company's* purchases equaled 70 percent of its cost of goods sold in 2005, its average payment period is

P 382,000 = P 382,000 = 94.1 days

.70 X P 2,088,00 P 4,060

360

This figure is meaningful only in relation to the average credit terms extended to the firm. If *ATS Company's* suppliers, on the average, have extended 30-day credit terms, an analyst would give it a low credit rating. If the firm has been generally extended 90-day credit terms, its credit would be acceptable. Prospective lenders and suppliers of trade credit are especially interested in the average payment period, because it provides them with a sense of the bill-paying patterns of the firm.

Total Asset Turnover

The total asset turnover indicates the efficiency with which the firm uses its assets to generate sales. The higher a firm's total asset turnover, the more efficiently its assets have been used. This measure is probably of greatest interest to management, because it indicates whether the firm's operations have been financially efficient. Total asset turnover is calculated as follows:

Total asset turnover = Sales / Total assets

The value of ATS Company's total asset turnover is 2005 is P 3,074,000 / P 3,597,000 = .85

The company turns an amount equal to its total assets .85 times a year.

Analyzing Debt

The debt position of the company shows the amount of other people's money being used in attempting to generate profits. The financial analyst is most concerned with long-term debts, because these commit the firm to paying interest, and eventually the principal, over the long-run. Because creditors' claims must be satisfied before earnings can be distributed to shareholders, present and prospective shareholders pay close attention to degree of indebtedness and ability to repay debts. Lenders are also concerned about the firm's indebtedness because the more indebted the firm, the more likely it will be unable to satisfy the creditor's claims. Management must be concerned with indebtedness.

In general, the more debt a firm uses in relation to its total assets, the greater its financial leverage. Financial leverage is the magnification of risk and return introduced through the use of fixed-cost financing such as debt and preferred stock.

The two general types of debt measures the degree of indebtedness and measures the ability to service debts. The degree of indebtedness measures the amount of debt relative to other significant balance sheet amounts. One of the most commonly used measures is the debt ratio.

The second type of debt measure, is the ability to service debt, assesses a firm's ability to make the contractual payments required on a scheduled basis over the life of a debt. Lease payments as well as preferred stock dividend payments also represent scheduled obligations. The firm's ability to pay certain fixed charges is measured using coverage ratios. Higher coverage ratios are preferred, but too high a ratio (above industry norms) may indicate unnecessarily low risk and returns. The lower the firm's coverage ratios, the more risky the firm is considered to be. Riskiness here refers to the firm's ability to pay fixed obligations. If a firm is unable to pay these obligations, it will be in default, and its creditors may seek immediate repayment. Two coverage ratios are : the times interest earned ratio and the fixed-payment coverage ratio.

Debt Ratio

The debt ratio measures the proportion of total assets financed by the firm's creditors. The higher this ratio, the greater the amount of other people's money being used in an attempt to generate profits. The ratio is calculated as follows:

Debt ratio = total liabilities / total assets

The debt ratio for ATS Company in 2005 is P 1,643,000 / P 3,597,000 = .457 = 45.7%

This shows that the company has financed close to half of its assets with debt. The higher this ratio, the greater the firm's degree of indebtedness and the more financial leverage it has.

Time Interest Earned Ratio

The times interest earned ratio, sometimes called the interest-coverage ratio, measures the firm's ability to make contractual interest payments. The higher the value of this ratio, the better able the firm is to fulfill its interest obligations. The times interest earned ratio is calculated as follows:

Earnings before interest and taxes

Times interest earned = interest

Applying this ratio to ATS Company yields the following 2005 value:

P 418,000 = 4.5

Time interest earned = P 93,000

The value of earning before interest and taxes is the same as the figure for operating profits shown in ATS Company' income statement. The firm's times interest earned ratio seems acceptable. As a rule, a value of at least 3.0 – and preferably closer to 5.0 is suggested. If the firm's earnings before interest and taxes were to shrink by 78% [(4.5 – 1.0) / 4.5], the firm would still be able to pay the P 93,000 in interest it owes. Thus, it has a good margin of safety.

Fixed – Payment Coverage Ratio

The fixed-payment coverage ratio measures the firm's ability to meet all fixed payment obligations. Like the times interest earned ratio, the higher this value, the better. Loan interest, principal payments on debt, scheduled lease payments, and preferred stock dividends are commonly included in this ratio. The formula for the fixed-payment coverage ratio is as follows:

Earnings before interest and taxes + lease payments

Interest + lease payments + [(principal payments+preferred stock dividends)X[(1/(1-T)]

Where T is the corporate tax rate applicable to the firm's income. The term 1/(1-T) is included to adjust the after-tax principal and preferred stock dividend payments back to a before-tax equivalent that is consistent with the before-tax values of all other terms. Applying the formula to ATS Company's 2005 data yields :

Fixed payment coverage ratio =

$$\frac{P\ 418{,}000 + P\ 35{,}000}{P\ 93{,}000 + P\ 35{,}000+[(71{,}000+P\ 10{,}000)\ X[(1/(1\text{-}0.32)]}$$

= P 453,000 / P 242,000 = 1.9

Earnings available are almost twice as large as its fixed-payment obligations. Thus, the firm appears able to safely meet its fixed payments.

Analyzing Profitability

There are many measures of profitability. As a group, these measures evaluate the firm's earnings with respect to a given level of sales, a certain level of assets, the owners' investment, or share value. Without profits, a firm could not attract outside capital. Present owners and creditors would become concerned about the company's future and attempt to recover their funds. Owners, creditors, and management pay close attention to generating profits due to the great importance placed on earnings in the marketplace.

Common-Size Income Statement

Common-size income statements for 2005 and 20054 for ATS Company are presented and evaluated in the table below. The statements reveal that the firm's cost of goods sold increased from 66.7 percent of sales in 2004 to 67.9 percent in 2005, resulting in a worsening gross profit margin. There is a decrease in total operating expenses, the firm's net profit margin rose from 5.8 percent of sales in 2004 to 7.5 percent in 2005. The decrease in expenses more than compensated for the increase in the cost of goods sold. A decrease in the firm's 2005 interest expense (3.0 percent of sales versus 3.5 percent in 2004) added to the increase in 2005 profits.

ATS Company Common- Size Income Statements

	For the years ended December 31		Evaluation
	2005	2004	1999-2000
Sales revenue	100.0%	100.0%	same
Less: Cost of goods sold	67.90	66.70	worse
(1) Gross Profit Margin	32.1%	33.3%	worse
Less: Operating expenses			
Selling expense	3.30%	4.20%	better
General & administrative expenses	6.30	7.30	better
Less: Expense	1.10	1.30	better
Depreciation Expense	7.80	8.70	better
Total Operating Expense	18.5%	21.5%	better
(2) Operating profit margin	13.60%	11.80%	better
Less: Interest Expense	3.00	3.50	better
Net Profits before Taxes	10.60%	8.30%	better
Less: Taxes	3.10	2.50	worse
(3) Net Profit Margin	7.50%	5.80%	better

Taxes as a percent of sales increased between 2004 and 2005 due to differing costs and expenses whereas the average tax rates (taxes +net profits before taxes) for 2004 and 2005 remained about the same – 32% and 29% profits.

Gross Profit Margin

The gross profit margin measures the percentage of each peso sales remaining after the firm has paid for its goods. The higher the gross profit margin, the better, and the lower the relative cost of merchandise sold. The opposite case is also true, as ATS Company example shows. The gross profit margin is computed as follows:

Sales – Cost of goods sold = Gross Profit

Gross Profit Margin = sales Sales

The value for ATS Company's gross profit margin for 2005 is

P 3,074,000 - P 2,088,000 = P 986,000 = 32.1%

P 3,074,000 P 3,074,000

This value is labeled (1) on the common-size income statement shown above.

Operating Profit Margin

This measures the percentage of each peso sales remaining after all costs and expenses other than interest and taxes are deducted. It represents the pure profits earned on each peso sales. Operating profits are pure because they measure only the profits earned on operations and ignore any financial and government charges (interest and taxes) A high operating profit margin is preferred. The operating profit margin is calculated as follows:

Operating Profits

Operating Profit Margin = Sales

The value for ATS Company's operating profit margin for 2004 is : P 418.000 / P 3,074,000 = 13.6%

This value is labeled (2) on the common-size income statement in the table shown above.

Net Profit Margin

The net profit margin measures the percentage of each peso sales remaining after all costs and expenses, including interest and taxes, have been deducted. The higher the firm's net profit margin, the better. The net profit margin is a commonly cited measure of the firm's success with respect to earnings on sales. Good net profit margins differ considerably across industries. A net profit margin of 1 percent or less would not be unusual for a grocery store, whereas a net profit margin of 10 percent would be low for a retail store. The net profit margin is calculated as follows:

Net profits after taxes

Net profit margin = sales

ATS Company's net profit margin for 2004 is : P 231,000 / P 2,074,000 = 7.5%

This value is labeled (3) on the common-size income statement in the table above.

Return on Total Assets (ROA)

The return on total assets (ROA) also called the return on investment (ROI), measures the firm's overall effectiveness in generating profits with its available assets. The higher the firm's return on total assets, the better. The return on total assets is computed as follows :

Net profits after taxes

Return on total assets = total assets

ATS Company's return on total assets in 2004 is : P 231,000 / P 3,597,000 = 6.4%

To assess the company's 6.4 percent return on total assets, appropriate cross-sectional and time-series data that would be required.

Return on Equity (ROE)

The return on equity (ROE) measures the return earned on the owners' investment in the firm. The higher this return, the better off are the owners. Return on equity is computed as follows :

Net profits after taxes

Return on equity = stockholders' equity

The ratio for ATS Company in 2005 is : P 231,000/P 1,954,000 = 11.8%

To evaluate ATS Company's 11.8 percent return on equity, appropriate cross- sectional and time-series data would be required.

Earnings Per Share (EPS)

The firm's earnings per share (EPS) are generally of interest to present of prospective stockholders and to management. The earnings per share represent the number of peso earned on behalf of each outstanding share of common stock. Earnings per share are calculated as follows :

*_Net Income_*

Earnings per share = EPS = Common shares outstanding

The value of ATS Company's earnings per share in 2005 is P 221,000/ P 76,262 = P 2.90

Price / Earnings (P/E) Ratio

The Price/Earnings ratio is commonly used to assess the owner's appraisal of share value. The P/E ratio measures the amount investors are willing to pay for each dollar of the firm's earnings. This ratio shows the degree of confidence that investors have in the firm's future performance. The higher the P/E ratio, the greater the inventor confidence. The P/E ratio is computed as follows :

Market price per share of common stock

Price/earnings (P/E) ration = earnings per share

If ATS Company's common stock at the end of 2005 was selling at 32% (i.e. P 32.25), using the earnings per share (EPS) of P 2.90 from the income statement in the table , the P/E ratio at year-end 2005 is : P 32.25? P 2.90 = 11.1

Thus, the investors were paying P 11.10 for each P 1.00 of earnings.

Note that EPS calculations is based on earnings after preferred dividends – that is, on the net income available to common stockholders. Calculations are as follows:

<u>Dividends paid to common stockholders</u>

Dividends per share =DPS Common shares outstanding

<u>Total common equity</u>

Book value per share = BVPS = Common shares outstanding

<u>Net Income + Depreciation + Amortization</u>

Cost flow per share = CFPS = Common shares outstanding

The Du Pont Equation

Using Artuz Company as the model illustration, the various expense items are listed and then summed to obtain its total cost, which is subtracted from sales to obtain the company's net income. When we divide net income by sales, we find that 3.8 percent of each peso sales is left for stockholders. The profit margin is low or trending down, one can examine individual expense items to identify and then correct problems. The right side of those figures in the table lists the various categories of assets, totals them and then divides sales by total assets to find the number of times Artuz Company turns its assets over each year.

The company's total assets turnover ratio is 1.5 times. The profit margin times the total assets turnover is called the Du Pont equation and it gives the rate of return on assets (*ROA)*

ROA=Profit margin x Total asset turnover

=Net income x Sales

Sales x Total Assets

= 3.8% x 1.5 = 5.7%

Artuz Company made 3.8 percent, or 3.8 cents, on each peso sales, and were turned over 1.5 times during the year. The company earned return of 5.7 percent on its assets.

If the company were finance only with common equity, the rate of return on assets (ROA) and the return on equity (ROE) would be the same because the total assets would equal the common equity:

ROA = Net Income = Net Income = ROE

Total Assets Common equity

This equality holds if and only if Total assets = Common equity, that is, if the company uses no debt. Artuz Company does use debt, so its common equity is less than total assets. The return to the common stockholders (ROE) must be greater than the ROA of 5.7 percent. To find the ROE, multiply the rate of return on assets

(ROA) by the equity multiplier, which is the ratio of assets to common equity.

Equity multiplier = Total assets

Common equity

Firms that use a large amount of debt financing (a lot of leverage) will necessarily have a high equity multiplier – the more the debt, the less the equity, hence the higher the equity multiplier. Artuz Company's return on equity (ROE) depends on its ROA and its use of leverage.

ROE = ROA x Equity multiplier

= Net Income x Total assets

Total assets Common equity

5.7% x P 2,000/P 896

5.7% x 2.23

=12.7%

We can combine equations 1 and 2 to form the extended Du Pont equation which shows how the profit margin, the assets turnover ration and equity multiplier combine to determine the ROE.

ROE = (Profit margin) (Total assets turnover)(Equity multiplier)

= Net Income x Sales x Total Assets

Sales total assets Common equity

ROE = (3.8%)(1.5)(2.23)

= 12.7%

The 12.7 percent rate of return could, of course, be calculated directly : both and the total assets cancel, leaving net income/ common equity = P 113.5/P89 = 12%. The Du Pont equation shows how the profit margin, the assets turnover, and the use of debt interest to determine the return on equity.

Review Questions

1. What additional information is needed to assess the reasonableness of the firm's average collection period and average payment period ratios?

2. What is financial leverage? What ratio can be used to measure the firm's degree of indebtedness? What ratios are used to assess the firm's ability to service debts?

3. What is a common-size income statement? Which three ratios of profitability are found on this statement?

4. What would explain a company's having a high gross profit margin and a low net profit margin?

1. Distinguish return on total assets (ROA) from return on equity (ROE), and earnings per share 9EPS). Which measure is probably of greatest interest to owners ? Why?

1. What is the price/earnings (P/E) ratio? How does it relate to investor confidence I the firm's future ? Is the P/E ratio a true measure of profitability?

Problems: Solutions in Appendix D

1. The earnings per share (EPS) Of *Wallex Technologies, Inc.* was P 4 last year, and it paid a Php 2 dividend. Total retained earnings increased by P 12million during the year, when book value per share at year-end was P 40. Wallex has no preferred stocks and no new common stock was issued during the year. If Wallex' year-end debt (which equals its total liabilities) was P 120 million, what was the comparative year-end debt/assets ratio?

2. *Kerdex & Company* has the following data (in million pesos)

:

Cash & marketable securities	100.00
Fixed Assets	283.50
Sales	1,000.00
Net Income	50.00
Quick ratio	2.0X
Current ratio	3.0X
DSO	40.55 days
ROE	12%

Kerdex has no preferred stock – only common equity, current liabilities, and long-term debt.

a. Find Kerdex's accounts receivable (A/R); current liabilities; current assets; total assets; ROA; common equity, and long-term debt.

b. You may find Kerdex's accounts receivable = Php111.1 million. If Kercex could reduce its DSO from 40.55 days to 30.4 days while holding other things constant, how much cash would it generate? If this cash were used to buy back common stock (at book value), thus reducing the amount of common equity, how would this affect; ROE, the ROA, and the total debt/total assets ratio?

3, The current assets of *Eastwood Products,Inc.* equal to Php 3million. The company's current ratio is 1.5, and its quick ratio is 1.0. What is the firm's level of current liabilities? What is the firm's level of inventories? *(liquidity ratios)*

4. *Bread & Butter Enterprises* has a DSO of 40 days. The company's average daily sales are Php 20,000. What is the level of its

accounts receivable? Assume there are 365 days in a year. (*Days sales outstanding)*

5. *Brad & Saints, Ltd.* has as an equity multiplier of 2.4. The company's assets are financed with some combination of long-term debt and common equity,. What is the company's debt ratio? (*Debt ratio)*

6. *D & D Dealers* has an ROA of 10 percent, a 2 percent profit margin, and a return on equity equal to 15 percent. What is the company's total assets turnover? What is the firm's equity multiplier? (*Du pont analysis)*

7. Your are given the following relationship for the *Brewer Corporation*. Assume the following data: *(ratio calculations)*

Sales/Total assets 1.5 X

Return on assets (ROA) 3%

Return on equity (ROE) 5%

Calculate Brewer's profit margin and debt ratio.

8. The current assets of *Percy & Tom Company* is P 1,312,500 and P 525,000 in current liabilities. Its initial inventory level is P 375,000, and it will raise funds as additional notes payable and use them to increase inventory. How much can *Percy & Tom Company's* short term debt (notes payable) increase without pushing its current ratio below 2.0? What will be the firm's quick ratio after Percy has raised the maximum amount of short-term funds? *(liquidity ratio)*

9. *Kent & Haley Company* had a quick ratios of 1.4, a current ratio of 3.0, an inventory turnover of 6 times, total current assets of P 810,000, and cash and marketable securities of P 120,000. What were Kent & Haley Company's annual sales and its DSO? *(ratio calculations)*

10. The *A.S. Corporation* has P 500,000 of debt outstanding, and it pays an interest rate of 10 percent annually; AS Corporation's annual sales are P 2million, its average tax rate is 30 percent, and its net profit margin on sales is 5 percent. If the company does not

maintain a TIE ratio of at least 5 times, its bank will refuse to renew the loan, and bankruptcy will result. What is AS Corporation's TIE ratio? *(time-interest-earned)*

11. *Jeff & Company* has the following data and industry averages :

a. Calculate the indicated ratios for Jess.
b. Construct the extended Du Pont equation for both Jeff and the industry.
c. Outline Jeff's strengths and weaknesses as revealed by your analysis.
d. Suppose Jeff had doubled its sales as well as its inventories, accounts receivable, and common equity during 2005. How would that information affect the validity of your ratio analysis? (Hint: Think about averages and the effects of rapid growth on ratios if averages are not used. No calculations are needed)

Jeff & Company : Balance Sheet as of December 31, 2005 (in thousands)

Cash	77,500.00	Accounts Payable	129,000.00
Receivables	336,000.00	Notes Payable	84,000.00
Inventories	241,500.00	Other Current Liabilities	117,000.00
Total Current Assets	655,000.00	Total current liabilities	330,000.00
Net Fixed assets	292,500.00		
		Long-term debt	256,500.00
		Common equity	361,000.00
Total assets	947,500.00	Total liabilities & equity	947,500.00

Jeff & Company : Income Statement for year ended December 31, 2005 (in thousands)

Sales	1,607,500.00
Cost of goods sold	1,392,500.00
Selling, general, & administrative expenses	145,000.00
Earnings before interest & taxes (EBIT)	70,000.00
Interest expense	24,500.00
Earnings before taxes (EBIT)	45,500.00
Income taxes (32%)	14,560.00
Net Income	30,940.00

Ratio	Jeff	Industry Average
Current assets/current liabilities		2.0x
Days sales outstanding		35 days
Sales/inventory		6.7x
Sales/fixed assets		12.1x
Sales/total assets		3.0x
Net income/sales		1.20%
Net income/total assets		3.60%
Net income/common equity		9.00%
Total debt/total assets		60.00%

Ratio	Jeff Industry Average
Current assets/current liabilities	2.0x
Days sales outstanding	35 days
Sales/inventory	6.7x
Sales/fixed assets	12.1x
Sales/total assets	3.0x
Net income/sales	1.20%
Net income/total assets	3.60%
Net income/common equity	9.00%
Total debt/total assets	60.00%

1. The balance sheet and sales information of *Lance Industries* using the following data are as follows:

Debt ratio : 50%

Quick ratios: 0.80 X

Total assets turnover:
1.5X

Days sales outstanding: 36.5 days

Gross profit margin on sales: (Sales- Cost of goods sold/Sales = 25%

Inventory turnover ratio: 5X

Balance Sheet		Accounts Payable	
Cash		Long-term debt	60,000.00
Accounts Receivable		Common stock	
Inventories		Retained earnings	97,500.00
Fixed assets		Total liabilities & equity	
Total assets turnover: 1.5X	300,000.00	Cost of goods sold	
Sales			

Chapter 8

CAPITAL BUDGETING & CASH FLOWS

Capital Budgeting Process

Capital budgeting is the process of evaluating and selecting long-term investments consistent with the firm's goal of owner wealth maximization. Firms typically make a variety of long-term investments, but the most common for the manufacturing firm is in fixed assets, which include property (land), plant, and equipment. These assets, often referred to as earning assets, generally provide the basis for the firm's earning power and value.

Long-term investments represent sizable outlays of funds that commit a firm to some course of action. The firm needs procedures to analyze and properly select those investments. It must be able to measure relevant cash flows and apply appropriate decision techniques. Fixed assets, as time lapses, may become obsolete or may require an overhaul; at these points, too, financial decisions may be required.

Firms typically make a variety of long-term investments, but the most common for the manufacturing firm is in fixed assets, which include property (land), plant, and equipment. These assets often referred to as earning assets, generally provide the basis for the firm's earning power and value.

Capital budgeting and financing decisions are treated separately. Once the proposed investment has been determined to be acceptable, the financial manager then chooses the best financing method.

Steps in Capital Budgeting Process

The capital budgeting process consists of five distinct but interrelated steps. It begins with proposal generation, followed by review and analysis, decision-making, implementation, and follow-up.

1. Proposal generation - Capital expenditures are made at all levels within a business organizations. Firms offer cash incentives or rewards for proposals that are ultimately adopted. Capital expenditure proposals typically travel from the originator to a reviewer at a higher level in the organization. Proposals that require large outlays will be much more carefully scrutinized than less costly ones.

2. Review and Analysis - Proposals are formally reviewed: to assess the appropriateness in light of the firm's overall objectives and plans and, more important; to evaluate their economic validity. The proposed costs and benefits are estimated and then converted into a series of relevant cash flows. Various capital budgeting techniques are applied to these cash flows to measure the investment merit of the potential outlay.

3. Decision-making - Capital budgeting determines the organization level at which the expenditure decision is made. Firms typically delegate capital expenditure authority on the basis of certain currency limits. The board of directors reserves the right to make final decisions on capital expenditures requiring outlays beyond a certain amount. Inexpensive capital expenditures, such as the purchase of a tools for P750 are treated as operating outlays not requiring formal analysis. Firms operating under critical time constraints with respect to production often give the plant manager the power to make decisions necessary to keep the production line moving.

4. Implementation - Funding is made available after a proposal has been approved and the implementation phase begins. For minor outlays, the expenditure is made and payment is rendered. For major

expenditures, greater control is required. Often the expenditures for a single proposal may occur in phases, each outlays requiring the signed approval of company officers.

5. Follow – up - This involves monitoring the results during the operating phase of a project. Comparison of actual cots and benefits with those expected and those of previous projects is vital. When actual outcomes deviate from projected outcomes, action may be required to cut the costs, improve benefits, or possibly terminate the project. Analysis of deviations of actual from forecast values provides data that can be used to improve the capital budgeting process, particularly the accuracy of cash flow estimates.

Principles of Capital Investment

A business firm incurs a current cash outlay for benefits when a business firm makes a capital investment to be realized in the future. A proposed investment is judged by its expected return.

The objective of capital budgeting is of course, the presentation and analysis of the rate of return on investment projects which necessitates the holding of constant the financing and dividend decisions of the firm. However, this does not alter the business-risk complexion of the firm as perceived by suppliers of capital.

This involves administrative framework of capital investments such as : generation of investment proposals; estimation of cash flows for the proposals; evaluation of cash flows; selection of projects based on an acceptance criterion; continual reevaluation of investment projects after their acceptance.

With respect to this point, post completion audits of projects are essential to provide information on forecasting biases to serve financial control purposes, and to guide future capital investment decisions as to which type of projects are desirable and which are not. Although many companies have capital budgeting systems, fewer have systematic post audits of projects accepted. Depending on the firm involved, investment proposals can emanate from various sources. For purposes of analysis, projects may be classified into one of five categories:

1. new products or expansion of existing products;
2. replacement of equipment or buildings;
3. research and development;
4. exploration;
5. other.

The fifth category comprises miscellaneous items, such as the expenditure of funds to comply with certain health standards or the acquisition of a pollution-control device. For a new product, the proposal usually originates in the marketing department. On the other hand, a proposal to replace a piece of equipment with model usually emanates from the operations area of the firm. Efficient administrative procedures are needed for channeling investment requests.

Most firms screen proposals at multiple levels of authority. For a proposal originating in the production area, the hierarchy of authority might run from : section chiefs to plant managers to the vice president of operations; to a capital expenditures committee under the financial managers; to the president to the board of directors. The approval of the proposal usually depends on its size. The greater the capital outlay, the greater the number of screens usually required . Plant managers may be able to approve moderate-sized projects on their own, but only higher levels of authority approve larger ones. Because from firm to firm, it is not possible to generalize The best procedure will depend on the circumstances.

The level and type of capital expenditure appear to be important to investors, as they convey information about the expected future growth of earnings. They find that an increase in capital expenditure intentions, relative to prior expectations, results in increased stock returns around the time of the announcement, and vice versa for an unexpected decrease. Thus, one of the most important tasks in capital budgeting is estimating future cash flows for a project. The final results are really as good as the accuracy of our estimates because cash, not income, is central to all decisions of the firm, we express whatever benefits we expect from a project in terms of cash flows rather than income. The firm invests cash now in the hope of receiving cash returns in a greater amount in the future. Only cash receipts can be reinvested in the firm or paid to stockholders in the form of dividends. In capital budgeting, good debtors may get credit, but effective managers get cash.

For each investment proposal, we need to provide information on expected future cash flows on an after-tax basis. The information must be provided on an incremental basis, in order to analyze the difference between the cash flows of the firm with and without the project. If a firm contemplates a new product that is likely to compete with existing products, it is not appropriate to express cash flows in terms of the estimated sales of the new product. To illustrate the information needed for a capital budgeting decision, consider the following situation. Dick & Jane Garments Company is considering the introduction of a new clothing line. To launch the product line, the company with the need to spend P 150,000 for special equipment and the initial advertising campaign. The marketing department envisions the product life to be 6 years and expects incremental sales revenue to be:

Year	1	2	3	4	5	6
Inflow	60,000.00	120,000.00	160,000.00	180,000.00	110,000.00	50,000.0(

Cash outflows include labor and maintenance costs, material costs, and various other expenses associated with the product. As with sales, these costs must be estimated on an incremental basis, In addition to these outflows, the company need to pay higher taxes if the new product generates higher profits, and this incremental outlay must be included. Cash outflows should not include interest costs on debt employed to finance the project. Such costs are embodied in the required rate of return . To deduct interest charges from net cash flows would result in double counting.

> Suppose that on the basis of these considerations, Dick & Jane Garments estimates total incremental cash outflows to be:

Year	1	2	3	4	5	6
Outflow	40,000.00	70,000.00	100,000.00	100,000.00	70,000.00	40,000.00

Depreciation is a non cash expense, that is why it is not included in these outflows. The expected net cash flows from the project are:

	Initial Cost	1	2	3	4	5
Cash inflow		60,000.00	120,000.00	160,000.00	180,000.00	110,0(
Cash outflow	150,000.00	40,000.00	70,000.00	100,000.00	100,000.00	70,00(
Net cash flow	(150,000.00)	20,000.00	50,000.00	60,000.00	80,000.00	40,00(

Thus, for an initial cash outflows of P 150,000 the company expects to generate net cash flows of P 20,000, P 50,000, P 60,000, P 80,000, P 40,000, and P 10,000 over the next 6 years. These cash flows represent the relevant information we need to judge the attractiveness of the project. The development of cash flow data of this sort is facilitated greatly by the use of a spreadsheet program.

The net cash flows for this example are plotted in the top panel and notice that the initial cash outlay, or investment, is followed by positive and increasing net cash flows through year 4, after which they drop off as the project becomes older. Many other patterns are possible, both with respect to the life of the project and to the annual cash flows. In the middle panel, the initial cash outlay is followed by a stream of eight equal net cash inflows. In the bottom panel, two distinct investment phases are shown. The first is at time 0 and continues into year 1 where there are heavy advertising and promotion expenses . In year 4, additional investment is needed to upgrade production capability and to promote the product some more. These outlays more than offset operating cash inflows, so there is net cash outflow for the year. In the next two years, the project generates net cash inflows. The project terminates at the end of year 7. At that time, a salvage value is realized that results in a higher net cash inflow than in year 6, These examples illustrate that the patterns of expected net cash flows can vary considerably over time, depending on the project.

Decisions and Replacement Decisions

In an example of replacement decision example involving taxes, we consider the purchase of a new machine to replace an old one, and we need to obtain cash-flow information to evaluate the attractiveness of this project. The purchase price of the new machine is P 18,500, and it will require an additional P 1,500 to install, bringing the total cost of P 20,000. We can sell the old machine for its depreciated book value of P 2,000. The initial net cash outflow for the investment project, therefore, is P 18,000. The new machine should cut labor and maintenance costs and effect other cash savings totaling P 7,100 a year before taxes for each of the next 5 years, after which it will probably not provide any savings, nor will it have a salvage value. These savings represent the net savings to the firm if it replaces the old machine with the new. With the difference the cash flows resulting from the two alternatives; continuing with the old machine or replacing it with a new one.

Funds and Capital Budgeting

Availability of funds for capital expenditures affects the firm's decisions. If a firm has unlimited funds for investment, making capital budgeting decision is quite simple; All independent projects that will provide returns greater than some predetermined level can be accepted. Firms are not in such a situation they instead operate under capital rationing. This means that they have only a fixed number of pesos or dollars available for capital expenditures and that numerous projects will compete for these currencies. Therefore the firm must ration its funds by allocating them to projects that will maximize share value.

Two basic approaches to capital budgeting decisions are available. The accept-reject approach involves evaluating capital expenditure proposals to determine whether they meet the firm's minimum acceptance criterion. This approach can be utilized when the firm has unlimited funds, as a preliminary step when evaluating mutually exclusive projects, or in a situation in which capital must be rationed.

The second method, the ranking approach, involves ranking projects on the basis of some predetermined measure, such as the rate of return. The project with the highest return is ranked first, and the project with the lowest return is ranked last. Ranking is useful in selecting the best of a group of mutually exclusive projects and in evaluating projects with a view to capital rationing.

Searching for Initial Investment

Initial investment refers to the relevant cash outflows to be considered when evaluating a prospective capital expenditure. Initial investment occurs at time zero – the time at which the expenditure is made,. The initial investment is calculated by subtracting all cash inflows occurring at time zero from all cash outflows occurring at time zero.

The cash flows that must be considered in determining the initial investment associated with a capital expenditure are the installed cost of the new asset, the after-tax proceeds (if any) from the sale of an old asset, and the change (if any) in net working capital. The format is as follows:

Initial cost of new asset =

Cost of new asset

=+ *Installation cost*

- *after-tax proceeds from sale of old asset =*

Proceeds from sale of old asset

"+- *tax on sale of old asset*

= *Change in net working capital / Initial investment*

Cash Flow Patterns : Conventional & Non-Conventional

Cash flow patterns associated with capital investment projects can be classified as conventional or non-conventional. A conventional cash flow pattern, constitutes an initial outflow followed by only a series of inflows. Example, a firm may spend P 500,000 today and a result to receive equal annual cash inflows of P1,000,000 each year for the next 8 years.

Non-conventional cash flow pattern is one in which an initial outflow is not followed by only a series of inflows. Example, the purchase of a machine may require an initial cash outflow of P1 million and may generate cash inflows of P250,000 each year for 4 years. In the fifth year after purchase, an outflow of P 400,000 may be required to overhaul the machine, after which it generates inflows of P 250,000 each year for 5 more years. Difficulties often arise in evaluating projects with non conventional patterns of cash flow.

Cash Flow Components

Decisions concerning the purchase of fixed assets must apparently be based upon the effect of future cash flows. Since a long time span is involved, estimates have considerable room for error. A project's cash flows will fall into one of three categories:

1. *Cash outlays for investment*; - determining the amount of cash outflow

involved in the purchase of a fixed or other long-term asset may appear to be simple. Care must be exercised. It is the net cash outflow that is figured out. Some offsetting cash inflows will often result from the purchase of an asset and will be received at approximately the same time that the payments for the investment are made. Tax rules are such that if the old machine is traded in rather than sold the book loss adds to the depreciable base of the new machine. The tax saving occurs during the life of the new machine and affects the cash inflows over the life of the new machine rather than the initial outflow.

Example:

In order to clarify the calculation of the initial outlay, consider that the company has a 50% marginal tax bracket. This company is considering the purchase of a new machine for P{90,000 which will be depreciated using the straight-line method down to a salvage value of zero in 10 year. The new machine will replace an existing machine originally purchased for P 30,000 ten years ago. The existing machine is being depreciated by the straight-line method down to zero over its expected life of 20 years. In order to put this machine in running order, it is necessary to pay transportation charges of P 1,500 and installation charges of P 7,500. Because the new machine will work faster than the old one, it will require an increase in goods-in-process inventory of P 11,250. Finally, the old machine can be sold for P 18,900 to a scrap dealer.

The installation cost of the new machine would the P 90,000 plus P 1,500 transportation and P 7,500 installation fees, for a total of P99,000. Additional outflows are associated with taxes incurred on the sale of the old machine and with increased investment in inventory. Although the old machine had a book value of P 15,000, it was sold for P 18,000. The increased taxes on resulting capital gain will be equal to selling price of the old machine less its depreciated book value times the firm's marginal tax rates (P 18000-P 15,000)(.50) or P 1,500. The effect of their assets in the block has been ignored. The increased in goods in process inventory of P 11,250 must also be considered part of the initial outlay, with an offsetting inflow of P 11,250 corresponding to the recapture of this inventory occurring at the termination of the project, In effect, the firm invests, P 11,250 in inventory now, resulting an initial cash outlay, and liquidates this inventory in 10 years resulting in a cash inflow at the end of the project. The total outlays associated with the new machine are P 99,000 for its installed cost, P 1,500 in increased taxes, and P 11,250 in investment in inventory, for a total of P 111,750. This is somewhat offset by the sale of old machine for P 18,000. Thus, the net initial outlay associated with this project is P 93,750. This is summarized as follows:

Outflows:		
Purchase price	90,000.00	
Shipping fee	1,500.00	
Installation fee	7,500.00	
Installation cost of machine		99,000.00
Increased taxes(P 18,000-P15,000)(.50)		1,500.00
Increased investment in inventory		11,250.00
Total outflows		111,750.00
Inflows:		
Salvage value of old machine		18,000.00
Net initial outlay		93,750.00

1. *Cash inflows from initial investments* - The amount of future cash inflows

expected from an investment may be difficult to calculate accurately. These flows may continue for a very long period, and apparently, the degree of accuracy in the estimate is somewhat function of time. By using cash flows rather than profit, one incorporates the same concept into capital budgeting. The cash flows can be calculated either before or after the added taxes resulting from the added taxable profit. Obviously a consistent approach must be adhered to either before or after tax figures must be used for all projects being compared and for both the cost of capital and cash flows. Because of the nature of tax regulations, using after-tax figures throughout will make the calculations simpler and reduce the chances fro inaccuracy.

The added cash flow expected from a project may come from increase in revenues or from reduction in expenses. There is really little analytical difference between a machine that will increase the net annual cash flow and a machine that will reduce the annual operating cost. The pertinent figure is the expected net incremental cash flow. The source is quite irrelevant except in terms of risk.

The net incremental cash will be received throughout the year. There is a difference in present value between an expected inflow of P 1 each day for a year and an expected for P 365 at the end of the year. This difference will be ignored for the sake of simplicity, and the assumption will be made that all cash inflows are expected at the end of each year.

Cash outflows related to the cost of money will be treated different from other cash outflows. The cost of capital will be used either as a hurdle rate that must be exceeded by the anticipated rate of return or as the rate of discount. If cash outflows connected with the financing of a project were deducted from anticipated net incremental inflows, this would constitute a double counting.

Example 2 in relation to example number 1, assuming that purchasing the machine is expected to reduce salaries by P 18,000 per year and fringe benefits by P 1,500 annually, because it will take only one man to operate, whereas the old machine requires to operators. In addition, the cost of defects will fall from P 9,000 per year to P 1,500. However, maintenance expenses will increase by P 1,500 annually,. The annual depreciation on this new machine is P 9,900 per year, while the depreciation expense lost with the sale of the old machine is P 1,500 for each of the next 10 years. Annual depreciation on the new machine is determined by taking its depreciable value – that is, the cost of the new machine plus any expenses necessary to put it in operating order –subtracting out the salvage value, and dividing by the machine's expected life. For the new machine these calculations are reflected as follows:

New machine purchase price	90,000.00
Transportation charges	1,500.00
Installation fee	7,500.00
total depreciable value	99,000.00
Less: Salvage value	-
Divide by expected life	99,000/10
Equals: Annual depreciation	9,900.00

Since the depreciation on the old machine is P 1,500 per year, the increased depreciation will be from P 1,500 per year to P 9,900 per year, or an increase of P 8,400 per year. Although this increase in depreciation expenses is not a cash flow item, it does affect cash flows by reducing the book profits, which in turn reduces taxes.

In order to determine the annual net cash flows resulting from the acceptance of the project, the net savings before taxes using both book profit and cash flows must be found. The additional taxes are then calculated based upon the pre-tax book profit. For this example, the table below shows the determination of the differential cash flows on an after-tax basis, thus the different cash flows over the project's life are P 17,700

Calculation of the Differential Cash Flow

	Book Profit	Cash Flow
Savings:		
Reduced salary	18,000.00	18,000.00
Reduced fringe benefits	1,500.00	1,500.00
Reduced defects		
(P9,000-P 1,500)	7,500.00	7,500.00
Costs:		
Increased maintenance expenses	(1,500.00)	(1,500.00)
Increased depreciation		
expenses(P 9,900-P1,500)	(8,400.00)	
Net savings before taxes	18,600.00	27,000.00
Taxes (32%)	(5,952.00)	(8,640.00)
Net cash flow after taxes	12,648.00	18,360.00

1. *Terminal cash flow* - When an asset's economic life is terminated there is frequently some value left in the asset. The asset may still be useable in its current form. For example, a pump on a depleted oil well may transfer the pump and saves the purchase price of another pump or if the firm sells the pump to another firm there is a cash inflows created. In the transfer case this case inflow is in the form of a cost savings and in the case of the sale the cash salvage cash flow before tax created. Alternatively, if the asset is worn out there may be some scrap value associated with it. If, for example, the pump is worn out and beyond repair it may still have value as scrap metal. The sale of the asset as asset creates a salvage cash flow before tax in the year of abandonment. Additionally the firm will recover any increased net working capital that was committed to the project in the initial time period.

Example 3

The depreciated book value of the machine at the termination date will be equal to zero. However, there will be a cash flow generated from the liquidation of the P 11,250 in work-in-process inventory. Therefore, the expected total terminal cash flow equals P 11,250. If we are to draw a cash flow diagram it would have an initial outlay of P 93,750 differential cash flows during years 1 through 10 of P 17,700, and an additional terminal cash flow at the end of year 10 of P 11,250. The cash flow occurring in year 10 is P 28,950, the sum of the differential cash flow in year 10 of P 17,700, and the terminal cash flow of P 11,250.

```
17,700   17,700   17,700   17,700   17,700   17,700   17,700
  |        |        |        |        |        |        |
  \/       \/       \/       \/       \/       \/       \/
 ____________________________________________________________
|
\/|        |        |        |        |        |        |
  1        2        3        4        5        6        7
```

Net cash flows do not cover all possible cash flows, while determining the incremental after tax, as they do set up a framework under which almost any situation can be.

All benefits expected from a proposed project must be measured on a cash flow basis. Cash inflows represent currencies that can be spent, not merely, accounting profits. A simple technique for converting after-tax net profits into operating cash inflows follows. The basic calculation requires adding any non cash charges deducted as expenses on the firm's income statement back to net profits after taxes. The most common non-cash charge found on income statements is depreciation. It is the only non cash charge that will be considered.

Example:

Stockwood Industries's estimates of its revenue and expenses (excluding depreciation) with and without the proposed new machine described in the preceding example, are given below. Both the expected usable life of the proposed machine and the remaining usable life of the present machine is 5 years. The amount to be depreciated with the proposed machine is calculated by summing the purchase price of P19 million and the installation costs of P100,000. table (1)

Year	Revenue	Expenses (excl. of depn)
With proposed machine	(1)	(2)
1	126,000,000.00	115,000,000.00
2	126,000,000.00	115,000,000.00
3	126,000,000.00	115,000,000.00
4	126,000,000.00	115,000,000.00
5	126,000,000.00	115,000,000.00
With present machine		
1	110,000,000.00	99,500,000.00
2	110,000,000.00	105,500,000.00
3	110,000,000.00	111,500,000.00
4	110,000,000.00	112,500,000.00
5	110,000,000.00	106,000,000.00

Depreciation Expense for Proposed and Present Machines for Bronson & Company (table(2)

	Year Cost	Applicable MACRS depn %	Depreciation [(1)x(2)]
	(1)	(2)	(3)
	With proposed machine		
1	20,000,000.00	0.20	4,000,000.00
2	20,000,000.00	0.32	6,400,000.00
3	20,000,000.00	0.19	3,800,000.00
4	20,000,000.00	0.12	2,400,000.00
5	20,000,000.00	0.12	2,400,000.00
6	20,000,000.00	0.05	1,000,000.00
Total		100%	20,000,000.00
	With present machine		
1	12,000,000.00	12%(year-4 depn)	1,440,000.00
2	12,000,000.00	12(year 5-depn)	1,440,000.00
3	12,000,000.00	5 (year 6 depn)	600,000.00
4			-
5			-
6			-

**Because the present machine is at the end of the third year of its cost recovery at the time the analysis is performed, it has only the final 3 years of depreciation.*

The proposed machine is to be depreciated un MACRS (modified accelerated cost recovery system) using a 5-year recovery period. The resulting depreciation on this machine for each of the 6 years, as well as the remaining 3 years of depreciation on the present machine are computed in the above table.

The operating cash inflows in each year can be calculated using the income statement format in subsequent table below. Substituting the data of the previous tables above 1 & 2 into this format and assuming a 40% tax rate. It demonstrates the calculation of operating cash inflows for each year for both the proposed and the present machine. Because the proposed machine is depreciated over 6 years, the analysis must be performed over the 6-year period to fully capture the tax effect of its year-6 depreciation. The resulting operating cash inflows are shown in the final row of this table below for each machine.

Calculation of Operating Cash inflows using the Income Statement Format:

Revenue

-Expenses (excluding depreciation)

Profits before depreciation and taxes

-depreciation

Net profits before taxes

- Taxes

Net profits after taxes

+ Depreciation

Operating cash inflows

Calculation of Operating Cash Inflows for Bronson & Company's proposed and present machines:

	YEAR			
	1	2	3	4
With proposed machine				
Revenue	126,000,000.00	126,000,000.00	126,000,000.00	126,000,00
-expenses(excl depn)	115,000,000.00	115,000,000.00	115,000,000.00	115,000,00
Profits before depn and taxes	11,000,000.00	11,000,000.00	11,000,000.00	11,000,000
-Depreciation	4,000,000.00	6,400,000.00	3,800,000.00	2,400,000.(
Net profits before taxes	7,000,000.00	4,600,000.00	7,200,000.00	8,600,000.(
-Taxes (rate=32%)	2,240,000.00	1,472,000.00	2,304,000.00	2,752,000.(
Net profits after taxes	4,760,000.00	3,128,000.00	4,896,000.00	5,848,000.(
+Depreciation	4,000,000.00	6,400,000.00	3,800,000.00	2,400,000.(
Operating cash inflows	8,760,000.00	9,528,000.00	8,696,000.00	8,248,000.(
With present machine				
Revenue	110,000,000.00	115,000,000.00	120,000,000.00	120,000,00
-expenses(excl depn)	99,500,000.00	105,500,000.00	111,500,000.00	112,500,00
Profits before depn and taxes	10,500,000.00	9,500,000.00	8,500,000.00	7,500,000.(
-Depreciation	1,440,000.00	1,440,000.00	600,000.00	
Net profits before taxes	9,060,000.00	8,060,000.00	7,900,000.00	7,500,000.(

-Taxes (rate=32%)	2,899,200.00	2,579,200.00	2,528,000.00	2,400,00
Net profits after taxes	6,160,800.00	5,480,800.00	5,372,000.00	5,100,00
+Depreciation	1,440,000.00	1,440,000.00	600,000.00	
Operating cash inflows	7,600,800.00	6,920,800.00	5,972,000.00	5,100,00

Installed cost of new asset

The cost of new asset is the net outflow its acquisition requires. Installation costs are any added costs necessary to place an asset into operation. They are considered part of the firm's capital expenditure. The installed cost of new asset, calculated by adding the cost of the asset to its installation costs, equals its depreciable value.

After-Tax proceeds from Sale of Old Asset

The proceeds from sale of old asset are the net cash inflows it provides. This amount is net of any costs incurred in the process of removing the asset. Included in these removal costs are cleanup costs, such as those related to removal and disposal of chemical and nuclear wastes. These costs may not be trivial The proceed from the sale of an old asset are normally subject to some type of tax. This tax on sale of old asset, depends on the relationship between its sale price, initial purchase price, and book value. The actual tax treatment is dictated by government tax laws, procedures, and forms, all of which are periodically revised. An understanding of : book value and basic tax rules is necessary to determine the tax on sale of an asset.

Book value The book value of an asset is its strict accounting value. It can be computed as follows:

Book value = installed cost of asset – accumulated depreciation

Example

Hiedelberg Industries, Inc. , a small electronics company, 2 years ago purchased a machine tool with an installed cost of P 450,000. The asset was being depreciated under using a 5 –year recovery period. It shows that 20 and 32% of the installed cost would be depreciated in years 1 and 2, respectively. In other words, 52%(20% + 32%) of the P450,000 cost, or P 234,000 (.52 x P 450,000), would represent the accumulated depreciation at the end of year 2. Substituting equation allows us to obtain:

Book value = P 450,000 –P234,000 = P 216,000

Tax rules - In the US, there are four potential tax situations which occur when selling an asset. It depends on the relationship between the asset's sale price, its initial purchase price, and its book value. This application may or may not be applied in the Philippines, however, the BIR under the NIRC has guidelines or tax rules in this aspect. The three key forms of taxable income and their associated tax treatments are defined and summarized as follows:

Taxable Income

Capital gain

Recaptured depreciation

Loss on sale of asset

Definition

Portion of the sale price that is in excess of the initial purchase price.

Portion of the sale price that is in excess of book value and represents a recovery of previously taken depreciation.

Amount by which sale price is less than book value.

Tax treatment

Regardless of how long the asset has been held, the total capital gain taxed as ordinary income.

All recaptured depreciation is taxed as ordinary income.

If asset is depreciable and used in business, loss is deducted from ordinary income.

If asset is not depreciable or is not used in business, loss is deductible only against capital gains.

Tax rate

40%

40%

40% of loss is a tax savings.

40% of loss is a tax savings.

Example:

The old asset purchased 2 years ago for $100,000 *by Harrison Industries* has a current book value of $48,000. What will happen if the firm now decides to sell the asset and replace it? The tax consequences depend on the sale price. In the light of the asset's original purchase price of $100,000 and its current book value of $48,000. The taxable consequences of each of these sale prices is described separately.

		Sale Price	
		$110,000	$70,00
	$110,000———]	capital gain($10,000)	
Initial Purchase Price	$100,000——-]		
	$70,000————-	recaptured depreciation($52,000)	
			recaptu depreci ($22,0(
book value————>	$48,000	______________	
	$30,000———>	——————————————	

The sale of asset for more than its initial purchase price. If *Harrison* sells the old asset for $110,000, it realizes a capital gain of $10,000, which is taxes as ordinary income. The firm also experiences ordinary income in the form of recaptured depreciation, which is the portion of the sale price that is above book value, and below the initial purchase price. In this case, there is recaptured depreciation of $ 52,000($100,000-$48,000. Both the $10,000 capital gain and the $52,000 recaptured depreciation under $110,000 sale price in the above table. The taxes on the total gain of $ 62,000 are computed as follows:

	Amount	Rate	Tax [(1) x(2)]
	(1)	(2)	(3)
Capital gain	10,000.00	0.40	4,000.00
Recaptured depreciation	52,000.00	0.40	20,800.00
Totals	62,000.00		24,800.00

These taxes should be used in computing the initial investment in the new asset in the basic format determining initial investment. In effect, the taxes raise the amount of the initial investment in the new asset by reducing the proceeds from sale of the old asset.

The sale of the asset for more than its book value but less than its initial purchase price. If *Harrison* sells the old asset for $70,000, there is no capital gain. However, the firm still experiences again in the form of recaptured depreciation of $ 22,000 ($70,000-$48,000) under the $70,000 sale price in the above table. This amount is taxed as ordinary income . Because the firm is assumed to be in the 40% tax bracket, the taxes on the $22,000 gain are $ 8,800. This amount in taxes should be used in calculating the initial investment in the new asset.

The sale of asset for its book value. If the asset is sold for $48,000, its book value , the firm breaks even. There is no gain or loss, as shown under the $48,000 sale price in in the above table. Because no tax results from selling an asset for its book value, there is no effect on the initial investment in the new asset.

The sale of the asset for less than its book value. IF Harrison sells the asset for $30,000, it experiences a loss of $18,000 ($48,000-$30,000), as shown under the $30,000 sale price in the above table. If this is a depreciable asset used in the business, the loss may be used to offset ordinary operating income. If the asset is not depreciable or not used in the business, the loss can be used only to offset capital gains. In either case, the loss will save the firm $7,200 ($18,000 x.40) in taxes. If current operating earnings or capital gains are not sufficient to offset the loss, the firm may be able to apply these losses to prior or future years' taxes.

Change in Net Working Capital

Net working capital is the net amount by which a firm's current assets exceed its current liabilities. At this point it is important to know that changes in net working capital is often associated with capital expenditures decisions. If a firm acquires new machinery to expand its level of operations, levels of cash, accounts receivable, inventories, accounts payable, and accruals will increase. Increases in cash, accounts receivable, and inventories are uses of cash (cash outflows or investments), whereas increases in accounts payable and accruals are sources of cash (cash inflows or financing). As long as the expanded operations continue, the increased investment in current assets (cash, accounts receivable, and inventories) and increased current liability financing (accounts payable and accruals) would be expected to continue.

The difference between the change in current assets and the change in current liabilities would be the change in net working capital. Current assets increase by more than current liabilities, resulting in increased net working capital, which would be treated as an initial outflow. If the change in net working capital were negative, it would be shown as an initial inflow. The change in net working capital-whether an increase or a decrease – is not taxable because it merely involves a net buildup or reduction of current accounts.

Example:

Bronson & Company, food and beverage distributor, is considering expanding its operations. It acquired a variety of new capital equipment, financial analysts expected that the changes in current accounts summarized below will be maintained over the life of the expansion. Current assets are expected to increase by P100,000, and current liabilities are expected to increase by P 450,000, resulting in P 650,000 increase in net working capital. In this case, the increase would represent an increased net working capital investment and be treated as a cash outflow in calculating the initial investment:

Calculation of Change in Net Working Capital for *Bronson & Company*

Current Account		Change in balance
Cash	200,000.00	
Accounts receivable	500,000.00	
Inventories	400,000.00	
(1) Current assets		1,100,000.00
Accounts payable	350,000.00	
Accruals	100,000.00	
(2) Current liabilities		450,000.00
Changes in net working capital[(1)-(2)]		650,000.00

Illustrative Examples:

1.

JAS Company is purchasing an asset to replace an existing asset. The purchase price if P 800,000 plus an additional P 90,000 to transport and install it. It will operate much more quickly than the asset it replaces and therefore will tie up additional inventory worth P 120,000. The firm has an existing asset that can be sold for P 100,000 but it will cost P 40,000 to remove it so that it can be delivered to the buyer. The book value of the existing asset is P 90,000. What is the net initial outlay for the new asset? Tax rate is 32%.

Outflows:		
Purchase price	800,000.00	
Transport and Installation cost	90,000.00	
Initial cost of machine		890,000.00
Increased investment in inventory		120,000.00
Total outflows		1,010,000.00
Inflows:		
Salvage value of old machine (P 100,000-P40,000)		60,000.00
Tax savings@32%on short term capital less of (P90,000-60,000)= P 30,000@32%=9,600		9,600.00
Net cash outlay		940,400.00

2.

W & R Industries,Inc. is using a machine whose original cost was P 685,000. The machine is 5 years old and is expected to last an additional ten years. It is being depreciated on a straight line basis over its fifteen years life to an expected zero salvage. It can be sold currently for P 230,000. A replacement is being contemplated. The new machine has a cost of P 620,000 and will have zero salvage value at the end often years. The machine will produce savings (before interest and depreciation) of P 88,000 per year. The tax rate is 40%. Determine the cash flows associated with this replacement.

Outlays:	
Purchase price	620,000.00
Sale of old machine	(230,000.00)
Tax savings@40%on short term capital of	
P326,667(P685,000-P228,333-P130,000)	(130,666.00)
Net cash outlay	259,334.00
Cash benefits:	
Savings	88,000.00
Incremental depreciation	(23,000.00)
Taxable income	65,000.00
Less: taxes	26,000.00
Earnings after taxes	39,000.00
Add back depreciation	23,000.00
Cash flow (1-10 yrs.)	62,000.00

Effect of Depreciation

A machine of this sort has a useful life in excess of 1 year, we cannot charge its cost against income for tax purposes but must depreciate it. We then deduct depreciation from income in order to compute taxable income. These classes of property have periods, or depreciable lives, of 3,5,7,10,15,20,271/2, and 39 years. A general description falls into the 5-year property class for cost recovery (depreciation) purposes.

As a result, the annual depreciation charge is 20 percent of the total depreciable cost of P 20,000, or P 4,000 a year. Assume, additionally that the corporate income tax rate is 40 percent. Assume that the old machine has a remaining depreciable life of 5 years, that there is no expected salvage value at the end of this time, and that the machine also is subject to straight-line depreciation. The annual depreciation charge on the old machine is 20 percent of its depreciated book value of P 2,000, or P 400 a year. Because we are interested in the incremental impact of the project, we subtract depreciation charges on the old machine from depreciation charges on the new one to obtain the incremental depreciation charges associated with the project.

Below is the information cited, we now are able to calculate the expected net cash flow (after taxes) resulting from the acceptance of the project.

	Book Account	Cash Flow Account
Annual cash savings	7,100.00	7,100.00
Depreciation on new machine	4,000.00	
Less: Depreciation on old machine	400.00	
Additional depreciation charge	3,600.00	
Additional income before taxes	3,500.00	
Income tax (32%)	1,120.00	1,120.00
Additional income after taxes	2,380.00	
Annual net cash flow		5,980.00

Evaluating Capital investment

While our objective is to assume the risk or quality of all investment projects of the firm and that the acceptance of any proposal or group of investment proposals does not change the relative business risk of the firm. The investment decision will be either to accept or to reject the proposal. There are four methods of capital budgeting:

1. Average rate of return;
2. Payback;

3. Internal rate of return;
4. Net Present Value

The first two are approximate methods for assessing the economic worth of the project. For simplicity, we assume throughout that the expected cash flows are realized a the end of each year.

Average Rate of Return

This accounting measure represents the ratio of the average annual profits after-taxes to the investment in the project. In the previous example of the new machine, the average annual book earnings for the 5- year period are P 2,100, and the initial investment in the project is P 18,000. therefore;

Average rate of return = P 2,100/P 18,000 = 11.67%

If income were variable over the 5 years, an average would be calculated and employed in the numerator. Once the average rate of return is its simplicity; it makes use of readily available accounting information. Once the average rate of return for a proposal has been calculated; it may be compared with a required, or cutoff rate of return to determine if a particular proposal should be accepted or rejected. The principal shortcomings of the method are that it is based on accounting income rather than on cash flows and that it fails to take account of the timing of cash inflows and outflows. The time value of money is ignored: Benefits in the last year ar valued the same as benefits in the first year.

Payback Period

The payback period of an investment project tells us the number of years required to recover our initial cash investment. It is the ratio of the initial fixed investment over the annual cash inflows for the recovery period. For our example:

Payback period = P 18,000 / P 5,700 = 3.16 years

If the annual cash inflows are not equal, the job of calculation is somewhat more difficult. Suppose annual cash inflows are P 4,000 in the first year, P 6,000 in the second and third years, and P 4,000 in the fourth and fifth years. In the first 3 years, P 16,000 of the original investment will be recovered, followed by P 4,000 in the fourth year. With an initial cash investment of P 18,000, the payback period is 3 years + (P 2,000/P 4,000) or 3 ½ years.

If the payback period calculated is less than some maximum acceptable payback period, the proposal is accepted; if not, it is rejected. If the required payback period were 4 years, the project would be accepted. The major shortcoming of the payback method is that it fails to consider cash flows after the payback period; consequently, it cannot be regarded as a measure of profitability. Two proposals costing P 10,000 each would have the same payback period if they both had annual net cash inflows of P 5,000 in the first 2 years; but one project might be expected to provide no cash flows of P 5,000 in the first 2 years; but one project might be expected to provide no cash flows after 2 years, whereas the other might be expected to provide cash flows of P 5,000 in each of the next 3 years. Thus, the payback method can be deceptive as a yardstick of profitability. The method does not take account of the magnitude or timing of cash flows during the payback period. It considers only the recovery period as a whole.

Payback period affords management limited insight into the risk and liquidity of a project. The shorter the payback period, supposedly, the less risky the project and the greater its liquidity. The company that is deficient of cash may find the method to be very useful in gauging the early recovery of funds invested. There is some merit to its use in this regard but the method does not take into account the dispersion of possible outcomes – only the magnitude and timing of the expected value of these outcomes relative to the original investment. It cannot be considered an adequate indicator of risk. When the payback method is used, it is more appropriately treated as a constraint to be satisfied than as a profitability measure to be maximized.

Internal Rate of Return (IRR)

The internal rate of return is probably the most used sophisticated capital budgeting technique for evaluating investment alternatives. It is considerably more difficult than NPV to calculate by hand. The internal rate of return (IRR) is the discount rate that equates the present value of cash inflows with the initial investment associated with a project. The IRR, in other words, is the discount rate that equates the NPV of an investment opportunity with Php 0 (because the present value of cash inflows equals the initial investment). It is the compound annual rate of return that the firm will earn if it invests in the project and receives the given inflows. IRR is found by solving equation :

NPV = n CF t -1]

Σ (1+k)

t=1

= n

Σ (CF x PV1 Fkt) – 1]

1

When IRR is used to make accept-reject decisions, the decision criteria are as follows:

1. If the IRR is greater than the cost of capital, accept the project.
2. if the IRR is less than the cost of capital, reject the project.

This criteria guarantee that the firm earns at least its required return. Such an outcome should enhance the market value of the firm and therefore the wealth of its owners.

IRR calculations

The IRR can be found either by using trial-and-error techniques or with the aid of a sophisticated financial calculator or a computer. Calculating IRR for an annuity is considerably easier than calculating it for a mixed stream of operating cash inflows. The steps involved in calculating the IRR in each case are illustrated by the following examples: Using the table below:

Rexthione Electromagnetic Company Capital Expenditures

	Project A	Project B
Initial Investment	42,000.00	45,000.00
Year	Operating Cash Inflows	
1	14,000.00	28,000.00
2	14,000.00	12,000.00
3	14,000.00	10,000.00
4	14,000.00	10,000.00
5	14,000.00	10,000.00
Average	14,000.00	14,000.00

The two –step procedure for finding the IRR of an annuity can be demonstrated by using the projects of *Rexthione Electromagnetic Company.*

Step 1. Dividing the initial investment of P 42,000 by the annual cash inflow of P 14,000 results in a payback period of 3.000 years (P 42,000/P14,000 = 3.000)

Step 2. The PVIFA factors closest to 3.000 for 5 years are 3.058 (for 19%) and 2.991 (for 20%). The value closest to 3.000 is 2.991; therefore, the IRR for project A, to the nearest 1% is 20%. The actual value, which is between 19 and 20% could be found by using a calculator or computer or by interpolation; it is 19.86%(Note: for our purposes, values rounded to the nearest 1% will suffice.) Project A with an IRR of 20% is quite acceptable, because this IRR is above the firm's 10% cost of capital.

Steps for calculating the Internal Rates of Return (IRRs) of Annuities and Mixed Streams

For an Annuity

1. *Calculate the payback period for the project;*

2. *Find, for the life of the project, the present value interest factor closest to the payback value. (Use the given example above, which shows the present value interest factors for a P1 annuity, PVIFA) The discount rate associated with that factor is the internal rate of return (IRR) to the nearest 1%.*

For a Mixed Stream

1. Find the average annual cash inflow by dividing the sum of the annual cash inflows by the number of years in the project's life.

2. Divide the average annual cash inflow into the initial investment to get an average payback period (or present value interest factor for a P1 annuity, PVIFA) The average payback is needed to estimate the IRR for the average annual cash inflow.

3. Find the discount rate associated with the present value interest factor PVIFA for the life of the project that is closest to the average payback period. The result will be a very rough approximation of the IRR based on the assumption that the mixed stream of cash inflows is an annuity.

4. Adjust subjectively the IRR obtained in Step 3 by comparing the pattern of average annual cash inflows (in Step 1) to the actual mixed stream of cash inflows. If the actual cash flow stream seems to have higher inflows in the earlier years than the average stream, adjust the IRR up. If the actual cash inflows in the earlier years are below the average, adjust the IRR down. The amount of adjustment up or down typically ranges from 12 to 3 percentage points, depending upon how much the actual cash inflow stream's pattern deviates from the average annual cash inflows. For small deviations, an adjustment of around 1 percentage point may be best, whereas for large deviations, adjustments of around 3 percentage points are generally appropriate. If the average cash inflows seem fairly close to the actual pattern, make no adjustment in the IRR.

5. Calculate the net present value of the mixed stream project using the IRR from Step 4. Be sure to use the present value interest factors for P 1, PVIF, treating the estimated IRR as the discount rate.

6. If the resulting NPV is greater than zero, subjectively raise the discount rate; if the resulting NPV is less than zero, subjectively lower the discount rate,. The greater the deviation of the resulting NPV from zero, the larger the subjective adjustment. Adjustments of 1 to 3 percentage points are used for relatively small deviations, whereas larger adjustments are required for relatively large deviations.

7. Calculate the NPV using the new discount rate. Repeat step 6. Stop as soon as two consecutive discount rates that cause the NPV to be positive and negative, respectively, have been found. Whichever of these rates causes the NPV to be closer to zero is the IRR to the nearest 1%.

Step 5. - By using the present value interest factors (PVIF) for 19% and the correct year from *Rexthione Electromagnetic Company*, we calculate the net present value of the mixed stream as follows:

Year	Cash inflows (1)	Project B PV interest factor, PVIF (2)	PV @ 19% [(2)x(2)] (3)
1	28000	0.84	23,520.00
2	12000	0.706	8,472.00
3	10000	0.593	5,930.00
4	10000	0.499	4,990.00
5	10000	0.419	4,190.00
Present value of cash inflows			47,102.00
-Initial investment			45,000.00
Net present value (NPV)			2,102.00

Step 6 & 7. Because the net present value of P 2,102, calculated in Step 5, is greater than zero, the discount rate should be subjectively increased. Because the NPV deviates by only about 5% from the P 45,000 initial investment, let's try a 2 percentage point increase, to 21%.

Year	Cash inflows (1)	Project B PV interest factor, PVIF (2)	PV @ 21% [(2)x(2)] (3)
1	28000	0.826	23,128.00
2	12000	0.683	8,196.00
3	10000	0.564	5,640.00
4	10000	0.467	4,670.00
5	10000	0.386	3,860.00
Present value of cash inflows			45,494.00
-Initial investment			45,000.00
Net present value (NPV)			494.00

These calculations indicate that the NPV of P 494 for an IRR of 21% is reasonably close to, but still greater than, zero. Thus a higher discount rate should be tried. Because we are so close, let's try a 1 percentage point increase, to 22%. As the following calculations show, the net present value using a discount rate of 22% is –P256.

		Project B	PV @ 22%
	Cash	PV interest	
	inflows	factor, PVIF	[(2)x(2)]
Year	(1)	(2)	(3)
1	28000	0.82	22,960.00
2	12000	0.672	8,064.00
3	10000	0.551	5,510.00
4	10000	0.451	4,510.00
5	10000	0.37	3,700.00
Present value of cash inflows			44,744.00
-Initial investment			45,000.00
Net present value (NPV)			(256.00)

Because 21 and 22% are consecutive discount rates that give positive and negative net present values, we can stop the trial-and-error process . The IRR that we are seeking is the discount rate for which the NPV is closest to P0. For project B, 22% causes the NPV to be closer to P 0 than 21%, so we will use 22% as the IRR. If we had used a financial calculator or a computer or interpolation, the exact IRR would be 21.65%' as indicated earlier, for our purposes the IRR rounded to the nearest 1% will suffice. It is interesting to note that the IRR suggests that project B, which has an IRR of approximately 22 percent, is preferable to project A, which has an IRR of approximately 20 percent. This conflicts with the rankings of the projects obtained in an earlier example using NPV. These two techniques have no guarantee, the NPV and IRR- will rank projects in the same order. Both methods should reach the same conclusion about the acceptability or non acceptability of projects.

Net Present Value

The net present value method is a discounted cash-flow approach to capital budgeting. With the present-value method all cash flows are discounted to present *value, using the required* rate of return. The net present value of an investment proposal is

$$NPV = \sum_{T=0}^{n} \frac{A}{(1+k)^t}$$

Where k is the required rate of return. If the sum of these discounted cash flow is zero or more, the proposal is accepted; if not, it is rejected. Another way to express the acceptance criterion is to say that the project will be accepted if the present value of cash inflows exceeds the present value of cash outflows. The reason behind the acceptance is the same as that behind the internal-rate-of-return method. If the require rate of return is the return investors expect the firm to earn on the investment proposal, and the firm accepts a proposal with a net present value greater than zero, the marked-price of the stock should rise. The firm is taking on a project with a risk of return greater than that necessary to leave the market price of the stock changed.

Because the net present value give explicit consideration to the time value of money, it is considered a sophisticated capital budgeting technique. All such techniques in one way or another discount the firm's cash flows at a specified rte. This rate – often called the discount rate, required return, cost of capital, or opportunity cost –refers to the minimum return that must be earned on a project to leave the firm's market value unchanged.

The net present value is found by subtracting a project's initial investment (II) from the present value of its cash inflows (CF) discounted at a rate equal to the firm's cost of capital (k):

NPV = present value of cash inflows – initial investment

By using NPV, both inflows and outflows are measured in terms of present pesos. Because we are dealing only with investments that have conventional cash flow patterns, the initial investment is automatically stated in terms of today's pesos. If it were not, the present value of a project would be found by subtracting the present value of outflows from the present value of inflows.

When NPV is used to make accept-reject decisions, the decision criteria are as follows:

1. if the NPV is greater than P0, accept the project.
2. if the NPV is less than P 0, reject the project.

If the NPV is greater than P0, the firm will earn a return greater than its cost of capital. Such action should enhance the market value of the firm and therefore the wealth of its owners.

The net present value (NPV) approach can be illustrated by using the information below:

Rexthione Electromagnetic Company Capital Expenditures

	Project A	Project B
Initial Investment	42,000.00	45,000.00
Year	Operating Cash Inflows	
1	14,000.00	28,000.00
2	14,000.00	12,000.00
3	14,000.00	10,000.00
4	14,000.00	10,000.00
5	14,000.00	10,000.00
Average	14,000.00	14,000.00

If the firm has a 10% cost of capital, the net present values for projects A (an annuity) and B (a mixed stream) can be calculated in the table below:

Project A	
Annual cash inflow	14,000.00
X Present value annuity interest factor, PVIFA	3,790.00
Present value of cash inflow	53,074.00
- Initial investment	42,000.00
Net present value (NPV)	11,074.00

Project B

Year	Cash inflows (1)	PV interest factor, PVIF (2)	Pres. Value [(2)x(2)] (3)
1	28000	0.909	25,452.00
2	12000	0.826	9,912.00
3	10000	0.851	7,510.00
4	10000	0.683	6,830.00
5	10000	0.621	6,210.00
Present value of cash inflows			55,914.00
-Initial investment			45,000.00
Net present value (NPV)			10,914.00

0. If the projects were being ranked, however, project A would be considered superior to B, because it has a higher net present value (P 11,074 vs. P 10,914).

Problem

Jade Industries,Inc. chose the better of two equal-risk, mutually exclusive, capital expenditure projects – A and J. The relevant cash flows for each project are shown in the following table. The firm's cost of capital is 14%.

	Project A	Project J
Initial investment (II)	28500	27000
Year (t)	Cash inflows (CF)	
1	10,000.00	11,000.00
2	10,000.00	10,000.00
3	10,000.00	9,000.00
4	10,000.00	8,000.00

a. Calculate each project's payback period.

b. Calculate the net present value 9NPV) for each project.

c. Calculate the internal rate of return (IRR) for each project.

d. Summarize the preferences dictated by each measure calculated above, and indicate which project you would recommend. Explain why.

e. Draw the net present value profiles for each project on the same set of axes, and explain the circumstances under which a conflict in rankings might exist.

DEPRECIATION

Accounting depreciation refers to the reported charges as per the book keeping practices of the corporation. Accounting depreciation may coincide with a physical depreciation but the rate of accounting depreciation is usually much higher than that of actual physical deterioration. The discrepancy in the rates depends on the type of asset and the firm's policies, but the flow of accounting charges is bound on the one hand by legal conventions and on the other by the physical deterioration of the asset. Some depreciation allowances are added to the pool of funds as a source, fast growing corporations have gone to the legal limits and used depreciation along with retained earnings as a steady source of internally generated funds.

Economic depreciation refers to the rate of decrease in the revenues from the use of a specified asset. Since revenues are determined by the market, economic depreciation refers to the gradual obsolescence of an asset, as the demand for the commodity it produces diminished due to changes in market tastes and preferences. Rates of economic depreciation, as determined by the market, may be equal to or greater than the rates of physical and accounting depreciation. It is the liquidation (market) value of an asset that is important rather than its book value. Typically, in a developed economy, economic depreciation is higher than the physical or accounting types since both shifting market preferences and technological progress combine to reduce the liquidating value of an asset. When economic and accounting depreciations are equalized by continual adjustment of the asset's book value, the ex post rate of return on assets is equal to the discount factor (cost of borrowing)

Kinds of Depreciation:

1. Economic depreciation- is a depreciation which is caused by obsolescence or inadequacy of the asset to perform well.

2. Physical depreciation is a depreciation of asset which is caused by the wearing and tearing and deterioration over a period of time. Depreciable amount is the cost of an asset or other amount substituted for cost less its residual value.

3. Residual value is the estimated amount that an entity would currently obtain from disposal of the asset after deducting the estimated cost of disposal if the asset were already of age and condition expected at the end of its useful life.

Useful life is the period over which an asset is expected to be available for use by the entity or the number of production or similar units expected to be obtained from the asset by the entity . It can be expressed by the time in years, units of output or production, service hours or working hours.

Depreciation Methods

The factors to be considered in computing the periodic depreciation of an asset are its, cost , estimated residual value, and estimated period of usefulness. The estimated residual value of a depreciable asset, which is the amount expected to be realized upon its eventual disposition, is frequently termed scrap, salvage, or trade-in value. The excess of cost over the estimated residual value is the amount that is to be charged to depreciation expense during the life of the asset. The quantitative relationship between the residual value and the cost of an asset varies considerably among types of assets and among enterprises.

Property, Plant & Equipment are depreciated in the following methods :

1. Straight line method The formula for computing is as follows:

Annual depreciation = Cost minus Residual value
Life in years

Illustration : The following data is available :

Equipment 125,000

Residual value 5,000

Life 5 years

Depreciation table appears as follows :

Year	Particular	Depreciation	Accumulated Depreciation	Book Value
				P
	Acquisition cost			125,000
1	Depreciation 1st	24,000	24,000	101,000
2	2nd year	24,000	48,000	77,000
3	3rd year	24,000	72,000	53,000
4	4th year	24,000	96,000	29,000
5	5th year	24,000	120,000	5,000

1. To obtain the amount of depreciation, divide 120,000 (125,000 – 5,000) by 5 years equals 24,000 or 20% x P 120,000 = 24,000.

2. The balance of accumulated depreciation for the 1st year is added each year's depreciation. (please see the table)

3. A Cost of P 125,000 minus column b equals the book value and so on.

At the end of the 5th year a life of the asset, the book value should equal the residual value. At the end of the accounting period, the journal entry is prepared as follows :

Depreciation 24,000

Accumulated deprecation 24,000

The balance sheet when prepared at the end of the 1st year would show the following :

Equipment P 125,000

Less : Accumulated Depreciation 24,000

Book Value or Carrying amount

Composite Method Under this method assets are dissimilar on a nature and have different physical characteristics and vary widely in useful life, grouped as a single unit.

Illustration:

Asset Cost Residual Value Depreciable Cost Life in years Annual Depreciation

Building 850,000 50,000 800,000 20 40,000

Machine 300,000 30,000 270,000 10 27,000

Equipment 240,000 40,000 200,00 8 25,000

1,390,000 120,000 1,270,000 92,000

The composite life is obtained by dividing the total depreciable cost by total annual depreciation, thus, 1,270,000 / 92,000 = 13.8 years. The composite rate is obtained by dividing the total annual depreciation by total cost thus, 92,000/1,390,000 = 7%. The journal entry to record the annual depreciation is :

Depreciation 92,000

Accumulated depreciation 92,000

If the equipment is retired and sold after 8 years for 30,000, the entry is :

Cash 30,000

Accumulated depreciation 210,000

Equipment 240,000

The remaining cost of assets in group is1,150,00 (1,390,000 – 240,000) while the annual depreciation is no longer 92,000 nut 80,500. obtained by multiplying the composite rate of 7% to 1,150,000.

On the ninth year the amount of annual depreciation is 80,500.

Sum of year's digits (SYD) This method is obtained by multiplying the depreciable cost by a series of fractions whose numerator is the digit in the life of the asset and the denominator is the sum of the digits in the life of the asset. The fractions are taken by getting the sum of the digits in the life the asset. Example; if the asset has a life of 2 years, the sum of the digits would be 3, that is 1 plus 2. Hence, the depreciation would be 2/3 for the first year and 1/3 for the second year.

Illustration :

Machinery 500,000

Residual value 50,000

Estimated life 4 years

SYD = 4 (4+1/ 2) 10

<u>Year Particular Depreciation Accumulated Depn Book Value</u>

Acquisition .cost 500,000

1 4/10 x 450,000 180,000 180,000 320,000

2 3/10 x450,000 135,000 315,000 185,000

3 2/10x450,000 90,000 405,000 95,000

4 1/10x450,000 45,000 450,000 50,000

Double- declining balance method This is a method where a fixed rate is multiplied by the declining book value of the asset to get the annual depreciation. The straight line rate is doubled to get the fixed rate. This is also known as 200% declining balance method.

Illustration

Cost of the asset 500,000

Date of Acquisition Jan 1, 2006

Residual value 50,000

Estimated life 5 years

Straight line rate (100%/5 yeas) 20 %

Double declining rate (20% x 2) 40%

Year Particular Depreciation Accumulated.Depn Book Value

50,000

2006 40% x 500,000 200,000 200,000 300,000

2007 40% x 300,00 120,000 320,000 180,000

2008 40% x 180,000 72,000 392,000 108,000

2009 40% x 108,000 43,200 435,000 64,800

2010 40% x 50,000 14,800 450,000 50,000

Under this method residual value is ignored in the first year. The rate of 40% is multiplied by the total cost of P 500,000. In the last year, 2010, the fixed rate of 40% is no longer multiplied by the preceding book value. It is simply the difference between the preceding book value of 64,800 and residual value of 50,000.

150% Declining Balance The fixed rate is twice or 200% of the straight line rate. The fixed rate is 150% of the straight line rate. Example:

Cost of asset 600,000

Residual Value 50,000

Date of acquisition Jan 1, 2000

Life 5 years

Straight line rate 20 %

Fixed rate (150% x 20%) 30%

The depreciation for 2006 is as follows :

30% x P 600,000 = 180,000

Declining Balance method The depreciation is obtained by multiplying a fixed or uniform rate by the declining book value or undepreciated cost of the asset in order to arrive at the annual depreciation . The formula is :

Rate = 1- n/RV/ Cost " n" is the life of the asset.

The value of the asset cannot be reduced to zero and that the formula cannot be used unless there is a residual value. Thus, a residual value must always be assigned to the asset. In the absence of any residual value a nominal amount of P 1 is assumed.

Illustration

Cost of the asset 600,000

Salvage value 60,000

Estimated life 5 years

Substituting the formula : Rate = 1- 5/60,000/600,000

= 1- 5/ .10

At table of logarithms must be used to get the fifth root of .10. thus, the 5th root of .10 is .632. Thus the fixed rate is = 1- .632 = .368 or 36.8 %

The table for deprecation is shown like this

Year Particular Depreciation Accumulated Dep Book Value

600,000

1 36.8% x 600,000 220,800 220,800 379,200

2 36.8% x 379,200 139,456 360,346 239,654

3 36.8% x 239,654 88,193 448,339 151,461

4 36.8% x 151,461 55,738 504,277 95,723

5 36.8% x 95,723 35,226 540,000 60,000

Note that on the 5th year, the accumulated depreciation is rounded-off to be exact for the difference in book value.

Exercises

1. Equipment was acquired on Jan 1, 1979 at a cost of P 1,200,000 shows an accumulated depreciation of P 240,000 on Jan. 1, 1984. Appraisal estimate shows that the equipment will last only an additional 15 years and present replacement value is considered to be P 1.8M. What is the original life of the equipment?

a. 25 years c. 20 years

b. 15 years d. answer not given

2. On Jan 1, 1984 a new building was purchased at a cost of P 6M. Depreciation was regularly provided at 2% per year. On Jan 1, 1994, the building was appraised by an independent appraiser at P 9M and a condition per cent of 75 and salvage value of P 600,000. The depreciation on the building that should be reported for the year 1984 is:

a. P230,000 c. P 140,000

b. P 210,000 d. not given

3. A machinery costing P 500,000 had been appraised at P 1,000,000. The accumulated depreciation on cost is P 200,000 and appraised value, P500,000. the original life of the asset is 10 years. What is the age of the asset at the time of appraisal ?

a. 4 years c. 6 years

b. 5 years e. not given

What is the amount of annual depreciation that should be reported in the Income Statement?

a. P 100,000 c. P 75,000

b. P 125,000 e. P 50,000

4. The company purchased a patent for P 100,000 on May 6, 1982. On this date, the patent has a remaining life of 14 years but it is considered unlikely that the patent will extend beyond 10 years. Early in Jan, 1984, P 30,000 is paid to settle an infringement suit. How much is the patent amortization for 1984?

a. P 13,600 c. P 3,600

b. P 10,000 d. P 13,000

5. During 1979, Traxco Machinery Company spent P 176,000 on Research & Development cost for an invention. The invention was patented on Jan. 2, 1980 at a nominal cost that was expensed in 1980. The patent had a legal life of 17 years and an estimated life of 8 years. In Jan. 1984, Traxco paid P 16,000 for legal fees in a successful defense of the patent. Amortization for 1984 should be:

a. 0 c. P 4,000

b. P 1,231 d. P 26,000

6. A building was constructed and finished on Jan 1, 1986. The total cost is P 860,000. It was estimated to last up to Jan. 1,2026 with a salvage value then at P 60,000. Depreciation is on a straight line method. On Feb. 1 1986 repairs costing P 100,000 were made on the building. On Jan. 1, 1991, the life of the building was changed and it was estimated to last up to Jan. 1, 2021 and the salvage value remains the same. On Jan. 1, 1993 the building was sold for P 750,000. The depreciation change for 1991 is :

a. P 20,000 c. P 23,334

b. P 22,857 d. P 25,715

How much is the gain or loss as a result of the sale of the building for P 750,000?

a. (P10,000) c. P50,000

b. (P 37,500) d. P 13,334

7. The following data were taken from the books of AT & S Company:

Machinery Equipment

Date of Acquisition Jan. 1, 1986 July 1, 1986

Amount P 28,000 P 7,000

Estimated Residual value P 3,000 P 1,000

Estimated years & useful life 10 years 5 years

On Oct. 1, 1989, the above machinery was sold for P 20,000. The equipment can no longer be used on March 31, 1989 and the company received P 2,500 from insurers in settlement of claim in full.

What was the gain or loss from sale of machine?

a. (P500) c. P 1,375

b. P 1,000 d. not given

What was the gain or loss upon retirement of Equipment ?

A (P 500) c. P 800

b. (P 800) d. not given

8. JR Shop acquired a machine on July 1, 1988 at a cost of P 50,000 with an estimated life of 5 years & salvage value of P 5,000. Calculate the depreciation that would be charged to expense in the above machine in 1988 using the sum-of-year's digit method?

a. P 3,750 c. P 15,000

b. P 7,500 d. not given

For 1989 using the SYD method:

a. P 13,500 c. P 15,000

b. 12,000 d. not given

1988 using the declining balance method at a rate double the straight line :

a. P 6,000 c. P 18,000

b. 9,000 d. not given

1989 Using the decline balance at a rate double the straight line rate:

a. P 4,500 c. P 12,600

b. 9,000 d. 16,000

9. On Dec.1, 2002 H company acquired a new delivery truck in exchange for an old delivery truck that it had acquired in 2001. The old truck was purchased for P 70,000 and had a book value of P 33,000. On the date of exchange the old truck had a market value of P 30,000. In addition, paid P 35,000 cash for the new truck which had a best price of P 80,000.

At what amount should H company record the new truck for financial purposes.

a. P 65,000 c. 70,000

b. 65,000 d. 80,000

What is the gain or loss to be recognized on the exchange?

a. P1,500 c. (P3,000)

b. (2,500) d. P 4,000

10. DS Stores acquired an equipment making payment of P 43,716. The payment was analyzed as follows :

Price of equipment P 44,160

Charges for extra equipment 248

Sales disc. 3% of94,408 1,332

Insurance for 1 year 976

P 43,716

The old equipment cost P 40,000 and had a book value of P 2,000 on the date of the trade.

What is the cost of the new equipment?

a. P 45,740 c. P 45,716

b. P 44, 740 d. P 46,716

What is the gain (loss) on the exchange ?

a. P 1,000 c. not determinable

b. (P1,000) d. 0

11. S Corp. paid Mr. Paz for land and a building the amount of P 220,000 and assume a mortgage loan of P 200,000. 75% of the purchase price is for the building and 25% is for the land. For remodeling and painting the sum of P 95,000 was paid. Salvage materials recovered in the remodeling were sold for P 6,000 and landscaping cost P 6,000.

The land shall be recorded at a cost of.

a. 101,000 c. 105,000

b. 112,500 d. 106,000

Retiring of Plant Assets

Plant assets are retired and discarded when no longer useful. If fully depreciated, equipment acquired at a cost of P 2,000 is discarded as worthless, the following entry is made:

1-Mar Accumulated Depreciation 121.1 2,000.00

Equipment 2,000.00

To write off equipment discarded 121

If the equipment had not been fully depreciated, it would have been necessary to record a loss at the time of its disposal. Assume that the balance in the accumulated depreciation account as of the preceding December 31, the end of the fiscal year, is P 1,000 and the equipment is depreciated at the rate of 10%. The entry to record the depreciation for the 3 months of the current year is as follows:

1-Mar Depreciation Expense – Equipment 714 50.00

Accumulated Depreciation - Equipment 121.1 50.00

To record 3 months' depreciation on equipment

Discarded

The equipment is then removed from the accounts and the loss is recorded by the following entry:

1-Mar Depreciation Expense – Equipment 121.1 1,050.00

Loss on Disposal of Plant Assets 912 950.00

Equipment 121 2,000.00

To write off equipment discarded

Losses and gains on the disposal of plant assets are non operating items and are reported in the Other Expense and Other Income sections of the Income Statement. A plant asset that has been depreciated for the full period of its estimated life but that is still useful to the enterprise should not be removed from the accounts. This is true even though the asset has no residual value and the accumulated depreciation is exactly equal to the cost. Otherwise the accounts would contain no evidence of the continued existence of useful plant assets and the control function of the ledger would be impaired. The cost and the accumulated depreciation data on such assets may be needed in reporting for income tax purposes.

The balance of each asset account, together with the balance of the related account for accumulated depreciation may be presented in different ways in the financial statements as follows:

JAMA ENTERPRISES
Balance Sheet
December 31,2002

ASSETS

Total Current Assets...				P355,500
		Accumulated	Book	
Plant Assets:	Cost	Depreciation	Value	
Land	P450,000.00		450,000.00	
Buildings	250,000.00	10,000.00	240,000.00	
Office Equipment	17,500.00	1,750.00	15,750.00	
Factory Equipment	350,000.00	12,000.00	338,000.00	
Total plant assets	1,067,500.00	23,750.00		1,043,750.00

Choosing a Depreciation Method

The choice in the method of depreciating assets constitutes many factors. Generally, the most important factor is the effect of the method on the timing of income taxes paid.

If income tax rates are constant and the firm has taxable income over the depreciable file then the total income taxes paid is identical regardless of the depreciation method employed. However, given the choice of paying now and later the time value of money effect encourages one to choose the postponement. In fact, this postponement is achieved by depreciation methods which result in higher depreciation charges (and thus lower taxable incomes and taxes) in the early years of an asset, as in the sum-of-the-year's-digits and declining balance method.

The choice between depreciation methods for income tax purposes can be quite important to the firm. Among the factors which should be considered in this decision are : the expected trend of income tax rates and variability of the firm's earnings; whether or not the firm issues to be carried forward to future years, and the effect on future after-tax earnings reported to the shareholders or owners.

Problems Solving

1. *GE Enterprises* has an asset that currently generates annual revenues of P 2,295,000 and incurs annual cost of P 945,000. These costs do not include P 162,000 of depreciation. If replacement machine is purchased, the revenue would rise to P 2,565,000 and the cost would drop to P 864,000 but depreciation on the new machine would be 216,000 per year. The company is in the tax bracket of 32%. What are the annual after-tax cash flows on each machine?

2.

The Raven Industries,Inc. is considering the purchase of a machine tool to replace an existing tool that has a book value of P 26,000 and can be sold for P 14,000. The salvage value of the old machine in four years is zero, and it is depreciated on a straight line method. The proposed machine will perform the same function that the old machine is performing; however improvements in technology will enable the firm to gain cash benefits (before depreciation and taxes) of P 66,000 per year in materials, labor, and overhead. The new machine has a four year life, costs P 116,000 and can be sold for an expected P 18,000 at the end of the fourth year. Assuming straight line depreciation and a 32% tax rate, compute the cash flows associated with this replacement.

3.

L &M Polyvinyl Inc. is considering replacing one of its plastic molding machines with a new and efficient machine. The old machine has a book value of P 40,000 and can be sold to net P 16,000 or it can be sold in five year to P 10,000 net. The old machine is being depreciated on a straight line method at P 8,000 a year down to a zero book value. The existing machine can run for 5 more years, producing annual revenues of P 120,000 with cash expense of P 60,000. The replacement machine will cost p 100,000 plus additional P 40,000 to transport it to factory and install it It will generate revenues of P 180,000 but will have cash expenses of P 80,000. It will be depreciated using the straight line method over a 5-year period at which time it will have a book value of P 40,000 and a cash salvage value of P 50,000.. The replacement machine will require additional working capital of P 10,000 to be tied up permanently. The company is in the 32% tax bracket. What is the differential after-tax cash flow stream?

4.

AJAM Industries,Inc. is planning to replace an exiting plant with a new machine that performs a particular manufacturing operation more efficiently. The following data determine the cash flows associated with the replacement:

Current situation:

Two full-time machine operators-salaries	35,000 each/per year
Cost of maintenance	3,500 per year
Cost of defects	25,000 per year
Original cost of old machine	38,500.00
Expected life	15 years
Age	5 years
Expected salvage value	
Depreciation method	straight line
Tax rate	32%
Current market value of old machine	38,500.00
Proposal	
Fully automated machine no operator	
Cost of machine	85,000.00
Installation fee	7,500.00
Transportation fee	6,000.00
Cost of maintenance	13,500.00
Cost of defects	7,500.00
Expected life	10 years
Salvage value	
Depreciation method	straight line
Increase in inventory	14,500.00

5.

The Birchstock Industries,Inc. is considering a new product line to supplement its range line. It is anticipated that the new product line will involve cash investments of P 700,000 at time 0 and P 1.0million in year 1. After-tax cash inflows of P 250,000 are expected in year 2, P 300,000 in year 3, P 300,000 in year 3, P 350,0000 in year 4, and P 400,000 each year thereafter through year 10. Although the product line might be viable after year 10, the company prefers to be conservative in all calculations at that time.

a. If the required rate of return is 15 percent, what is the net present value of the project? Is it acceptable?

b. What is internal rate of return?

c. What would be the case if the required rate of return were 10 percent?

d. What is the project's payback period?

Chapter 9

TIME VALUE OF MONEY

Time Value of Money In Finance

Time and money are inextricably related. One of the principal ideas in finance is the relationship between time and money. Called the time value of money, this economic principle recognizes that the passage of time affects the value of money. It advises you that if offered a currency either today or next time, you'd be better off to take that money today. You will have the use of money now, which you can put to some productive use for the whole period.

The timing of cash flows, both outflows and inflows – has important economic consequences, which financial managers explicitly recognize as the time value of money. Time value is based on the belief that dollar or peso today is worth more than it that will be received in some future date. There are two views involved in the study of time value of money in finance : future value and present value, and the computational aids to streamline time value calculation.

The timing of cash outflows and inflows has important economic consequences, which financial managers explicitly recognize as the time value of money since financial managers and investors are always confronted with opportunities to earn positive rates of return on their funds, whether through investment in attractive projects or in interest-bearing securities or deposits.

Time value is based on the belief that a dollar today is worth more than a dollar or a peso that will be received at some future time.

Distinction between Future Value from Present Value

By using either future value or present value techniques, financial values and decisions can be assessed. Thus, these techniques will result in the same decisions differently. Future value techniques typically measure cash flows at the end of a project's life; present value techniques measure cash flows at the commencement of a project's life (time zero). Future value is cash you will receive at a given future date, and present value is just like cash in hand nowadays.

To portray cash flows, a time line can be used with a given investment. It is a horizontal line on which time zero appears at the leftmost end and future periods are marked from left to right. A time line covering five periods may be shown as follows:

(10,000.00)	3,000.00	5,000.00	4,000.00	3,000.00	2,000.
0	1	2	3	4	5

end of year

A time line covering five periods is given above the line; the negative values represent cash outflows ($10,000 at time zero) and the positive values represent cash inflows ($3,000 inflow at the end of year 1, $5,0000 inflow at the end of year 2, and so on) Time lines allow the analyst to fully understand the cash flows associated with a given investment.

Because money has a time value, all of the cash flows associated with an investment, such as those given above must be measured at the same point in time. Typically, that point is either the end or the beginning of the investment's life. The future value technique uses compounding to find the future value of each cash flow at the end of the investment's life and then sums those values to find the investment's future value.

The present value technique uses discounting to find the present value of each cash flow at time zero and then sums these values to find the investment's value today. Financial managers make decisions at time zero and tend to rely primarily on present value technique, although future value and present value result in the same decisions.

Financial aids in calculations

Time consuming computations are often constituted in obtaining future and present values. The concepts and mathematics in these calculations should be understood through practical application of these important time value techniques . The use of financial tables or computers or calculators as computational aids would be of great aids in the calculations.

Concept of Future Value

The future value of a present amount is found by applying compound interest over a specified period of time. Savings institutions advertise compound interest returns at a rate of x percent interest compounded annually, semiannually, quarterly, monthly, weekly, daily , or even continuously. The concept of future value with annual compounding is illustrated as follows:

If Johnny places P5,000 in a savings account paying 8% interest compounded annually, at the end of 1 year he will have P5,400 in the account – the initial principal of P5,000 plus 8% in interest. The future value at the end of the first year is calculated by using equation 1:

Future value at end of year 1 = P 5,000 x (1+.08) = P 5,400.00

If Johnny were to leave this money in the account for another year, he would be paid interest at the rate of 8% on the new principal of P 5,400. at the end of this second year 2 (P5,400) plus 8% of the P 5,400(P432) in interest. The future value at the end of the second year is computed by using equation 2 as follows:

Future value at end of year 2 = P5,400 x (1+.08)
= P 5,832.00

Substituting the expression between the equal signs in equation 1 for the P5,400 in equation 2 gives us equation 3 as follows:

Future value at end of year 2 = P 5,000 x (1 + .08)x(1 + .08)

=P 5,000 x $(1+.08)^2$
= P 5,832.00

Interest Calculations

Calculations of interest may be based on interest rates which are either simple or compound.

Simple Interest

To compute for the interest, it is necessary to know the principal, the rate of interest and the term of the loan. The principal is the sum of money borrowed; the rate of interest is the percent of the principal which is charged for its use for one period of time, and the term of the loan is the number of periods during which the principal is used. Thus, the simple interest (S) on any principal (P) is found by multiplying together the principal, the rate of interest per annum (i) and time expressed in years (n).

Thus; S = P x I x n

Example 1

Bank X pays 10% on twelve months fixed deposit. What will be the interest on P 10,000 in fixed deposit for a year?

S = Px I x n

S = P 10,000 x .10 x 1 = P 10,000

The accumulated value at the end of the year is found by adding the interest to the principal. That is;

Accumulated value = Principal + Interest

If the accumulated value is designated by the symbol (V) then;

V = P + S

V = P + P. i . n

V = P (1 + i. n)

Equation (2) is the formula for the accumulated value at simple interest of a principal (P) bearing interest at the rate of I and n years.

Example 2.

Calculate the accumulated value for Example 1

V = P (1 + i.n.)

V = P 10,000 (11+ .10 x 1)

= P10,000 (1.10)

= P 11,000

To find the accumulated value of a principal invested at simple interest we use the formula, V = P (1 + i.n.) If the accumulated value is known and we wish to compute the present value (principal) we solve equation 2 for P. Thus, by transformation of equation 2, we find that;

$$P = \frac{V}{(1+i.n)}$$

Equation 3 is the formula for the present value of a future sum of money at simple interest

Example 3

What is the present value of P 11,000 due in one year's time fi money can be invested 10% per annum?

$$P = \frac{V}{(1 + i.n)}$$

$$P = \frac{P\ 11{,}000}{(1+10x\ I)}$$

$$P = \frac{P\ 11{,}000}{1.10}$$

= P 10,000

Thus, P 10,000 now and P 11,000 in one year's time at a rate of interest of 10% per annum are equivalent.

Compound Interest

Compound interest is similar to receiving interest on interest. The interest earned by the invested capital in any period is accumulated so that simple interest in the next period is paid not only on the original principal but also on the accumulated interest of all the previous periods during which interest was paid.

Example 4

What will P 1,000 amount to in 4 years if interest is 10% per annum compounded annually? Calculations for the above example are tabulated below:

Year amount deposited at beginning of year	Interest charge for year	Amount deposited at end of year
1 1,000.00	P 1,000 x 0.10 = 100	2,000.00
2 2,000.00	P2,000 x 0.10 = 200.00	2,200.00
3 2,200.00	2,200 x 0.10=220.00	2,420.00
4 2,420.00	P 2,420 x 0.10 = 242.00	2,662.00

The simple interest is much more often encountered in practice than simple interest. The compounding formula is derived by using the simple interest formula over and over again. Let us use the same symbols as those found in the simple interest formula. An amount paying interest compounded annually will grow to a future sum, V, accounting to the formula.

Equation 4:

$V = P+Pi$

$FV1 = P(1+i)$ for one year

For 2 years we have

Equation 5:

$FV2 = P(1+i)(1+i)$

$FV2 = P(1+i)^2$

At the end of n years the original sum deposited will grow to

Equation 6 :

$FVn = P(1+i)^n$

Example 5

Calculate the accumulated value for example 4 by using equation 6

$FV = P(1+i)^n$

$FV4 = P\ 1{,}000\ (1+.10)^4$

P 1,000 (1.4641)

= P 1,464.10

Thus, at the end of 4 years, we will have P 1,464.10

As the determination of future value can be quite time consuming when an investment is held for a number of years. Tables have been compiled for values pf (1+i)*n*. An abbreviated compound interest table appears in Table -1. In this table, the compounding factors represent the value of 1 compounded at rate I at the end of the nth year. To compute the future value of an initial investment we need to determine the table value and multiply the times of the initial investment.

Example 6

If we invest P 50,000 in the bank where it earns 8% annually. How much will it be worth at the end of 5 years?

Using table 1 in the row n = 5 and column I = 8%, we find a value of P 1,469. Substituting this in equation 6. we find

$FV\,n = P(1+i)^n$

$FV5 = P\ 50{,}000\ (1+.08)^5$

= P 50,000 (1.4693)

= P 73,465.00

Example 7

How many years will it take for an initial investment of P 10,000 to grow to P 51,156 if it is invested at 10% compounded annually?

Substituting the known values in equation 6, we find

$FV_n = P(1+i)^n$

$P\ 51{,}156 = P\ 10{,}000(1+.10)^n$

$5.1156 = (1+.10)^n$

Looking at the table value, we find 5.1156 in the 10% column, as it occurs in the n = 19. Thus, it will take 19 years for an initial investment of P 10,000 to grow to P 51,156.00 if it is invested at 10% compounded annually.

Example 8

At what rate P 20,000 be compounded annually for it to grow to P 50,545 in 17 years?

Substituting into equation 6, we get:

$FV\,n = P(1+i)^n$

$P\ 50{,}545 = P\ 20{,}000(1+i)^{17}$

$5.0545 = (1+i)^{17}$

By looking at the n = 17 row for a table value of 5.0545, we find this in the i= 10% column. Thus, we must invest at 10% if we want the initial investment of P 20,000 to accrue to P 50,545 in 17 years.

Table -1

Compound Sum of One Peso

n	1%	2%	3%	4%	5%	6%	7%	8%	9%	10%
1	1.0100	1.0200	1.0330	1.0400	1.0500	1.0600	1.0700	1.0800	1.0900	1.1
2	1.0201	1.0404	1.0609	1.0816	1.1025	1.1236	1.1449	1.1664	1.1181	1.2
3	1.0305	1.0612	1.0927	0.1249	1.1576	1.1910	1.2250	1.2597	1.2950	1.3
4	1.0406	1.0824	1.1255	1.1699	1.2155	1.2625	1.3108	1.3605	1.4116	1.4
5	1.0510	1.1041	1.1593	1.2067	1.2763	1.3382	1.4026	1.4693	1.5386	1.6
6	1.0615	1.1261	1.1941	1.2653	1.3401	1.4185	1.5007	1.5869	1.6771	1.7
7	1.0721	1.1870	1.2299	1.3159	1.4071	1.5036	1.6058	1.7138	1.8280	1.9
8	1.0829	1.1717	1.2668	1.3656	1.4775	1.5939	1.7182	1.8509	1.9926	2.1
9	1.0937	1.1951	1.3038	1.4233	1.5513	1.6895	1.8385	1.9990	1.1719	2.3
10	1.1046	1.2190	1.3439	1.4802	1.6289	1.7809	1.9672	2.1589	2.3674	2.5
11	1.1157	1.2434	1.3842	1.5395	1.7103	1.8993	2.1049	2.3316	2.5804	2.8
12	1.1268	1.2682	1.4258	1.6010	1.7959	2.0122	2.2522	2.5182	2.8127	3.1
13	1.1381	1.2936	1.4685	1.6651	1.8857	2.1329	2.4098	2.7196	3.0658	3.4
14	1.1495	1.3915	1.5126	1.7317	1.9799	2.2609	2.5785	2.9372	3.3417	3.7
15	1.1610	1.3459	1.5589	1.8009	2.0789	2.3966	2.7590	3.1722	3.6425	4.1
16	1.1726	1.3728	1.6047	1.8750	2.1829	2.5404	2.9522	3.4259	3.9703	4.5
17	1.1843	1.4002	1.6529	1.4479	2.2920	2.6928	3.1588	3.7000	4.3276	5.0
18	1.1962	1.4283	1.7024	2.0258	2.4066	2.8543	3.3799	3.9960	4.7171	5.5
19	1.2081	1.4568	1.7535	2.1069	2.5270	3.0256	3.6165	4.3157	5.1417	5.1
20	1.2202	1.4860	1.8061	2.1911	2.6523	3.2071	3.8697	4.6610	5.6044	6.7

Compounding Interest for Non-annual Periods

The compounding of interest is frequently less than a year as we adjust the compound interest formula to reflect the increase number of times the compounding will occur in the year. Frequently, the interest is earned and begins, in turn, to earn further interest, the greater the effective annual compound rate of interest.

Example: If interest is compounded quarterly, the amount on deposit at the end of 3 months would be:

Equation 7:

$FV_n = P(1 + i/4)$

Equation 8

The balance at the end of 6 months is:

$FV_n = P(1+i/4)(1+i/4)$ or $FV_n = P(1+i/4)^2$

Equation 9

And at the end of 1 year:

$FV_n = P(1+i/4)^4$

Equation 10

If interest is compounded *m* times per year, the amount on deposit at the end of *n* years will be:

$FV_m = P(1+i/m)^m$

The number of times per year interest is compounded may range from once to continuously. The interest rate is usually stated on the annual basis and is known as the nominal rate. When the nominal rate is compounded more than once a year a higher rate of return results, known as the effective rate. The effective rate compound once a year yields the same return as the nominal rate compounded in times per year. If we let the effective rate be j and the nominal rate be I, the relationship between j and I is given by:

$(1+J) = (1+ i/m)m$, or $j=(1+i/m) - 1$

Example 9:

What would be the effective rate if a nominal rate of 12% compounded 4 times a year?

A nominal rate of 12% compounded four times a year yields an effective rate of 12.55 percent:

$(1+0.1255) = (1+0.12/4)$ or $j= 1.1255 - 1=12.55\%$

Fractional Periods

When a problem includes fractional periods, it is usual in practice to use simple interest for the fraction of an interest period.

Example 10:

Harvey & Truman invest P 10,000 in each in a joint account. In return for their investment interest will accumulate at the rate of 8% per annum compounded annually. It is agreed that none of them will withdraw their investment until after the third year. After 3 ½ years. Harvey decides to withdraw his investment . how much will he receive?

Find the compound interest for the first 3 years and add to this simple interest for the half year to solve it . In 3 years the investment would have grown for :

$FV_3 = P\ 10,000(1.08)^3$

$FV_3 = P\ 10,000\ (1.25971)$

$= P\ 12,597.10$

To find the amount of repayment to Harvey:

FV_m = P 12,597.10 (1+ ½ x 0.08)

FV_m = P 12,597.10 (1.04)

= P 13,100.98

Interpolation

The principal, accumulated value and number of compounding periods are known in many and we compute the rate of interest. An approximate rate of interest may be found by interpolation. Interpolation assumes that the values in the tables vary uniformly. This is not exactly correct but it is sufficiently accurate for most purposes. Thus, since 2 ¼% is halfway between the 2% and 2 ½ % , it is expected that $(1.025)_m$ is approximately halfway between $(1.02)^n$ and $(1.050)^n$.

Present Value Discounting

Present value is the exact opposite or mirror image of future value. While future value shows how much a sum can become at some future date, present value shows what the value is today (at present) of future sums of money. This process of reducing future income payments to their present value is called *discounting.* The value today of the sum to be received in the future is called its present value.

Single Payment

Finding the present value (discounting) of a single payment is the reverse of compounding an initial sum over the same period of time.

Dividing both sides of Equation-6, FV = $P (1+i)^n$ by $(1+i)^2$ where FV is the future sum, P is the amount deposited, and I and n are defined as above, we have

$\underline{FV_n}$

$P = (1+i)_n$

Rearranging terms and substituting PV for P we have present value:

$$PV = \frac{FV_n}{(1+i)^n}$$

Example -11`

At what nominal rate of interest compounded quarterly will P 10,000 amount be P 14,000 in 5 years time?

$FV_n = P(1+i)^{20}$

Then;

$$(1+i)^{20} = \frac{P\ 14{,}000}{P\ 10{,}000} = 1.4000$$

Now it is necessary to find the value of I for which $(I - i)^{20}$ is equal to 1.4000. Looking through table we fail to find = 20 a value of 1.4000. However, we may find the approximate interest rate by linear interpolation which will result in a rate sufficiently accurate for most practical purposes.

In order to find the interest rate we follow along the line n= 20 until we find an entry slightly smaller than 1.4000 and one slightly greater, which we use to set up the following table.

	i			$(1+i)^{20}$	
	0.015			1.3469	
		x	0.0531		
0.0025	?			1.4000	
					0.0679
	0.0175			1.4148	

The interpolation process is performed as follows:

$$\frac{X}{0.0025} = \frac{0.0531}{0.0679}$$

$X = 0.00196$

Therefore, the rate of interest per compounding period is 0.015 + 0.00196 = 1.696%. The nominal rate compounded quarterly is 4i X 1.696 = 6.78%

As the mathematical procedure for determining the present value is exactly the inverse of determining the future value, we also find that the relationships among P, 1, and n are just opposite of those we observed with the future value. The present value of a future sum of money in inversely related to both number of years until the payment will be received at the opportunity rate.

Present Value Tables

In calculating present values, discount tables have been designed to provide convenience and accurate computations. Discount tables consist of discount factors. The discount factor is multiplied by the future sum to convert the sum to a present value.

Present value = (Future sum at period n)(Discount factor for i% per period and an periods)

PV = (FV_n)(DF I,n)

To determine the present value of a sum of money to be received at some future date, we ought to determine only the appropriate table value and multiply it by the future value.

Example 13

If the time value of money is 10% per year, calculate the present value of P 200,000 to be received twelve years in the future.

By referring to table – 2 below, in the n= 12 now, and I = 10% column, we find the value of [$1/(1+.10)^{12}$]is 0.31683. Substituting this value into equation 14, we find

PV = P 200,000 (0.31683) = P 63,366.00

Table -2

Present Value of One Peso at the end of n years.

n	1%	2%	3%	4%	5%	6%	7%	8%
1	1.01000	1.02000	1.03300	1.04000	1.05000	1.06000	1.07000	1.08000
1	0.99010	0.98039	0.97007	0.96154	0.95238	0.94340	0.93558	0.92593
2	0.98030	0.96117	0.94260	0.92456	0.90703	0.89000	0.87344	0.85734
3	0.97059	0.94232	0.91514	0.88900	0.86384	0.83962	0.81630	0.79383
4	0.96098	0.92285	0.88849	0.85480	0.82270	0.79209	0.76290	0.73503
5	0.95147	0.90573	0.86261	0.82193	0.78353	0.74726	0.71299	0.68058
6	0.94204	0.88797	0.83748	0.79031	0.74622	0.70496	0.66634	0.63017
7	0.93272	0.87056	0.81309	0.75992	0.71068	0.66506	0.62275	0.58349
8	0.92348	0.85349	0.78941	0.73069	0.67684	0.62741	0.58201	0.54027
9	0.91434	0.83675	0.76642	0.70259	0.64461	0.59190	0.54393	0.50025
10	0.90529	0.82035	0.74409	0.67556	0.61391	0.55839	0.50835	0.46319
11	0.89632	0.80426	0.72242	0.64958	0.58468	0.52679	.47a9	0.42888
12	0.88745	0.78849	0.70138	0.62460	0.55684	0.49627	0.44401	0.39711
13	0.87866	0.77303	0.68095	0.60057	0.53032	0.46884	0.41496	0.36770
14	0.86996	0.75787	0.66112	0.57747	0.50507	0.44230	0.38782	0.34046
15	0.86135	0.74301	0.64186	0.55526	0.48102	0.41726	0.36245	0.31524
16	0.85282	0.72845	0.62317	0.53391	0.45811	0.39365	0.33873	0.29189
17	0.84438	0.71416	0.60502	0.51337	0.43630	0.37137	0.31657	0.27027
18	0.83602	0.70016	0.58739	0.49363	0.41552	0.35034	0.29586	0.25025
19	0.82774	0.68643	0.57029	0.47464	0.39573	0.33051	0.27651	0.23171
20	0.81954	0.67297	0.55367	0.45639	0.37689	0.31180	0.25842	0.21455

A wise investor who can earn 10% per year on his own money would be indifferent between receiving P 63,366.00 now or P 200,000 12 years from now because the amounts are time equivalent. For if the investor had the P 63,366 today he could invest at 10% and have P 200,000 in 12 years. This equivalence is what is implied when we say that the present value of the future P 200,000 payment is P 63,366.00.

Annuity

An annuity is a series of payments of a fixed amount for a specified number of years. While the process of compounding and determining the present value of an annuity can be dealt with by using the methods ,may be quite time-consuming, especially for large annuities.

Formulas and tables are modified and developed in order to deal directly with annuities.

Compound Value of an Annuity

The compound value of an annuity is the total amount one would have at the end of the annuity period if each payment is invested at a certain interest rate and is held to the end of the annuity period. Thus, the procedure can be generated as :

Equation 15

$FV_a = [\, A \sum n \, (1+i)^t \,]$

Where FV_n = the future value of the annuity at the end of the nth year.

A = the annuity value deposited at the end of each year.

I = the annual compound interest rate.

n = the number of years for which the annuity will last.

Example 14

A promised to pay P 1,000 a year for three years is a three-year annuity. If you were to receive such an annuity and were to deposit each annual payment at the end of each year in a savings account paying 8% interest. How much would you have at the end of three years?

Compounding each of these values, we find that we will have P 3,246.40 at the end of three years.

FV_n = P 1,000(1+.08)^2+ P 1,000 (1+.08) + P 1,000

= P 1,000 (1.08)^2 + P 1,000 (1.08) + P 1,000

= P 1,166.40 + P 1,080 + P 1,000

= P 3,246.40

Pre calculated compound annuity tables

There are pre calculated compound annuities in table -3 . As in the case of the compound interest tables. By selecting the interest rate and the number of periods for which the funds are invested. We read the amount to which p 1 deposited annually for a n periods will grow at the specific interest rate. Reexamining the previous example 14, in which we determined the value of P 1,000 deposited at the end o each of the next 3 years in the bank at 8%, we can read from table-3. the factor of 3.264 which implies:

FV_n = P 1,000 x 3.2464

= P 3,246.40 – the same answer we obtained earlier;

Rather than asking how much we will accumulate if we deposit an equal sum in a saving account each year, a more common is how much we must deposit each year in order to accumulate a certain amount of savings. This problem frequently occurs with respect to saving for large expenditures and pension funding obligations.

Example 15

How much must be deposited in a 10% saving account at the end of each year in order to accumulate P 350,000 at the end of 10 years?

10

P 350,000 = AΣ (1+.10)

i= 1

<u>P 350,000</u>

15.937 = A

A = P 21,962

Thus, we must deposit P 21,962 per year for 10 years at 10% in order to accumulate P 350,000.

Table – 3

Annuity Compound Factor

n	1%	2%	3%	4%	5%	6%	7%	8%	9%
1	1.0000	1.0000	1.0000	1.0000	1.0000	1.0000	1.0000	1.0000	1.0
2	2.0100	2.0200	2.0300	2.0400	2.0500	2.0600	2.0700	2.0800	0.0
3	3.0300	3.0600	3.0910	3.1220	3.1530	3.1840	3.2150	3.2460	3.2
4	4.0600	4.1220	4.1840	4.2460	4.3100	4.3750	4.4400	3.5060	4.5
5	5.1010	5.2040	5.3090	5.4160	5.5260	5.6370	5.7510	5.8670	5.9
6	6.1520	6.3080	6.4680	6.6330	6.8020	6.9750	7.1530	7.3360	7.5
8	8.2860	8.5830	8.8920	9.2140	9.5490	9.8970	10.2600	10.6370	11.
9	9.3690	9.7550	10.1590	10.5830	11.0270	11.4910	11.9780	12.4880	13.
10	10.4620	10.9500	11.4640	12.0060	12.5780	13.1810	13.8160	14.8470	15.
11	11.5670	12.1690	12.8080	13.4860	14.2070	14.9720	15.7840	16.6450	17.
12	12.6830	13.4120	14.1920	15.0260	15.9170	16.8700	17.8880	18.9770	20.
13	13.8090	14.6800	15.6180	16.6270	17.7130	18.8820	20.1410	21.4950	22.
14	14.9470	15.9740	17.0860	18.2920	19.5990	21.0150	22.5500	24.2150	26.
15	16.9700	17.2930	18.5990	20.0240	21.5790	23.2760	25.1290	2.0000	29.
16	17.2580	18.6390	20.1570	21.8250	23.6570	25.6730	27.8880	30.3240	33.
17	18.4300	20.0120	21.7620	23.6980	25.8400	20.2130	30.8400	33.7500	36.
18	19.6150	21.4120	23.4140	25.6450	28.1320	30.9060	33.9990	37.4500	41.
19	20.8110	22.8410	25.1170	27.6710	30.5390	33.7600	37.3790	41.4460	36.
20	22.0190	24.2970	26.8700	29.7780	33.0660	36.7860	40.9950	45.7620	51.

Example 16

How much would a depositor receive with P 1,000 at the end of the next 3 years, and is worth to us if given an appropriate discount rate or opportunity rate of 10%? He can simply substitute the appropriate values into equation 13 :

PV = P 1,000 [1/ (1+.10)] + P 1,000 [1 / (1+ .10)^2] + P 1,000 [1/ (1+.10)^3]

= P 909.09 + P 826.45 + P 751.32

= P 2,486.86

Thus, the present value of this annuity is P 2,486.86

The Present Value of an Annuity

The present value of an annuity is the lump sum one would need to have on hand today in order to be able to withdraw equal amounts each year and end up with a balance exactly equal to zero at the end of the annuity period.

The mathematics involved, this procedure can also be generalized to :

Equation 16

N <u>*1*</u>

$PV_a = A\Sigma (1+i)^1$

i=1

where A = the annuity received at the end of each year.

1= the annual interest or discount rate

PV_a = the present value of the future annuity

n = the number of years for which the annuity will last.

Pre calculated present value of annuity tables

Simplifying the process of determining the present value of an annuity, tables are provided at the back of this book for various combinations of I and n; an abbreviated version is given in the table as follows:

Table -4

Present Value of One Peso per Year for n Years

n	1%	2%	3%	4%	5%	6%	7%	8%	9%
1	0.9901	0.9804	0.9701	0.9615	0.9524	0.9434	0.9356	0.9259	0.91
1	0.9901	0.9804	0.9709	0.9615	0.9524	0.9434	0.9346	0.9259	0.91
2	1.7040	1.9416	1.9135	1.8831	1.8594	1.8334	1.8080	1.7833	1.75
3	2.9410	2.8839	2.8286	2.7751	2.7233	2.6730	2.6243	2.5771	2.53
4	3.9020	3.8077	3.7171	3.6299	3.5459	3.4657	3.3872	3.3121	3.23
5	4.8535	4.7134	4.5897	4.4518	4.3295	4.2123	4.1002	3.9927	3.88
6	5.7955	5.6014	5.4172	5.2421	5.0757	4.9173	4.7665	4.6229	4.48
7	6.7282	2.4720	6.2302	6.0020	5.7863	5.5824	5.3893	5.2064	5.03
8	7.6517	7.3254	7.0196	6.7327	6.4632	6.2098	5.9713	5.7466	5.53
9	8.5661	8.1522	7.7861	7.4352	7.1078	6.8017	6.5152	6.2469	5.98
10	9.4714	8.9825	8.7326	8.1109	7.7217	7.3601	7.0236	6.7101	6.41
11	10.3677	9.7868	9.2526	8.7604	8.3064	7.8868	7.4987	7.1389	6.80
12	11.2552	10.5753	9.9539	9.3850	8.8632	8.3838	7.9427	7.5361	7.16
13	12.1338	11.3483	10.6349	0.9986	9.3935	8.8527	8.3576	7.9038	7.48
14	13.0038	12.1062	11.2960	10.5631	9.8986	9.2950	8.7454	8.2442	7.78
15	13.8651	12.8492	11.9379	11.1183	10.3796	9.7122	9.1079	8.5595	8.06
16	14.7180	13.5777	12.5610	11.6522	10.8377	10.1059	9.4466	8.8514	8.31
17	15.5624	14.2918	13.1660	12.1656	11.2740	10.4772	9.7632	9.1216	8.54
18	16.3984	14.9920	13.7514	12.6592	11.6895	10.8276	10.0591	9.3719	8.75
19	17.2281	15.2684	14.3237	13.1339	12.0853	11.1581	10.3556	9.6036	8.95
20	18.0457	16.3514	14.8774	13.8903	12.4622	11.4699	10.5940	9.8181	9.12

The product of the annuity discount factor (ADF i,n) and the annuity payment is the present value of the annuity at the stated time value of money:

Equation 17

(PVa =) (ADF I,n)

This is the same answer we calculated when we discounted each cash flow back to the present.

Example 17

How would an investor find the present value of the following cash flow, given the 20% rate?

Cash	1	2	3	4	5
Flow	100,000.00	200,000.00	300,000.00	400,000.00	500,000.00

Given a 20% discount rate, the investor would simply discount the flows back to the present and total them by adding in the positive flows and subtracting the negative ones. For example, this is:

PV = 1[P 100,000)(.83333)+(P200,000)(.69444)-(P300,000)(.57870)+(P500,000)(.48225)+(P400,000)(.40188)]

=P 450,488

The present value of this series is P 450,488

Perpetuities

A perpetuity is an annuity or series of periodic payments that runs indefinitely, differing, therefore from the annuities in terms of duration only. The most common example of a perpetuity is the establishment of an endowment, although bonds lacking any maturity also qualify. The value of a perpetuity is determined by dividing the yearly payment by the rate of return being received on the principle. The present value of a perpetuity of Pesos. A per year can be portrayed as:

Equation 18;

PV (perpetuity) = A + A + ... A

(1+i) (1+i)^2 (1+i)^m

m A

= Σ (1+i) ^{t}

t=1

m 1A

A = Σ (1+i) ^{t}

t=1

equation 19

by examining expression (16) we see that

m

A = Σ = 1

t=1 t

Hence,

Equation 20

PV (perpetuity) = Peso A

i

Example 18

If X is to pay Y P 11,000 each year in perpetuity, how much does it worth if discount rate is 15%? Substituting into equation 20, the present value of the payment is:

PV (perpetuity) = P 11,000 = P 68,750

0.16

Problems Solving:

1. *Mr Sandoval* needs P200,000 to buy a second hand machine for his fabrication business in ten years. How much must be deposited at the end of each year in the bank at 10% compound interest in order to have the machine available?

2. Find the effective rate of interest for :
   (a) 8% compounded semi annually ;
   (b) 8% compounded quarterly;
   (c) 8% compounded monthly.

   1. If P 50,000 is put in savings account yielding 6% compounded annually and other P 30,000 in ten years. Using equation-6 we obtain:

4. *Shrex Manufacturing* needs P 100,000 for a 3- year-period. A local bank will provide a 3-year discount loan at a stated rate of 10%. Determine how much Sherex must borrow in order to have use of the P 100,000. Calculate the effective rate of interest on the loan.

5. A sinking fund was established for *Norseman Industries* to ration a P 1,000,000 bond issue which matures in 15 years. How much do they have to put into the fund at the end of each year to accumulate the P 1,000,000, assuming the funds were compounded at 7% annually?

6. *Vikings International* is due to receive *P 500,000* a year for next 5 years and P 250,000 at the end of the sixth year. Money is worth 12%. What is the present value of the stream?

7. What is the present value of cash flows of P 1,000 per year indefinitely : (a) at an interest rate of 8% and (b) at an interest rate of 10%?

8. *Rich Bank* pays 8 % interest, compounded quarterly, on its money market account. The managers of *Millionaire Bank* want its money market account to equal Rich Bank's effective annual rate, but interest is to be compounded on a monthly basis. What nominal, or quoted, rate must *Millionaire Bank* set?

9. *Future values*

Mark Anthony has $ 10,000 that he can deposit in any of three savings accounts for a 3-year period. *City Bank* compounds interest on an annual basis, *Town Bank* compounds interest twice each year, and *Promdi Bank* compounds interest each quarter. All three banks have a stated annual interest rate of 4%.

a. What amount would Mark have at the end of the third year, leaving all interest paid on deposit, in each bank?

b. What effective annual rate (EAR) would he earn in each of the banks?

c. On the basis of your findings in a and b, which bank should Mark deal with? Why?

d. If a 4th bank – *Avenue Bank,* also with a 4% stated interest rate – compounds interest continuously, how much would Mark have at the end of the third year? Does this alternative change your recommendation in c? Explain why or why not.

10. *Future values of annuities.*

Julius wants to choose the better of two equally costly cash flow streams – annuity A and annuity B. A is an annuity due with a cash inflow of $ 9,000 for each of 6 years. B is an ordinary annuity with a cash inflow of $ 10,000 for each of 6 years. Assume that Julius can earn 15% on his investments.

a. Which annuity, on a purely intuitive basis, do you think is more attractive? Why?

b. Find the future value at the end of year 6, FVA6 for both annuities – A and B.

c. use your finding in b to indicate which annuity is more attractive. Why? Compare your finding to your intuitive response in a.

Chapter 10

COST OF CAPITAL

Factors that determine the Cost of Capital

We consider the elements in the business environment that cause a company's cost of capital to be high or low. The primary factors to be examined are:

1. General Economic Conditions

The general economic conditions determine the demand for and supply of capital within the economy, as well as the level of expected inflation. This represents the rate of return on risk- free investments, such as the interest rate on short-term government securities. As the demand for money in the economy changes relative to the supply, investors change their required rate of return. For example, if the demand for money increases without an equivalent increases in supply, creditors will raise in the purchasing power of the money, investors require a higher rate of return to compensate for this anticipated loss.

2. **Risk and Cost of Capital**

If an investor is purchasing a security where the risk of the investment is significant, the opportunity for additional returns is necessary to make the investment attractive. The risk elements is composed of five aspects that closely inter-twined: business risk, financial risk, purchasing power risk, money rate risk (also called interest rate risk), and market (or liquidity)risk.

Business risk is the variability in return on assets and is affected by the company's investment decisions.

Financial risk refers to the change in the purchasing power of money measure by price level changes.

Money rate risk refers to the premium in yield demanded by suppliers of capital to cover the risk of an increase in future interest rates.

Market (or liquidity) risk refers to the ability of a supplier of funds to sell his holdings quickly.

Flotation Costs Flotation costs represent a financial market-distortion which makes the new issues more expensive form of financing. They are the cost of marketing new securities. They include all costs involved in moving new securities from the issue to the ultimate investor. They include legal fees, printing expenses, sales commissions, and profit to the underwriting syndicate, among other things. Flotation costs are called because they are incurred in floating new securities. The sometimes called *underwriting costs or issuance costs.*

Because they increase the cost of firm's capital when they are incurred, flotation costs here are involved. This costs reduce the cash proceeds from the sale of a security. Example, a firm issues an equity share of P 100, if flotation costs are 2%, the issuing firm will receive only P 98 on per equity share. Reduction of proceeds when flotation costs are incurred is not accompanied by a reduction in the return to the capital suppliers. Consider a corporation that issues a P 1,000 bond that promises 12% return. The issue promises to pay P 120 interest each year, that is:

.12 X P1,000 = P 120

Without flotation costs, the corporation is to earn only 12% before taxes on his assets to pay the bondholder, other things equal. But when flotation costs are introduced, the situation changes.

Assume that it costs P 20 to market each bond. This mean that the firm gets proceeds of only 980 (P 1,000 – P 20) But the bondholders are still expecting a P 120 return for each bond. Ignoring the tax affects momentarily, the corporation must earn P 120 over the net proceeds of P 980, that is:

Equation 1:

P 120 = 12.24%

P 980

Flotation costs can be included in the cost of capital buy adjusting the market rate of return. The cost of capital including flotation costs is figured as:

Market rate of return

Cost of Capital = 1- flotation cost percentage

In the example above, the market rate of return was 12.0 per cent and if the flotation costs are increased to 2.50%, then by using the equation – 1. we get

Before –tax cost of debt = .120 / 1-.025 = .120 / .975 = 12.31%

Taxes

In capital budgeting, all cash flows are evaluated on an after-tax basis. In order to be consistent with this capital budgeting framework, the cost of capital, which is to discount the cash flows in determining net present values and benefit-cost ratios, and as the cut-off rate for internal rates of return must also be measured on an after tax basis. The specific cost of capital that actually requires any type of tax adjustment is the cost of debt.

Components of Cost of Capital

The overall cost of capital of a firm is comprised of the costs of the various components of financing.

Debt, preference shares, retained earnings, and equity shares are presented in determining the specific costs of each of these sources. The techniques presented tend to develop precisely computed values of specific as well as weighted average costs, which is important to recognize that the resulting values are at best rough approximations due to the numerous assumptions and forecasts that underlie them.

Cost of Debt

The cost of capital for debt is the return that potential investors require of the firm's debt securities, such as its bonds. The cost of debt has two basic components; one is the annual interest and the other arises from the amortization of discounts or premium paid or received when the debt is initially issued.

Since the interest payments and the return of principal remain constant regardless of the change in investor's required rate of return, only the bond price and the cost of debt can change, a financial manager can pinpoint the exact cost of debt after the price change by computing *kd in generalize equation:*

$$P_n = \sum_{T=1}^{n} \frac{IP}{(1+k_d)^t} + \frac{P_{nt}}{(1+k_d)^n}$$

P_n = the observed market price of the bond

IP_t = the interest payments on the principal

P_n = the return of principal

K_d = the cost of debt (after-tax)

n = the number of years until the bond matures.

Since interest is tax-deductible expense, consider the after-tax cost of debt, especially if we qualify its impact on firm's after-tax profitability or compare it to the cost of other types of securities which a company can offer whose cash flow streams are not – deductible, such as preference and equity shares. The after-tax cost of debt is computed by adjusting the pre-tax for the tax rate such that:

$K_d = k_t (1 - t)$

Where;

k_d = the after-tax cost of debt

k_i = the pre-tax cost of debt

t = the tax rate

The general formula for effective rate is:

Effective rate = interest rate (1.0 – tax-rate)

In many instances, individuals or corporation may borrow from more than one source. The amounts of loans and their interest rates often differ quite appreciably. As a result, the average interest rate must be computed. Since the amounts of the loans differ, a weighted average must be taken.

Example -1

Drake Equipment,Inc. has the following outstanding debts:

Debt	Amounts	Pre-tax Interest rate
Bonds, Series A	1,000,000.00	12.0%
Mortgage	2,000,000.00	15.0%
Bonds, Series B	4,500,000.00	16.6%
Bonds, Series C	5,000,000.00	18.0%
	12,500,000.00	

Determine the weighted average pre-tax interest rate

Solution : First, determine the proportion of each type of debt. This is accomplished by dividing the amount of each debt by the total debt. In this example, the total is P 12,500,000.

Debt	Amounts	Pre-tax Interest rate
Bond, Series A	1mil / 12.5mil	0.08
Mortgage	2 mil / 12.5 mil	0.16
Bond, Series B	4.5mil / 12.5mil	0.36
Bond, Series C	5mil/12.5mil	0.40
		1.00

Next, multiply the properties of each type of debt by its interest rate (expressed in decimal form) then add the sum to obtain the weighted average cost of debt. These computations in tabular form are depicted as follows:

Debt	Amounts	Proportion	Pre-tax Interest rate	Weighted costs Rate (cost)
Bonds, Series A	1,000,000.00	0.08	0.120	0.00960
Mortgage	2,000,000.00	0.16	0.150	0.02400
Bonds, Series B	4,500,000.00	0.36	0.166	0.05976
Bonds, Series C	5,000,000.00	0.40	0.180	0.07200
		1		0.16536

Assuming Drake Equipment Company has a marginal income tax-rate of 40%. Determine the after-tax weighted average cost of debt.

Solution:

The weighted average pre-tax cost of debt (interest rate) is 16.536%. Applying equation 2, the after tax cost of debt may be computed as follows:

$k_d = k_t (1-t)$

$= .16536(1-.40)$

$= .066144 = 6.6144\%$

The after-tax weighted average cost of debt is 6.6144%

Flotation costs (F) for new issues of debt accelerates the cost. The greater the flotation cost, other things being equal, the higher the cost of debt. The following formulation accounts for the incidence of flotation cost and tax-effects.

$$k_d \ \frac{k_t (1-t)}{(1-F)}$$

Example 3

Referring to example 2, the after-tax weighted average cost of debt for Drake Equipment, assuming the flotation for bonds to be 2%,

Solution:

To determine the after-tax weighted average cost of debt, equation 4 is to be applied to take the incidence of flotation costs. By using equation 4, we get;

$$k_d = \frac{16536(1-.40)}{(1-.02)}$$

$= 6.1984$

Yield to Maturity (YTM)

Yield to maturity provides the calculation of the k_d which is synonymous with the cost of debt. Using the present-value tables, we compute the k_d or resort to approximation method"

The formula for yield to maturity is:

$$\text{Approximate YTM} = \frac{\text{Average Annual Return}}{\text{Average Investment}}$$

[C+(M-P)/n] [12/(M+P)]

Where;

C = the annual coupon

M = the maturity or the par value of the bond

P = the purchase price

N = the number of years remaining to maturity

Example 4

Grander Company issued bonds with par value of P 1,000 at 12% at 10% discount for 10 years,. Compute the YTM:

Solution:

Substituting the information of bond into the equation (5), we have:

YTM = [(120+(1000-900)/10] [2/(1000 + 900)]

= 130/950 - 13.68%

Cost of Preference Share

The cost of preference share is represented by a fixed dividend payment carrying a higher order of precedence than equity share dividends, but not the binding contractual obligation as of interest on debt. Preference share, being a hybrid security, has neither the ownership privilege of equity nor the legally enforceable provisions of debt. The cost of preference share is found by dividing the annual preference share dividend by net proceeds from the sale of preference share. The net proceeds represent the amount of money to be received minus flotation costs.

$$k_p = \frac{D}{P_p - F}$$

Where,

k_p = the cost of preference share

D = the preference share dividend

P_t = the market price of preference share

F = the flotation or selling costs.

For example, if:

(i) D = P 20; P_t = P 100

Then,

k_p = <u>P20</u>

P 100

= 20%

If;

(ii) F – P 2

Then;

k_p = <u>P 20</u>

P 100 – P 2

= 20.41

IF, the preference is selling at a premium, say, P 110;

k_p = <u>P 20</u>

P 110- P 2

= P 20 / P 100 = 18.52

If, the preference share is selling at a discount , P90 , for example:

k_p - P20 / P 90 – P 2 = P20/P88 = 22.73

Example 5:

In 2007 ,*Cyril Enterprises* issued preference shares for P 100 per share. The share pays a yearly dividend of P 18.60. Cyril Enterprises received P 98 for each share. What is the cost of the 2007 issue of preference share ?

Solution:

The selling price was P 100 and the amount *Cyril Enterprises* received was only P 98, because the flotation cost was P 2. Using equation 6, the cost is computed below:

k_p = P 18.60/ P100-P2 = P 18.60/P98.00 = 18.98%

While the preference shares do not legally bind the firm to pay dividends and meet other indenture agreements, its additional cost overshadows these advantages of the preference shares.

Cost of Retained Earnings

The cost of retained earnings is closely related to the cost of equity shares. If earnings are not retained they will be paid out to the equity shareholders as dividends. Retained earnings are often fully subscribed issue of new equity, since they increase the shareholders' equity in the same way that a new issue of equity shares would. The cost of retained earnings must be viewed as the opportunity cost of the foregone dividends to the existing equity shareholders.

If the firm is unable to earn as much on its retained earnings as other firms with a comparable level of risk, the shareholders will prefer to receive these earnings in the form in dividends, so that they can invest in other firms. It assumes that the shareholders cannot earn as much on the money through reinvestment when the company retain earnings.

The value of an equity share depends, ultimately on the dividends paid on the share:

Equation 7

$P_a = D_1 /(1+k_r)\ ^1D^2/ (1+k^r))\ ^2...$

Where;

P_a = the current price of the share

D_t = the dividends expected to be paid at the end of year t

k_r = the required rate of return

If dividends are expected to grow at a constant rate, equation 7 reduces to

$P_a = D_1 / k - g$

Where; g = growth rate

The expected and required rates of return must be equal, we solve k, to obtain the required rate of return on equity;

$P_a = D_1 / P_a + \text{expected } g$

To illustrate, consider a firm expected to earn P 24 a share and to pay a P 12 dividend during the coming year. The company's earnings, dividends and share prices have all been growing at about 12 % a year, and this growth rate is expected to continue indefinitely. If the current price of the equity share is P 100, then k_t would be computed as :

k_t = P 12 / P 100 + 12% = 24%

IF the firm refrains from meeting investment and pays all its earnings in dividends, it will cut its growth rate to zero. The price of the share will not fall. Investors still get the required 24%rate of return on their shares.

= P24/ P 100+0 = 24%

Cost of Equity

The cost of equity can be stated as the rate at which investors discount the expected dividend of the firm in order to determine the market price of an ownership interest in the firm. The cost of new shares of equity can easily be computed by determining the percentage reduction in the current market price attributable to flotation costs, which consists of under pricing and under writing fees. Let F represent the percentage reduction in the current market price expected as a result of under pricing and underwriting charges on a new equity-issue, the cost of the new equity issue k_e can be illustrated as :

$k_e = D_1 / P_a (1\text{-}F) + g$

F is the percentage cost of selling the issue, so P_a (1-F) = P_a (1-F) = P_a is the net price received by the firm

Example

The market price of Jason Company equity share is P 285 per share and the flotation costs are P 5 per share. If the dividend is P 35, and has been growing at an annual rate of 18%, what is the cost of equity capital?

Solution:

Using equation 11, the cost of equity share is :

k_e = P35 / P 285 –P 5 + g

= P 35/ P 280 + .18 = .125+.18 = .305

The cost equity capital is 30.5g

Weighted Average Cost of Capital

The weighted average cost of capital summed up the after tax cost of the entire capital structure. It is used as the discount rate in calculating the net present value of investment proposals, Any projects with internal rates of return less than the weighted-average cost cannot be accepted.

The calculation of the weighted average cost of capital (WACC) is done by multiplying the specific cost of each form of financing by its proportion in the firm's capital structure and summing the weighted values. As an equation, the weighted average cost of capital, k_a, can be specified as follows:

$k_a = (w_i \times k_i) + (w_p \times k_p) + (w_5 \times k_{r\ or\ n})$

where;

wi = proportion of long-term debt in capital structure

wp = proportion of preferred stock in capital structure

w 5 = proportion of common stock equity in capital structure

$w_1 + w_p + w_5 = 1.0$

Three important points should be noted :

1. for computational convenience, it is best to convert the weights to decimal form and leave the specific costs in percentage terms.

2. the sum of weights must equal 1.0 Simply stated, all capital structure components must be accounted for;

3. The firm's common stock equity weight, w_s is multiplied by either the cost of retained earnings, k, or the cost of new common stock, k_n. Which cost is used depends on whether the firm's common stock equity will be financed using retained earnings, k_r, or new common stock, k_n.

Example:

The *D Corporation* has the costs of various types of capital :

Cost of debt, k_i = 5.6%

Cost of preferred stock, k_p = 10.6%

Cost of new common stock, k_n = 14.0%

The company uses the following weights in computing its weighted average cost of capital:

Sources of Capital	
Long-term debt	40%
Preferred stock	10%
Common stock equity	50%
Total	100%

Calculation of the Weighted average cost of capital for D Corporation.

Sources of capital	Weight	Cost	Weighted Cost [(1)x(2)]
	(1)	(2)	(3)
Long-term debt	0.40	0.06	2.2%
Preferred stock	0.10	0.11	1.1
Common stock equity	0.50	13.0	6.5
Totals	1		9.8%

Weighted average cost of capital = 9.8%

Computation of Weighted Average Cost of Capital

This is found by weighing the cost of specific type of capital by the historical, target, or marginal proportions of each type of capital used. Historical weights are based on the firm's existing capital structure, target weights are based upon the proportion of the various types of capital the firm wishes to maintain, whereas marginal weights consider the actual proportions of each type of capital expected to be used in financing a given project.

Book Value Weights

The book value weights in computing the firm's weighted average cost of capital assumes that new financing will be raised using exactly the same proposition of each type of financing as the firm currently has in its capital structure. The calculation involved can be illustrated by a simple example.

Book value weights use accounting values to measure the proportion of each type of capital in the firm's financial structure. Market value weights measure the proportion of each type of capital at its market value. Market value weights are appealing, because the market values of securities closely approximate the actual dollars to be received from their sale. Moreover, because the costs of the various types of capital are computed by using prevailing market prices, it seems reasonable to use market value weights. The long-term investment cash flows to which the cost of capital is applied are estimated in terms of current as well as future market values.

Market value weights are clearly preferred over book value rights.

Table – 2 shows an example of computing the weighted average cost of capital. Column lists the type of capital-bonds, preference shares, retained earnings, and equity shares. Column 2 contains the book value of each capital source. These figures will be used to determine the relative importance of each capital source. The values in column 3 are calculated by dividing the amount of each type of capital by the total figure. For example, bonds contribute 30 % of the capital; (i.e. P 30,000,000/P 100,000,000= .50). The weight must sum to unity , 1.0 .

The Weighted Average Cost of Capital
(Book Value Rights)

Capital Component	Book Value	Book Value Weight (2)+100,000,000	Before-tax Cost	After-tax Cost	Weighted Cost of Capital
1	2	3	4	5	6
Bonds	50,000,000.00	0.50	0.15	0.075	0.0375
Preference Shares	7,500,000.00	0.08	0.12	0.12	0.0096
Retained Earnings	18,000,000.00	0.18	0.21	0.21	0.0378
Equity Shares	40,000,000.00	0.40	0.24	0.24	0.0960
Total	115,500,000.00	1		WACC	0.1809

Tax rate = 50%

Column 4 contains the before-tax cost of each type of capital. The figure in column 5 contains the after-tax cost of each type of capital. This figure is computed by applying the tax rate to the before-tax cost. The only type of capital in Table 2 whose cost is tax-deductible is debt. Applying the 50 per cent tax rate to the before-tax cost of debt of .15 leaves an after tax cost of .075.

Market Value Rights

The use of market value weights for computing the firm's weighted average cost of capital is theoretically more appealing than the use of book value weights since the market value of the securities closely approximate the actual to be received from their debt. Since the cost of the various types of capital are calculated using prevailing market prices, it seems only reasonable to use market value of a firm's sources of equity financing (i.e. preference, retained earnings, and equity) than to use book values. The weighted average cost of capital based on the market value weights is greater than the weighted average cost of capital based on book value weights, since it is not unusual for preference and equity shares to have market values that are above their book value. Since these sources of long-term funds have higher specific costs than debt, the overall cost of capital normally increases when market value instead of book value weights are used.

The Marginal Weights and Cost of Capital

The use of marginal weights involves weighting the specific costs of various types of financing by the percentage of the total financing expected to be raised via each method. The proportion of each type of financing in the firm's capital structure would remain the same using historical weights. The firm is trying to develop what is believed to be an optimal capital structure reflected by certain desired proportions of capital. The use of marginal weights is more attuned to the actual process of financing projects. It recognizes that the funds actually raised in discrete amounts, using the various sources of long-term funds.

The marginal cost of capital is computed by taking a weighted average of the marginal cost of each composition in proportion to the respective amounts of each that the firm will raise.

The Weighted-Average Cost of Capital

(Market Value Weights)

Capital Component

1	2	3	4	5	6
Bonds	28,500,000.00	0.26	0.15	0.075	0.0195
Preference Shares	4,500,000.00	0.04	0.12	0.120	0.0048
Retained earnings	18,000,000.00	0.16	0.20	0.200	0.0320
Equity shares	60,000,000.00	0.54	0.24	0.240	0.1296
Total	111,000,000.00	1.00			0.1859

tax rate = 50%

The table above is based upon market-value weights. Column 2 contains the market value of the firm's capital rather than its book value. The market value of bonds is computed by multiplying the number of bonds outstanding by each one's current market value. Each of the company's bond sells for P950, and there are 30,000 bonds outstanding, for a total market value of bonds P 28,500,000. There are 50,000 shares of preference , each with a market value of P 90, for a total value of P4,500,000. Likewise, there are 1,000,000 shares of equity, each with a market value of P 60, for a total of P 60,000,000. By definition retained earnings have no explicit market value, but again, the key to their valuation is taken from equity shares. Since equity shares are selling for 20% more than its book value (P 60million / P 50 million, we impute the same increased value to retained earnings, and increase their value by 20%, from P15million toP18million.

The use of market value weights in lieu of book value weights is dependent upon the availability of current and reliable market price for the firm's securities. If such market price are available, market-value weights may be used.

Example

A corporation plans to raise P 50,000,000 of new capital as follows:

Current liabilities : P 2,500,000 at 16% (assume no flotation or service charge)

Long-term debt: P 7,000,000 at 15% (flotation costs, ½%)

Preference shares : P 4,000,000, floatation costs (F) estimated at 2%; sold at P 32 per share with a stated dividend of P 2.50

Equity shares : P 40,000,000, floatation cost (F) estimated at 10% dividend P 2.50 per share; market price P 50 per share, anticipated growth rate of dividend, 12%.

The firm's marginal tax rate is 50%. Determine the cost of each component and the marginal cost of capital.

Solution:

Cost of long-term debt:

K_1 = $\underline{I(1-t)}$ = $\underline{P\ 1{,}050{,}000\ (1\text{-}05)}$ = $\underline{P\ 262{,}500}$ = .03769

P(1-F) = P7,000,00 (1-0.005) = P 6,965,000

Cost of preference:

K_p D_p / P_p (1-F) = P 2.50/P 32(1-0.02) =PO 2.50 / P 31.36 = 0.0797

Cost of new equity

K_e D_1 / P_0 (1-F) + g = P 2.50 / P 50(1-0.10) + 0.12

=P 2.50 / P 45 + 0.12 = 0.1786

Marginal Cost of Capital

	Market value	Market weights	After-tax cost	Weighted After-tax cost
Current liabilities	2,500,000.00	0.050	0.08000	0.0040
Long-term debt	7,000,000.00	0.125	0.03769	0.0047
Preference shares	4,000,000.00	0.075	0.07970	0.0060
New equity	40,000,000.00	0.750	0.17860	0.1340
	53,500,000.00	Marginal cost of capital =		0.1486
The marginal cost of capital is approximately 14.86%				

The Marginal Cost and Investment Decisions

The firm's weighted average cost of capital is a key input to the investment decision-making process. The firm should make only those investments for which the expected return is greater than the weighted average cost of capital. Of course, at any given time, the firm's financing costs and investment returns will be affected by the volume and investment undertaken. The concepts of a weighted marginal cost of capital and an investment opportunities schedule provide the mechanisms whereby financing and investment decisions can be made at the same time.

The Weighted Marginal Cost of Capital (WMCC)

The weighted average cost of capital may differ at any rime depending on the volume of financing the firm plans to raise. As the volume of financing increases, the costs of various types of financing will increase, raising the firm's weighted average cost of capital. It is useful to compute the weighted marginal cost of capital. Which its next dollar of total new financing. It is relevant to current decisions.

The WMCC is an increasing function of the level of total new financing, because the costs of the financing components –debt, preferred stock, and common stock – rise as larger amounts are raised. Increases in the component financing costs occur because the larger the amount of new financing, the greater the risk to the funds supplier. Funds suppliers require greater returns in the form of interest, dividends, or growth as compensation for the increased risk introduced as larger volumes of new financing are incurred.

Another factor that causes the weighted average cost of capital to increase is the use of common stock equity financing. New financing provided by common stock equity will be taken from available retained earnings until exhausted and then will be obtained through new common stock equity financing than the weighted average cost of capital will rise with the addition of more expensive new common stock.

To compute for WMCC, we calculate the *breaking points,* which reflect the level of total new financing at which the cost of one of the financing components rises. The following general equation can be used to find breaking points:

$Bp_i = AF_i / w_i$

Where;

BP_j = breaking point for financing source j

AF_i = amount of funds available from financing source j at a given cost

w_j = capital structure weight (historic or target, stated in decimal form) for financing source j.

Example:

When *DX Corporation* exhausts its P 300,000 of available retained earnings (k_r = 13.0%), it must use the more expensive new common stock financing (k_n = 14.0%) to meet its common stock equity needs. In addition, the firm expects that it can borrow only P 400,000 of debt at the 5.6% cost; additional debt will have possibilities from best (highest return) to worst (lowest return). As the cumulative amount of money invested in a firm's capital projects increases, its return (IRR) on the projects will decrease; generally , the first project selected will have the highest return, the next project the second highest, and so on. The return on investments will decrease as the firm accepts additional projects.

The Investment Opportunities Schedule (IOS)

A firm has certain investment opportunities available to it. These opportunities differ with respect to the size of investment, risk, and return. The firm's investment opportunities schedule is a ranking of investment possibilities from best (highest return) to worst (lowest return). As the cumulative amount of money invested in a firm's capital projects increases, its return (IRR) on the projects will decrease; generally, the first project selected will have the highest return, the next project the second highest, and so on. The return on investments will decrease as the firm accepts additional projects.

Investment Opportunities Schedule (IOS) for DY Corporation

Investment Opportunity	Internal rate of return (IRR) (1)	Initial Investment (2)	Cumulative investment (3)
A	15.0%	100,000.00	100,000.00
B	14.5%	200,000.00	300,000.00
C	14.0%	400,000.00	700,000.00
D	13.0%	100,000.00	800,000.00
E	12.0%	300,000.00	1,100,000.00
F	11.0%	200,000.00	1,300,000.00
G	10.0%	100,000.00	1,400,000.00

Using WMCC and IOS in Financing/Investment

As long as the project's internal rate of return is greater than the weighted marginal cost of new financing, the firm should accept the project, and the weighted marginal cost of capital will increase because greater amounts of financing will be required. The firm would therefore accept projects up to the point at which the marginal return on its investment equals its weighted marginal cost of capital. Beyond that point, its investment return will be less than its capital cost.

This is consistent with the maximization of net present value (NPV) because of conventional projects;

The NPV is positive as long as the IRR exceeds the weighted average cost of capital, k_a , the larger the resulting NPV. Therefore, the acceptance of projects beginning with those having the greatest positive difference between IRR and k_a down to the point at which IRR just equals k_a should result in the maximum total NPV for all independent projects accepted. Such an outcome is absolutely consistent with the firm's goal of owner wealth maximization.

By using tow functions in combinations, WMCC schedule and IOS, the firm's optimal capital budget ("X" in the figure) is determined . By raising $1.1 million of new financing and investing these funds in projects A,B,C,D and E, the firm should maximize the wealth of its owners, because these projects result in the maximum total net present value. Note that the 12.0% return on the last dollar invested (in project E) exceeds its 11.5% weighted average cost; investment in project F is not feasible because its 11.0% return is less than the 11.5% cost of funds available for investment.

At this point at which the IRR equals the weighted average cost of capital – ka – the optimal capital budget of $ 1,100,000 at point X in – the firm's size as well as its shareholders value will be optimized. In a sense, the size of the firm is determined by the market – the availability of and return on investment opportunities, and the availability and cost of financing.

Weighted Average Cost of Capital and IRR

15.5

15.0 A

14.5 B

14.0 C

13.5 |

13.0 | D

12.5

12.0 E

11.5 11.5% WMCC

11.0 F

10.5 10.3% G

10.0 9.80%

9.5 IOS

0 500 1000 1,500

1,100

X

Finding the Breaking Point

To compute the WMCC, we calculate the breaking points, which reflect the level of total new financing at which the cost of one of the financing components rises. The following equation can be used to find the breaking point.

$BP_j = AF_j / w_j$

where

BP_j = breaking point for financing source j

AF_j = amount of funds available from financing source j at a given cost

W_j = capital structure weight (historic or target, stated in decimal form) for financing source.

Key Definitions and Formulas for Cost of Capital

Variable Definitions

AF_j = Amount of funds available from financing source j at a given cost

B = bet coefficient or measure of non diversible risk

BP_i = breaking point for financing source j

D_1 = per share dividend expected at the end of year 1

D_p = annual preferred stock dividend (in dollars)

g = constant rate of growth in dividends

! = annual rate of growth in dividends

k_a = weighted average cost of capital

k_d = before-tax cost of debt

k_i = after-tax cost of debt

k_m = required return on the market portfolio

k_n = cost of new issue of common stock

k_p = cost of preferred stock

k_r = cost of retained earnings

ks = required return on common stock

n = number of years to the bond's maturity

N_d = net proceeds from the sale of debt (bond)

N_n = net proceeds from the sale of new common stock

N_p – net proceeds from the sale of preferred stock

P_0 = value of common stock

R_f = risk-free rate of return

T = firm's tax rate

W_i = proportion of long-term debt in capital structure

W_t = capital structure proportion (historic or target, stated in decimal form) for financing source i

W_s = proportion of common stock equity in capital structure.

Cost of Capital Formulas

Before-tax cost of debt:

$K_d = 1 + \$1,000 - N_d / n / N_d + \$1,000 / 2$

After-tax cost of debt:

$K_j = k_d \times (1 - 7)$

Cost of preferred stock:

$K_p = D_p / N_p$

Cost of common stock equity:

Using constant-growth valuation model:

$K_j = D_1 / P_o + g$

Using CAPM:

$K_s = R_f + [(b \times (k_m - R_f)]$

Cost of retained earnings:

$K_r = k_s$

Cost of new issues of common stock

$K_m = D_1 / N_n + g$

Weighted average cost of capital (WACC)

$K_a = (w_i \times k_i) + (w_p \times k_p) + (w_s \times k_{r \text{ or } n})$

Breaking point : $BP_j = AF_j / w_j$

Review Questions

1.

What is the weighted marginal cost of capital (WMCC)? What does the WMCC schedule represent? Why does this schedule increase?

2.

What is the weighted average cost of capital (WACC), and how is it calculated? Describe the logic underlying the use of target capital structure weights, and compare and contrast this approach with the use of historic weights.

3.

If retained earnings are viewed as an equivalent fully subscribed issue of additional common stock, why is the cost of financing a project with retained earnings less than the cost of using a new issue of common stock?

4

What is meant by net proceeds from the sale of bond? What are flotation costs and how do they affect a bond's net proceeds?

5.

How would you compute the cost of preferred stock? Why do we concern ourselves with the net proceeds from the sale of the stock interest of its sale price?

Problems Solving

1.

An issue of 15% unredeemable debenture is currently priced at P 120. Assume the rate of corporate tax is : a) zero b) 40%. Calculate the cost of debt.

2.

An issue of 12% preference shares, value of P 2100.00 has a current shares price of P 88,00 ex –dividend. Compute the cost of these preference shares for the company.

3.

In 2002, *Zenrex Industries* sold preference shares for P 70 per share. Zenrex paid a yearly dividend of P 8.60 per share. Zenrex received P 72 for each share. Determine the cost of the 2002 issue of preference.

4.

Alchester's market price is P 27 per share. If the dividend is P 3.50 and has been growing at an average rate of 4%, What is the cost of equity?

5.

A dividend of P2.40 per share is about to be paid by *AS Powers Company and has a current share price of P 20.50 the expected future growth in dividends is estimated at 12%. Find the cost of equity.*

6.

Last year, Audrey & Aubrey Company's cost of long-term debt was 10%. This rate was due to a 7% risk-free cost of long-term debt, a 2% business risk premium, and a 1% financial risk premium. The firm currently wishes to obtain a long-term loan.

a. If the firm's business and financial risk are unchanged from the previous period and the risk-free cost of long-term debt is now 8%, at what rate would you expect the firm to obtain a long-term loan?

b. If, as a result of borrowing, the firm's financial risk will increase enough to raise the financial risk premium to 3%, how much would you expect the firm's borrowing cost to be?

c. One of the firm's competitors has a 1% business risk premium and a 2% financial risk premium. What is that firm's cost of long-term debt likely to be?

7.

Warren Company is in the process of making an investment decision procedures. The two projects evaluated by the firm during the past month were projects 263 and 264. The basic variables surrounding each project analysis using the IRR decision technique and the resulting decision actions are summarized in the following table:

Basic variables	Project 253	Project 264
Cost	$64,000	$58,000
Life	15 years	15years
IRR	8%	15%
Least-cost financing		
Source	Debt	Equity
Cost (after-tax)	7%	16%
Decision		
Action	Accept	Reject
Reason	8%IRR>7% cost	15%IRR<16% cost

a.

Evaluate the firm's decision-making procedures, and explain why the acceptance of project 263 and rejection of project 264 may not be in the owners' best interest.

b.

If the firm maintains a capital structure containing 40% debt and 60% equity, find its weighted average cost using the data in the table.

c.

Had the firm used the weighted average cost computed in b, what actions would have been taken relative to projects 263 and 264?

d.

Compare and contrast the firm's actions with your findings in c. Which decision method seems more appropriate? Explain why.

Chapter 11

LEVERAGE

Leverage defined

Leverage is the results of the use of fixed- cost assets or funds to magnify returns to the firm's owners. It is the action of a lever and the mechanical advantage gained by it. It is the right piece that transmits and modifies force or motion when forces are applied at two points and it turns around a third.

In finance, the term leverage is used to describe the firm's ability to use fixed-cost assets or funds to magnify the returns to its owners. Generally, increases in leverage result in increased return and risk, whereas decreases in leverage result in decreased return and risk. The amount of leverage in the firm's capital structure which is the mix of long-term debt and equity maintained by the firm – can significantly affect its value by affecting return and risk.

Business Risk distinguished from Financial Risk

Business risk is sometimes called operating risk. It is the risk associated with the normal day to day operations of the firm. Financial risk is created by the use of fixed-cost securities (the its, debt and preference shares)

To distinguish the between business and financial risk, we examine the income statement of *Delvin Company* :

Table -1

Delvin Company

Income Statement

For the year ended Dec. 31, 2006

Net Sales	3,500,000.00
Cost of goods sold	1,100,000.00
Gross profit	2,400,000.00
Selling expenses	750,000.00
Earnings before interest and taxes (EBIT)	1,650,000.00
Interest	115,000.00
Earnings before taxes (EBIT)	1,535,000.00
Income taxes at 32%	491,200.00
Earnings after taxes (EAT)	1,043,800.00
Preferred dividends	130,000.00
Earnings available to equity shareholders(EATES)	913,800.00
Number of equity shares	320,000.00
Earnings per share (EPS)	2.86

The operating profit of the firm is viewed as earnings before interest and taxes which is the profit of the firm before deducting financing charges and taxes. Business risk is concerned with earnings before interest and taxes and financial risk is concerned with earnings available to equity share holders. The components of the business risk are: the chance that the firm will fail because of the inability of the assets of the firm to generate a sufficient level of earnings before interest and taxes; and the variability of such earnings. The two components of financial risk are payments of liability, and the variability of earnings available to equity shareholders caused by fixed financing charges (that is, interest expense and preferred dividends)

Fixed versus Variable Expenses

In making a decision regarding the use of fixed and variable expenses,

We would certainly know the level of sales at which the net income under both alternatives would be equal. The procedure used to determine this point is simple and we the following table below to illustrate an example.

Assuming that *Virco Company's* employees intend to work on commissions equal to 20% of sales rather than on salaries, i.e., work for zero salaries. It is also assumed that substitution will not effect the factors that influence sales. Should Virco Company accept the offer? Despite the reduction in business risk, however, it is not clear that Virco Company should choose the variable salaries alternative. A finance manager cannot consider risk alone. It is always risk in relations to return that is relevant. Is there anything to be gained from bearing the additional risk? To answer this question, let us compare the levels of net income for both alternatives for sales levels higher than 100,000 units. The table shows income based on 125,000 units and 150,000 units.

	Fixed salaries	Variable salaries
Net Sales (125,000 units @P10)	1,250,000.00	1,250,000.00
Cost of goods sold (75%)	937,500.00	937,500.00
Fixed salaries	200,000.00	
Variable salaries		250,000.00
Depreciation expense	30,000.00	30,000.00
Net Income	82,500.00	32,500.00
Net sales (150,000units @P10)	1,500,000.00	1,500,000.00
Cost of goods sold (75%)	1,125,000.00	1,125,000.00
Fixed salaries	200,000.00	
Variable salaries		300,000.00
Depreciation expense	30,000.00	30,000.00
Net Income	145,000.00	45,000.00

The level of net income for each alternative at any level of sales can be determined as follows:

Fixed Salaries: (Net sales -.75 net sales) – P 230,000 = net income

Variable Salaries: (Net sales - .95 net sales) – P 30,000 = net income

Setting the left hand side of the two equations equal to each other and solving for net sales will give the level of net sales at which the level of net income under each alternative will be equal. To demonstrate:

Net sales -.75 Net sales- P 230,000 = Net sales .95 net sales – P 30,000

.20 Net sales = P 200,000

Net sales = 1,000,000

By checking the veracity of the answer, it can be noted that the fixed salaries alternative will provide a higher level of net income at any sales level above P 1,000,000, while at any sales below P 1,000,000 net income will be higher under the variable salaries alternative.

	Fixed Salaries	Variable Salaries
Net sales	1,000,000.00	1,000,000.00
Cost of goods sold	750,000.00	750,000.00
Fixed salaries	200,000.00	
Variable salaries		200,000.00
Depreciation expense	30,000.00	30,000.00
Net income	20,000.00	20,000.00

Fixed Expenses and the Rate of Change of Net Income

The extent to which fixed expenses should be employed, manager must consider the effect that fixed expenses can have on the rate of change of net income over times. To illustrate this important point. We use a more convenient example of *Delvin Company*.

Assume that *Delvin Company* sold 100,000 units during 2006 at a price of P10 per unit. All expenses were variable and were equal to P 9 per unit. The following table shows the 2006 income statement *of Delvin Company, it is estimated that sales can be 50% higher(1250,000 units) pr 50% lowe (50,000units) during 2007.*

Delvin Company

Income Statement

Year Ended December 31, 2005

Net Sales	1,000,000.00
Expenses	900,000.00
Net Income	100,000.00

If sales are 50% higher, net income will be P 1,500,000 which is 50% higher than the level of net income earned in 2006. If sales are 50 % lower, net income will be P 50,000, which is 50% lower than the level of net income earned in 2006. The same rate of change for sales and net income is due to the fact that the firm has only variable expenses. To generalize, if a firm has only variable expenses, the rate of change of net income will always be identical to the rte of change of sales.

Assuming that on January 1, 2006, the *Delvin Company* installed a machine that created fixed expenses of P 100,000 per year but reduced variable expenses to P 7.50 per unit. The revised income statement for 2006 is as follows:

Delvin Company

Income Statement

Year ended December 31, 2006

Net Sales	1,000,000.00
Variable expenses	750,000.00
Fixed expenses	100,000.00
Net Income	150,000.00

The firm has achieved a higher level of net income by substituting fixed expenses for variable expenses. However, the breakeven point is 40,000 units versus zero units of all the variable expense. The firm has increased the level of income but has also increased the level of business risk. What happens to the level of income in 2007 if sales increases or decreases by 50% from 2006's level.

Delvin Company

Pro-forma Income Statement

Year ended December 31, 2007

Net Sales	500,000.00	1,500,000.00
Variable expenses (75%)	375,000.00	1,125,000.00
Fixed expenses	100,000.00	100,000.00
Net Income	25,000.00	275,000.00

If sales increases by 50%, net income will increase by 83.3 % (increase in net income of P 125,000 in 2007 divided by net income of P 150,000 in 2006.) If sales decline by 50% then net income will decline by 83.3 % (a decrease of P 125,000 in net income divided by net income of P 150,000 in 2006). The rate of change in net income is greater than the change in net sales and this will always be the case when a firm has fixed expenses. Given the existence of fixed expenses, if sales are growing at a certain rate, income will grow at a great rate, the use of fixed expenses creates the opportunity to magnify the rate of growth in net income. If sales are declining by a certain rate, income will decline at a greater rate.

Assuming the sales for *Delvin Company* increase by 50% (to 150,000 units) in 2007 and as a result net income increases by 83.3 % (to P 275,000). What happens to net income in 2007, if sales again increase by 50 % (to 225,000 units)? The pro-forma income statement for the year ended December 31, 2007 is as follows:

Delvin Company

Pro-forma Income Statement

Year ended December 31, 2007

Net Sales	2,250,000.00
Variable expenses (75%)	1,687,000.00
Fixed expenses	100,000.00
Net Income	463,000.00

If net sales further increases by 50% in 2007, net income will increase by 68 %(P 187,500/P275,000). Note that the net income will increase at a greater rate than sales but at a lower rate than the rate of growth in net income in 2002 (that is, 68 % versus DOL) declines as the level of sales moves further from the breakeven point. The degree of operating leverage is defined as the percentage change in net income that will be produced by each one percent change in sales at a given level of sales. Example, sales level of P1,000,000 for Delvin Company, the degree of operating leverage is 1.67. A change in sales from P1,000,000 level will produce a proportionate change in net income 1.67 times as large, if sales change by 10%, net income will change by 16.7 % (1.67 times 10per cent)

Breakeven Analysis

Breakeven analysis is sometimes called cost-volume profit analysis which is used by the firm; to determine the level of operations needed to cover all operating costs; and to evaluate the profitability associated with various levels of sales. The operating breakeven point is the level of sales necessary to cover all operating costs. At that point, earnings before interest and taxes equals 0.

In order to determine the operating breakeven point we divide the cost of goods sold and operating expenses into fixed and variable operating costs. Fixed costs are a function of time, not sales volume Variable costs vary directly with sales and are a function of volume, not time, shipping costs, are a variable cost.

A company's break-even point (BEP) is that level of activity, in units or dollars or pesos, at which total revenues equal total costs.

At breakeven, a company's revenues exactly cover its costs, thus, the company incurs neither a profit nor a loss on operating activities. Companies, however, do not wish merely to break-even on operations. The BEP is calculated to establish a point of reference. K

Finding the break-even point first requires understanding company revenues and costs. An important concept in break-even analysis is contribution margin (CM), which can be defined on either a per unit or total basis., CM per unit equals selling price per unit minus total variable cost per unit, which includes both production and selling and administrative costs. Unit contribution margin is constant because revenue and variable cost have been defined as being constant per unit. Total CM is the difference between total revenues and total variable costs for all units sold. This amount fluctuates in direct proportion to sales volume. On either a per unit or total basis, contribution margin indicates the amount of revenue remaining after all variable costs have been covered. This amount contributes to the coverage of fixed costs and the generation of profits.

Formula Approach to Breakeven

The formula approach to break even analysis uses an algebraic equation to calculate the break-even point. In this analysis, sales volume, rather than production activity, is the focus of the relevant range. The equation represents the variable costing income statement and shows the relationships among revenue, fixed costs, variable cost, volume, and profit as follows:

$R(X) - VC(X) - FC = P$

Where;

R = revenue (selling price) per unit

X = volume (number of units)

R(X) = total revenue

VC = variable cost per unit

VC (X) = total variable cost

FC = total fixed cost

P = profit

This equation is simply a formula representation of an income statement, P can be set equal to zero so that the formula indicates a break-even situation. At the point where P= $0, total revenues are equal to total costs, and break-even point (BEP) in units can be found by solving the equation for X.

R(X) – VC(X) – FC = $ 0.

R (X) – VC(X) = FC

(R-VC)(X) = FC

X = FC / (R-VC)

X = FC / CM

Break even volume equals total fixed cost divided by contribution margin per unit (revenue per unit minus the variable cost per unit) Break even point can be expressed either in units or dollars of revenue. One way to convert a unit break even point to dollars is to multiply the number of units by the selling price per unit. A short summary of revenue and cost assumptions is presented at this point to provide a foundation for BEP calculation and cost-volume profit (CVP) analysis.

Example 1

Cherix Company

Income Statement

For 2007

		Total	Per unit	Percentage
Sales (300,000 units)		180,000.00	8.00	100
Variable costs				
Production	111,600.00		3.72	62
Selling	72,000.00		0.24	4
Total variable cost		(1,188,000.00)	(3.96)	(66)
Contribution Margin		612,000.00	2.04	34
Fixed costs				
Production	160,200.00			
Selling and administrative	23,400.00			
Total fixed cost		(183,600.00)		
Income before income tax		428,400.00		

At this point, P = $ 0. total revenues are equal to total, and break even point (BEP) in units can be found by solving the equation for X.

Using the above operating information for *Cherix Company* ($ 6.00 selling price per; antenna, $ 3.96 variable cost per antenna, and $ 183,600 of total fixed costs), the BEP for the company is calculated as:

$ 6.00(X) - $ 3.96 (X) - $ 183,600 = $0.

$ 6.00(X) - $ 3.96(X) = $ 183,600

$ 2.04(X) = $ 183,600

X = $ 183,600 / $ 2.04

X = 90,000 antennas

Break-even point in sales dollars is $ 540,000 (90,000) antennas X $6 per antenna).

Another method of computing BEP is sales dollars requires the computation of a contribution margin (CM) ratio, which is computed as contribution margin divided by revenue; it indicates what proportion of revenue remains after variable costs have been covered. The contribution margin ratio represents that portion of the revenue dollar remaining to go toward covering fixed costs and increasing profits. The CM ratio can be computed using either per unit or total revenue and variable cost information. Dividing total fixed cost by the CM ratio gives the BRP in sales dollars. The contribution margin ratio allows the break-even point to be determined even if unit selling price and unit variable cost are not known. Subtracting the CM ratio from 100 percent gives the variable cost (VC) ratio, which represents the variable cost proportion of each revenue dollar.

The contribution margin ratio for *Cherix* Company is provided in the above table as 34 percent ($2.04/$6.00) Thus, break-even sales dollars are ($ 183,600/0.34) or $ 540,000. BEP in units can be determined by dividing the BEP in sales dollars by the unit selling price, or $ 540,000/$6.00 = 90,000 antennas.

The break even point provides a starting point for planning future operations. Substituting an amount other than zero for the profit (P) term in the break even formula converts break even analysis to cost-volume-profit analysis.

Sales –[(VC%)(sales)] = FC

(1-Vc%)Sales = FC

Sales = FC/(1-VC%)

Because (1-VC%) = CM%

Then Sales = FC/ CM%

Where VC% = the % relationship of variable cost to sales

CM% = the % relationship of contribution margin to sales

Thus, the variable cost ratio plus the contribution margin ratio is equal to 100%.

Assuming that *Cherry Blossoms Enterprises,* a small retailing business, has fixed operating costs of \$ 2,500, its sale price per unit is \$10, and its variable operating cost per unit is \$ 5. Applying equation 12.3 to these data yields:

Q = \$ 2,500 / \$ 10-\$5 = \$ 2,500/\$5 = 500 units

At sales of 500 units, the firm's EBIT should just equal \$0. The firm will have positive EBIT for sales greater than 500 units and negative EBIT, or a loss, for sales less than 500 units.

Sensitivity of Operating Breakeven Point

A firm's operating breakeven point is sensitive to a number of variables fixed operating cost (FC), the sale price per; unit (P), and the variable operating cost per unit (VC). The effects of increases or decreases in these variables can be readily seen by referring to equation (table) below. The sensitivity of the breakeven sales volume (Q) to an increase in each of these variables is summarized. An increase in cost (FC or VC) tends to increase the operating breakeven point, whereas an increase in the sale price per unit (P) will decrease the operating breakeven point.

Increase in variable	Effect on operating breakeven point
Fixed operating cost (FC)	Increase
Sales price per unit (P)	Decrease
Variable operating cost per unit (VC)	Increase

Assuming that Cherry Blossoms Enterprises wishes to evaluate the impact of several options: increasing fixed operating costs to \$3,000; increasing the sales price per unit to \$ 12.50; increasing the variable operating cost per unit to \$ 7.50, and simultaneously implementing all three of these changes. Substituting the appropriate data into equation above yields the following results:

1.

Operating breakeven point = $ 3,000/$10-$5 = 600 units

2.

Operating breakeven point = $ 2,500/$12.50 -0$5 = 3331/3 units

3.

Operating breakeven point = $2,500/ $10-$7.50 = 1,000 units

4.

Operating breakeven point = $3,000 / $ 12.50 -$ 7.50 = 600 units

We can see that the cost increases (actions 1 and 3) comparing the resulting operating breakeven points to the initial value of 500 units, raise the breakeven point, whereas the revenue increase (action 2) lowers the breakeven point. The combined effect of increasing all three variables (action 4) also results in an increased operating breakeven point.

Operating Leverage

This leverage is concerned with the relationship between the firm's sales revenue and its earnings before interest and taxes, or EBIT, (EBIT is a descriptive label for operating profits)

Operating leverage arises whenever a firm can expand output and sales without a proportionate increase in costs. Those that are directly related to the firm's production and sales, classified under operating profits, increase proportionately more than sales increase. If output decreases without an accompanying proportionate decrease in costs, the firm's operating profits shrink proportionately more than the decrease in sales.

Operating leverage is concerned with the relationship between sales and operating income (that is, earning before interest and taxes).

Operating leverage results from the existence of fixed operating costs in the firm's income stream. It is potential use of fixed operating costs to magnify the effects of changes in sales on the firm's earnings before interest and taxes.

Using the data for *Cherry Blossoms Enterprises (sales price, P = $ 10 per unit; variable operating cost, VC = $5 per unit, fixed operating cost, FC = $ 2,500). And this may be shown also in graphical form.*

The EBIT for Various Sales levels

	Case 2		Case 1
	-50%		50%
Sales (in units)	500	1,000	1,500
Sales revenue	5,000	10,000	15,000
Less: Variable operating costs	2,500	5,000	7,500
Less: Fixed operating costs	2,500	2,500	2,500
Earnings before interest and taxes			
EBIT	-	2,500	5,000
		-100%	100%

Sales revenue = $10/unit x sales in units

Variable operating costs = $ 5/units x sales in units

This illustrates two cases using the 1,000 unit sales level as a reference point:

Case 1 a 50% increase in sales (from 1,000 to 1,500 units) results in a 100% increase in earnings before interest and taxes (from $ 2,500 to $ 5,000)

Case 2 A 50% decrease in sales (from 1,000 to 500 units) results in a 100% decrease in earnings before interest and taxes from $ 2,500 to $0.

When a firm has fixed operating costs, operating leverage is present. An increase in sales results in a more-than-proportional increase, in EBIT; a decrease in sales results in a more-than-proportional decrease in EBIT.

Degree of Operating Leverage

The degree of operating leverage (DOL) is the numerical measure of the firm's operating leverage. It can be derived using the following equation:

DOL = percentage change in EBIT

Percentage change in sales

Whenever the percentage change in EBIT resulting from a given percentage change in sales is greater than the percentage change in sales, operating leverage exists. This means that as long as DOL is greater than 1, there is operating leverage.

Example:

Applying the equations above cases 1 and 2, which yields the following results:

Case 1: +100% / +50% = 2.0

Case 2: -100%/ -50% = 2.0

The result is greater than 1, operating leverage exists. For a given base level of sales, the higher the value resulting from applying the equation above, the greater the degree of operating leverage.

A more direct formula for calculating the degree of operating leverage at a base sales level, Q, is shown as:

DOL at base sales level Q = Q x {P-VC)

Q X (P-VC)-FC

Substituting Q = 1,000, P = \$10, VC = \$5, and FC = \$2,500 into equation which yields the following result:

DOL at 1,000 units = 1,000 X (\$10-\$5) = \$ 5,000 = 2.0

1,000 X(\$10-\$5)-\$2,500 \$ 2,500

Financial Leverage

This leverage is concerned with the relationship between the firm's EBIT and its common stock earnings per share. (EPS)

The presence of fixed financial costs in the firm's income stream. Financial leverage is the potential use of fixed financial costs to magnify the effects of changes in earnings before interest and taxes on the firm's income statement. The two fixed financial costs that may be found on the firm's income statement are ; interest on debt and preferred stock dividends. These charges must be paid regardless of the amount of EBIT available to pay them.

Cherry Blossoms Enterprises, expects EBIT of $ 10,000 in the current year. It has a $20,000 bond with a 10% (annual) coupon rate of interest and an issue of 600 shares of $ 4 (annual dividend per share) preferred stock outstanding. It also has 1,000 shares of common stock outstanding. The annual interest on the bond issue is $ 2,000 (.1`0 X $20,000) The annual dividends on the preferred stock are $ 2,400 ($ 4.00/share x 600 shares). The table below presents the EPS corresponding to levels of EBIT of $ 6,000, $ 10,000, and $ 14,000, the EPS corresponding to levels of EBIT of $ 6,000, $ 10,000, and $ 14,000, assuming that the firm is in the 40% tax bracket. Two situations are shown:

Case 1: A 40% increase in EBIT (from $ 10,000 to $ 14,000) results in a 100% increase in earnings per share (from $2.40 to $ 4.80).

Case 2: A 40% decease in EBIT (from $10,000 to $ 6,000) results in a 100% decrease in earnings per share (from $ 2.40 to $ 0.)

This results in a more than proportional increase in the firm's earnings per share, whereas a decrease in the firm's EBIT results in a more than proportional decrease in EPS.

	Case 2		Case 1
	-40%		40%
EBIT	6,000.00	10,000.00	14,000.00
Less: Interest (I)	2,000.00	2,000.00	2,000.00
Net profits before taxes	4,000.00	8,000.00	12,000.00
Less: Taxes (T =.40)	1,600.00	3,200.00	4,800.00
Net profits after taxes	2,400.00	4,800.00	7,200.00
Less: Preferred stock dividends (PD)	2,400.00	2,400.00	2,400.00
Earnings available fro common (EAC)	-	2,400.00	4,800.00
Earnings per share (EPS)	$0/ 1,000 = $0	$2,400/ 1,000 =	$4,800/1,000 =
		$2.40	$4.80
	———	———-	———————-
	-100%	—+100%	—

Financial Breakeven Point

Financial breakeven point exists when sufficient EBIT is earned to cover fixed financial changes, leaving EPS= P0. To find a financial breakeven point, we use the following equation:

Breakeven EBIT = 1+ Dp/ 1.0 – Tax Rate

When:

I = Interest Rate

D_p = Dividends to preference shares holder

T = Tax Rate

If Delvin Company takes P 800,000 a month to meet bond interest and P 400,000 [P 240,000/(I -0.40)] to net preferred stock dividends, the financial breakeven point is:

Breakeven EBIT = P 800,000 + P 240,000 / 1.0 -0.40

= P 800,000 + P 400,000 = P 1,200,000

If EBIT falls below the breakeven point of EBIT, EPS is negative; if EBIT levels exceed the financial breakeven point of EBIT; the EPS is positive.

Operating and Financial Leverage Combined

Interrelations between the decisions made regarding the level of fixed expenses to income and the amount of debt to be employed. In clarity, it is useful to examine the dual effect of operating and financial leverage on the rate of change of EPS.

Assume the following for the *De Gaulle Company*

1. Sales will be P 100,000 during the first year of operations.
2. All expenses are variable and are equal to 80 % of sales.
3. There are no taxes.
4. The firm employs no debt or preference shares.
5. There are 10,000 shares of equity.

EPS , therefore, can be calculated as shown in the table as follows:

De Gaulle Company
Pro-forma Income Statement
For Year One

Net Sale	100,000.00
Variable expenses	80,000.00
Fixed expenses	
Earnings before interest & taxes	20,000.00
Interest expense	-
Earnings before taxes	20,000.00
Income taxes	-
Earning after taxes	20,000.00
Preferred dividends	-
Earnings available to equity shareholders	20,000.00
Number of equity shares	10,000.00
Earnings per share	2.00

To see what happens to EPS as sales change, we examine the income statement. Let us assume a 10% increase and a 10% decrease in sales. A 10% decrease in sales produces a 10% decrease in EPS, while a 10% increase in sales produces a 10% increase in EPS.

De Gaulle Company
Pro-Forma Income Statement
For Year One (1)

	-10%	10%
Net Sale	90,000.00	110,000.00
Variable expenses	72,000.00	88,000.00
Fixed expenses		
Earnings before interest & taxes	18,000.00	22,000.00
Interest expense		-
Earnings before taxes	18,000.00	22,000.00
Income taxes	-	-
Earning after taxes	18,000.00	22,000.00
Preferred dividends	-	-
Earnings available to equity shareholders	18,000.00	22,000.00
Number of equity shares	10,000.00	10,000.00
Earnings per share	1.80	2.20

This is the case when a firm does not employ operating and financial leverage. In the absence of operating and financial leverage, a given percentage change in sales will produce an identical percentage change in EPS.

Assuming De Gaulle Company substitutes a part of fixed expenses by variable expenses, fixed expenses will be P 20,000 and variable expenses will be 60 % of sales instead of 80% of sales. The table below shows that at a sales level of P 100,000 earnings before interest and taxes and EPS will still be P 20,000 and P 2. 00 respectively.

De Gaulle Company
Pro-forma Income Statement
For Year One

	-10%	Given	10%
Net Sale	90,000.00	100,000.00	110,000.00
Variable expenses	54,000.00	60,000.00	66,000.00
Fixed expenses	20,000.00	20,000.00	20,000.00
Earnings before interest & taxes	16,000.00	20,000.00	24,000.00
Interest expense	`0	-	-
Earnings before taxes	16,000.00	20,000.00	24,000.00
Income taxes	-	-	-
Earning after taxes	16,000.00	20,000.00	24,000.00
Preferred dividends	-	-	-
Earnings available to equity shareholders	16,000.00	20,000.00	24,000.00
Number of equity shares	10,000.00	10,000.00	10,000.00
Earnings per share	1.60	2.00	2.40

A 10% increase in sales produces a 40% increase in EPS, while a 10% decrease in sales produces a 40% decrease in EPS.

De Gaulle Company
Pro-forma Income Statement
For Year One (1)

	-10%	Given	10%
Net Sale	90,000.00	100,000.00	110,000.00
Variable expenses	54,000.00	60,000.00	66,000.00
Fixed expenses	20,000.00	20,000.00	20,000.00
Earnings before interest & taxes	16,000.00	20,000.00	24,000.00
Interest expense	10,000.00	10,000.00	10,000.00
Earnings before taxes	6,000.00	10,000.00	14,000.00
Income taxes	-	-	-
Earning after taxes	6,000.00	10,000.00	14,000.00
Preferred dividends	-	-	-
Earnings available to equity shareholders	6,000.00	10,000.00	140,000.00
Number of equity shares	5,000.00	5,000.00	5,000.00
Earnings per share	1.20	2.00	2.80

We can calculate the combined degree of operating and financial leverage that is the percentage change in EPS produced by a given percentage change in sales at a certain level of sales. This combined sensitivity measure can be determined by calculating the percentage change in EPS produced by a 1 percent change in sales from a certain level. For example, it can easily be verified in the above table that a sales level of P100,000, the degree of operating time financial leverage is four. A given percentage change in sales from the P 100,000 level will produce a percentage change in EPS four times as large.

It is possible to ascertain the degree of combined leverage in a direct fashion without determining any percentage fluctuation or the separate leverage values. We need only to substitute the appropriate values into the following equation:

DCL = DOL X DFL

OR DCL = Q (SPPU – VEPU / Q (SPPU-VEPU) 0FE X EBIT / EBIT-F

By using the information in the last table above of the pro-forma income statement, we obtain the following:

DCL = 10,000 (P 10-P 6) / 10,000 (P 10-P6) – P20,000 X P 20,000 / P 20,000 – P 10,000

= P 40,000 / P 40,000 – 20,000 X P 20,000 / P 10,000

= P 40,000 / P 20,000 X P 20,000 / P 10,000 = 4 times

The total risk exposure that the firm assumes, it can be managed by combining operating and financial leverage in different degrees. When a firm is considering the substitution of fixed expense for variable expenses, or vice versa, it must take into account the extent to which financial leverage is employed. Moreover, when a firm is considering the addition of fixed cost securities, it must take into account the extent to which it is employing operating leverage. Second, the variability of sales is the key to the variability of EPS. If sales do not change, EPS, will not change, regardless of the level of operating and financial leverage. Some firms with large amounts of both operating and financial leverage have experienced stability of EPS operating and financial leverage have experienced stability of EPS over time because sales for these firms have been stable over time.

Total Leverage

This leverage is concerned with the relationship between the firm's sales revenue and EPS.

These three types of leverages are shown with its effects in fixed costs on the firm's operations.

Sales revenue

Less: Cost of goods sold

Gross profits

Less: Operating expenses

Earnings before interest and taxes(EBIT)

Less: Interest

Net profits before taxes

Less: Taxes

Net profits after taxes

Less: Preferred stock dividends

Earnings available for common stockholders.

Earnings per share (EPS)

Operating
Leverage

Financial
Leverage

Total Leverage

Total leverage may be defined as the potential use of fixed costs, both operating and financial, to magnify the effect of changes in sales on the firm's earnings per share. Total leverage can be viewed as the total impact of the fixed costs in the firm's operating and financial structure.

Skylink, Inc. a electrical cable manufacturer expects sales of 30,000 units at &6 per unit in the coming year and must meet the schedule on the following: variable operating costs of $2 per unit, fixed operating costs of $ 10,000, interest of $20,000, and preferred stock dividends of $14,000. the firm is in the 40% tax bracket and has 5,000 shares of common stock outstanding. The table below presents the levels of earnings per share associated with the expected sales of 30,000 units and with sales of 40,000 units.

As a result of a 50% increase in sales (from 30,000 to 40,000 units, the firm would experience a 300% increase in earnings per share (from $1.20 to $ 4.80). A 50% decrease in sales would, conversely, result in a 300% decrease in earnings per share. The linear nature of the leverage relationship accounts for the fact that sales changes of equal magnitude in opposite directions result in EPS changes of equal magnitude in the corresponding direction. At this point, it should be clear that whenever a firm has fixed costs – operating or financial – in its structure, total leverage will exist.

	——————————-50%	————————————	
Sales in units	20,000.00	30,000.00	DOL =
Sales revenue	100,000.00	150,000.00	=60%/50% =
Less: Variable operating costs	40,000.00	60,000.00	1.20
Less: Fixed Operating costs	10,000.00	10,000.00	
Earnings before interest and taxes			DTL =
(EBIT)	50,000.00	80,000.00	+300%/+50 =
	————————60%	——————————- —	6.00
Less: interest	20,000.00	20,000.00	
Net profits before taxes	30,000.00	60,000.00	DFL =
Less: Taxes (T= .40)	12,000.00	24,000.00	+300%/+60 =
Net	18,000.00	36,000.00	= 5.0

profits after taxes		
Less: Preferred stock dividends	12,000.00	12,000.00
Earnings available for common	6,000.00	24,000.00
Earnings per share (EPS)	$40,000/5,000	$ 76,000/5,000
	$8	$15.20
	\\——-—	—————-/
	300%	

Sales revenue = $ 5/ unit X sales in units

Variable operating costs = $2/unit x sales in units

The degree of total leverage (DTL) is the numerical measure of the firm's total leverage. It can be computed like operating and financial leverage. The following equation shows one approach for measuring DTL:

DTL = percentage change in EPS

Percentage change in sales

Whenever the percentage change in EPS resulting from a given percentage change in sales is greater than the percentage change in sales, total leverage exists. There is total leverage as long as the DTL is greater than 1.

A given formula for calculating the degree of total leverage in a more direct manner in a base level of sales, Q, is shown as follows:

Q x (P –VC)

DTL at base sales level Q = Q x(P-VC)-FC-1-(PD x 1/ 1-T)

Substituting Q = 20,000, P $5, VC = $2, FC = $10,000, I = $ 20,000,PD $ 12,000, and the tax rate (T= .40) yields the following result:

DTL at 20,000 units = 20,000 x ($5 - $2)

30,000 x ($ 5-$2)-$ 10,000 -$20,000 –($12,000 x 1/ I- .40)

= $ 60,000 /$10,000 = 6.0

Review Questions

1.

What is operating leverage? What causes It? How is the degree of operating leverage (DOL) measured?

2.

What is meant by the term leverage? How do operating leverage , financial leverage, and total leverage relate to the income statement?

3.

What is operating leverage? How is the degree of operating leverage (DOL) measured?

4.

How is the degree of financial leverage (DFL) measured? What is financial leverage?

5.

What is meant by break event point? How is it related to Cost volume profit analysis (CVP)

6.

How do you compute break even in sales and in dollars or pesos ?

Problems Solving

1.

Tetular Corporation recently sold 100,000 units at $7.50 each; its variable operating costs are $3.00 per unit, and its fixed operating costs are $ 250,000. Annual interest charges total $ 80,000, and the firm has 8,000 shares of $5 (annual divided) preferred stock outstanding. It currently has 20,000 shares of common stock outstanding. Assume that the firm has a 40% tax rate.

a. At what level of sales (in units) would the firm break even on operations (i.e., EBIT = $0)?

b. Calculate the firm's earnings per share. (EPS) in tabular form at (1) the current level of sales and (2) a 120,000 unit sales level.

c. Using the current$ 750,000 level of sales as a base, calculate the firm's degree of operating leverage (DOL).

d. Using the EBIT associated with the $ 750,000 level of sales as a base, calculate the firm's degree of financial leverage (DFL).

e. Use the degree of total leverage (DTL) concept to determine the effect (in percentage terms) of a 50% increase in the firm's sales from the $ 750,000 base level on its earnings per share.

2.

Newton Electronics has additional financing for $ 10,000. It currently has $ 50,000 of 12% (annual interest) bonds and 10,000 shares of common stock outstanding. The firm can obtain the financing through a 12% (annual interest) bond issue or the sale of 1,000 shares of common stock. The firm has a 40% tax rate.

a. Calculate two EBIT-EPS coordinates for each plan by selecting any two EBIT values and finding their associated EPS.

b. Plot the two financing plans on a set of EBIT-EPS axes.

c. On the basis of your graph in b, at what level of EBIT does the bond plan become superior to the stock plan?

3.

Daniel Moore wishes to estimate the number of flower arrangements she must sell at $24.95 to break even. She has estimated fixed operating costs of $ 12,350 per year and variable operating costs of $ 15.45 per arrangement. How many flower arrangements must Kate sell to break even on operating costs?

4.

Netzel Milk Company has collected the following data with respect to its capital structure, expected earnings per share, and required return:

Capital Structure debt ratio	Expected earnings per share	Required return, ks
0%	3.12	13%
10	3.90	15
20	4.80	16
30	5.44	17
40	5.51	19
50	5.00	20
60	4.40	22

a. Compute the estimated share value associated with each of the capital structures using the simplified method described in an equation.

b. Determine the optimal capital structure based on : maximization of expected earnings per share and; maximization of share value.

c. Which capital structure do you recommend? Why?

5.

Jumong Leather Corporation sells its single product for $ 129 per unit. The firm's fixed operating costs are $ 473,000 annually, and its variable operating costs are $ 86.00 per unit.

a. Find the firm's operating breakeven point in units.

b. X axis should be labeled as Sales units, and Y axis as Cost/(Revenues($) making a graph of the firm's sales revenue, total operating cost, and fixed operating cost functions on these axes. Label the operating breakeven point and the areas of loss and profit (EBIT).

6.

Billy John is opening a book and record store. He wants to estimate the number of CDs he must sell to break even. The CDs will be sold for $13.98 each, variable operating costs are $ 10.48 per CD, and annual fixed operating costs are $ 73,500.

a. find the operating breakeven point in CDs

b. If Billy estimates that at a minimum he can sell 2,000 CDs per month, should he go into the record business?

c. Calculate the total operating costs at the breakeven volume found in (a)

d. How much EBIT would Billy realize if he sells the minimum 2,000 CDs per month.

7.

Valentine Shoes, at the quarterly dividend meeting, declared a cash dividend of $1.10 per share for holders of record , July 1. The firm has 300,000 shares of common stock outstanding and has set a payment date of July 31. Prior to the dividend declaration, the firm's key accounts were as follows:

Cash $500,000 Dividends payable $ 0 Retained earnings 2,500,000

a. Show the entries after the meeting adjourned.

b. When is the ex dividend date?

c. After the July 31 payment date, what values would the key accounts have?

d. What effect, if any, will the dividend have on the firm's total assets?

e. Ignoring general market fluctuations, what effect, if any, will the dividend have on the firm's stock price on the ex dividend date?

8.

Arab Manufacturing Corp. sells a single product for P 3.00 with variable cost per unit of P1.80. If fixed costs are P 3,000,000, calculate the degree of operating leverage at sales levels of 3,000,000 units and 4,000,000 units.

9.

Referring to preceding problem. Assume Arab Manufacturing decides to automate their production process by replacing some of their manual production tasks. If fixed costs increased to P 3,330,000 because of the added depreciation while variable costs decrease to P 1.70 per unit because of the lower labor cost, what is the effect on the breakeven point? What would be the effect on operating profit at an output of 4,000,000 unit?

10.

SunSung Electronics Corporation sales are expected to be 50,000 units for the year and the selling price per unit is expected to be P 10 for all units. Total fixed expenses will be P 200,000. These expenses will remain fixed up to a sales level of 90,000 units. Variable expenses per unit will be P 4 for all units. There are no income taxes.

a. Calculate the breakeven point in units.

b. Assume a series of 10% increase and a series of 10% decreases in sales from the 50,000 units level and calculate the net income at each level of sales;

c. the annual rate of change of net income.

d. the net income to sale ratio

e. the degree of operating leverage at each sales level.

11.

Suppose SunSung Electronics Corporation requires a total of P 2,500,000 in funds and may select between two financing mixes; all equity or half equity and half debt at 15% effective interest rate. Suppose further that the firm can sell equity share for P 100 per share, has a tax rate of 40%, and expects EBIT of P 250,000. Determine the earnings per share (EPS) using each of the possible financial mixes.

12.

Dan Dimasupil had recently attended an orientation on the benefits of financial leverage. He represented his firm, D & D Enterprises which had assets of P 20 million financed entirely with 1,000,000 shares of equity currently selling at P20 per share. Dan is considering retiring some of the shares with borrowed funds, which he can obtain at an interest rate of 15%. He expects the company to earn P 5 million next year before interest and taxes. The company's tax rate is 32%.

a. What would be the effect of leverage on expected EPS and ROE? Why?

b. Dan is considering two alternative leverage ratios, 25% debt and 50% debt (per cent debt to total assets) Calculate expected EPS and ROE for each of these debt ratios at next year's expected EBIT.

c. D & D Enterprises' s EBIT could fall below P2million and in a good year could rise as high as P 8million. What effect this might have at the leverage ratios he was considering. Calculate expected EPS and ROE at the low and high EBIT levels for debt ratios of 0%, 25%, and50% and compare the results with those of part b.

13.

Assuming the firm is considering expanding assets by P 5million and has determined that it can financed the expansion either through a bond issue carrying a 15% interest rate or through a new issue of equity shares which can be sold to net the company P 20 per share. The firm currently has 40,000 shares issued and P 5 million with a 12% coupon. The tax rate is 50%.

a. Calculate the EPS for each alternative at EBIT levels of P 2 million and P 7.5million.

b. What can be said from this analysis regarding the choice between bonds and equity shares?

Chapter 12

BUSINESS RISK , FINANCIAL RISK & RISK ASSESSMENT

Business Risk

Business risk is defined as the risk of the business of being unable to cover its operating costs. The greater the firm's operating leverage – the use of fixed operating costs – the higher its business risk. There are two factors involved in business risk: revenue stability and cost stability. Revenue stability refers to the relative variability of the firm's sales revenues. Firms with reasonably stable levels of demand and with products that have stable prices have stable revenues. The result is low levels of business risk. Firms with highly volatile product demand and prices have unstable revenues that result in high levels of business risk. Cost stability refers to the relative predictability of input prices such as those for labor and materials. The more predictable and stable these input prices are, the lower the business risk; the less predictable and stable they are, the higher the business risk.

Regardless of their lines of business, and is not affected by capital structure decisions, business risk varies among firms. The level of business risk must be taken as a given. The higher a firm's business risk, the more cautious the firm must be in establishing its capital structure. Firms with high business risk tend toward less highly leveraged capital structures, and firms with low business risk tend toward more highly leveraged capital structure.

Assuming that *PeCola Company,* a soft drink company, is considering a capital structure decision. It has obtained estimates of sales and the associated levels of earnings before interest and taxes (EBIT) from its forecasting group. There is a 25% chance that sales will total $ 500,000, a 50% chance that sales will total $ 700,000, and chance that sales will total $900,000. Fixed operating costs total $ 200,000, and variable operating costs equal 50% of sales. These are shown as follows:

Probability of Sales	0.25	0.5	0.25
Sales revenue	500.00	700.00	900.00
Less: Fixed operating costs	300.00	200.00	200.00
less: Variable operating costs (50% of sales)	200.00	300.00	400.00
Earnings before interest and taxes (EBIT)	-	200.00	300.00

This shows that there is a 25% chance that the EBIT will be $0, a 50% chance that it will be $ 200,000, and a chance that it will be $300,000. The probabilities associated with the given levels should be accepted by the firm's authority when developing the firm's capital structure. These EBIT data effectively reflect a certain level of business risk that captures the firm's operating leverage, sales revenue variability, and cost predictability.

Financial Risk

Financial risk directly affects the firm's capital structure which is the risk to the firm of being unable to cover required financial obligations. Bankruptcy is the end result and penalty for failure to meeting financial obligations. The more fixed cost financing – debt (including financial leases) and preferred stock – a firm has in its capital structure, the greater its financial leverage and risk. Financial risk depends on the capital structure decision made by the management, and that decision is affected by the business risk the firm faces.

The total risk of a firm determines the probability of bankruptcy, that is, a combination of business and financial risk. Their combined impact can be shown by continuing the example of *PeCola Company*. Below shows the PeCola Company's current capital structure:

Current Capital Structure	
Long-term debt	-
Common stock equity (25,000 shares @$20)	500,000.00
Total capital	500,000.00

Assuming the firm has no current liabilities, its capital structure currently contains all equity as shown and the total amount of capital remains constant at $ 500,000, the mix of debt and equity associated with the seven debt ratios would be as follows:

Capital Structure with Alternative Debt Ratios for *PeCola Company*

Capital structure ($000)

Debt ratio	Total assets	Debt	Equity	Shares of outstanding common stock
		[(1)x(2)]	[(2)-(3)]	[(4)/ $20)]
(1)	(2)	(3)	(4)	(5)
0%	500	0	500	25.0
10	500	50	450	22.5
20	500	100	400	20.0
30	500	150	350	17.5
40	500	200	300	15.0
50	500	250	250	12.5
60		300	200	10.0

The firm assumed no current liabilities, its total assets equal its total capital of $500,000.

The $20 value represents the book value per share of common stock equity.

The table below calculates the earnings per share (EPS) for debt ratios of 0, 30, and 60%. A 40% tax rate is assumed.

Level of Debt, Interest Rate, and Currency (Dollar/Pesos) Amount of Annual Interest Associated with *PeCola Company's* alternative Capital Structure.

Capital Structure debt ratio	Debt $0	Interest rate on all debt	Interest $0 [(1)x(2)]
	(1)	(2)	(3)
0%	0%	0%	0%
10	50	9	4.50
20	100	9.5	9.50
30	150	10	15.00
40	200	11	22.00
50	250	13.5	33.75
60	300	16.5	49.50

The table below shows the resulting expected EPS, the standard deviation of EPS, and the coefficient of variation of EPS associated with each debt ratio.

Expected EPS, Standard Deviation, and Coefficient of Variation for Alternative Capital Structure for *PeCola Company*.

Capital Structure debt ratio	Expected EPS	Standard deviation of EPS	Coefficient of variation of EPS [(2)+(1)]
	(1)	(2)	(3)
0%	2.4	1.7	0.71
10	2.55	1.88	0.74
20	2.72	2.13	0.78
30	2.91	2.42	0.83
40	3.12	2.83	0.91
50	3.18	3.39	1.07
60	3.03	4.24	1.40

This summarizes the pertinent data for the seven alternative capital structures. The values shown for .30, and 60% debt ratios were developed in the table below, whereas computations of similar values for the other debt ratios(10,20,40 and 50%) are not shown. Because the coefficient of variation measures the risk relative to the expected EPS, it is the preferred leverage increases, so does its coefficient of variation of EPS. An increasing level of risk is associated with increased levels of financial leverage.

The relative risk of the two extremes of the capital structures evaluated below (debt ratios = 0% and 60% can described or portrayed by showing the probability distributions. The expected level of EPS increases with increasing financial leverage, as reflected in the dispersion of each of the distributions. The uncertainty of the unexpected EPS, is greater when higher degrees of financial leverage are applied, as well as the chance of experiencing negative EPS.

Calculation of EPS for Selected Debt Ratios ($000) for *PeCola Company*

Debt Ratio = 0%

Probability of EBIT	0.25	0.5	0.25
EBIT	0	100	200
Less: Interest	0	0	0
Net profits before taxes	0	100	200
Less: Taxes (T =.40)	0	40	80
Net profits after taxes	0	60	120
EPS (2.5 shares)	0	2.4	4.8
Expected EPS		2.4	
Standard deviation of EPS		1.7	
Coefficient of variation of EPS		0.71	

Debt Ratio = 30%

Probability of EBIT	0.25	0.5	0.25
EBIT	0	100.00	200.00
Less: Interest	15	15.00	15.00
Net profits before taxes	(15.00)	85.00	185.00
Less: Taxes (T=.40)	(6.00)	34.00	74.00
Net profits after taxes	(9.00)	51.00	111.00
EPS (17.50 shares)	(0.51)	2.91	6.34
Expected EPS		2.91	
Standard deviation of EPS		2.42	
Coefficient of variation of EPS		0.83	

Debt Ratio = 60%

Probability of EBIT	0.25	0.5	0.25
EBIT	0	100.00	200.00
Less: Interest	49.50	49.50	49.50
Net profits before taxes	(49.50)	50.50	150.50
Less: Taxes (T=.40)	(19.80)	20.20	60.20
Net profits after taxes	(29.70)	30.30	90.30
EPS (10.00 shares)	(2.97)	3.03	9.03
Expected EPS		3.03	
Standard deviation of EPS		4.24	
Coefficient of variation of EPS		1.40	

The nature of the risk-return trade-off associated with the seven capital structures under consideration can be clearly observed by planning the expected EPS and coefficient of variation relative to the debt ratio.

Risk and Cash Inflows

Risk refers to the chance that a project is unviable, that is, NPV < \$0 or IRR<cost of capital. Risk in capital budgeting refers to the degree of variability of cash flows. Projects with a small chance of acceptability and a broad range of expected cash flows are riskier than projects having a high chance of acceptability and a narrow range of expected cash flows. Risk stems almost entirely from cash inflows, because the initial investment is generally known with relative certainty. These inflows, of course, derive from a number of variables related to revenues, expenditures, and taxes.

Examples are: level of sales, cost of raw materials, labor rates, utility costs, and tax rates. Risk in the cash inflows actually results from the interaction of these variables. To assess the risk of a proposed capital expenditure, the analyst needs to evaluate the probability that the cash inflows will be large enough to provide for project acceptance.

Example:

Trident Enterprises, has a 10% cost of capital considers investing in either of two mutually exclusive projects, C and D, each requiring \$ 10,000 initial investment and expected to provide equal annual cash inflows over their 15-year lives. For either project to be acceptable according to the net present value technique, its NPV must be greater than zero.

Let CF equal the annual cash inflow and

II equal the initial investment, the following condition must be met for projects with annuity cash inflows, such as C and D, to be acceptable;

$NPV = [\ CF \times (PVIF_{k,n}\ )] - II$

Substituting k = 10%, n = 15 years,m and II = \$ 10,000, we can find the breakeven cash inflow – the minimum level of cash inflow necessary for *Trident Enterprises's* projects to be acceptable.

$[\ CF \times (\ PVIF_{10\%,15\ years})] - \$10,000 > \$0$

$CF \times (\ 7.606) > \$10,000$

$CF > \frac{\$\ 10,000}{7.606} = \$\ \underline{1,315}$

The projects to be acceptable, they must have annual cash inflows of at least \$ 1,315.

The risk of each project could be assessed by determining the probability that the project's cash inflows will equal or exceed this breakeven level. The various statistical techniques that would determine that probability are covered in more advanced courses. We simply assume that such a statistical analysis results in the following:

Probability of $CF_A > \$\ 1,315 \Rightarrow 100\%$

Probability of $CF_B > \$\ 1,315$ -> 65%

Project C is certain (100% probability) to have a positive net present value, whereas there is only a 65% chance that project B will have a positive NPV, project C is less risky than project D. The potential level of returns associated with each project must be evaluated in view of the firm's risk preference before the preferred project is selected. This identifies risk as it relates to the chance that a project is acceptable but does not address the issue of cash flow variability. Though project D has a greater chance of loss than project C, it might result in higher potential NPV's.

Appendix A

A. WORKING CAPITAL MANAGEMENT

***Problems*:**

A

The following checks were received by *Azenith Company* during January. Calculate the amount of opportunity costs for the company if the opportunity cost rate is 12% per annum.

Face Amount	Days delay
100,000.00	4
150,000.00	5
50,000.00	3
75,000.00	6

B.

A disbursement is currently made by *JJ Enterprises* from its concentration bank at a cost of P 100 per month for account maintenance and P10 per check processed. The controlled disbursement bank will charge P120 per month for account maintenance and P20 per check processed. The controlled disbursement account will add ½-day float to the disbursements. The company issues 100 checks of average face amount of P30,000 per day. The treasurer maintains an overnight portfolio of about P 500,000, on which she currently earns about 6% per annum. She estimates that she could earn an additional 25 basis points on the investments if she could invest earlier in the day. Transfers to the controlled disbursement account could be done at a cost of P20 per transfer. Determine the annual net benefit, or cost, of using the controlled disbursement account instead of the current system.

C.

Nero Company maintains a centralized billing system at its home office to handle average daily collections of P450,000. The total time for mailing, processing, and clearing has been estimated at 4 days.

a. if the company's opportunity cost on short-term funds is 15%, how much this time lag of 4 days costing the company?

b. If management has designed a system of lock-boxes with regional that would have reduced the float by 1 ½ days and home office credit department expense by P 52,000 annually, what is the largest total amount of required compensating balance that the firm should he willing to accept with the lock-box arrangement?

D.

JO is a manufacturer of Id cards and invitation cards. They sell to retail shops and stores in multistate area in the western part of the Philippines. Mr. Santos, the treasurer, is considering the use of a lockbox for the collection of their customer's remittance. Their customers fall into two categories: single outlets and regional chains. During a typical month they receive an average of 5,000 checks with an average face amount of P 300 from a customer and 2,000 checks with an average face amount of P2,500 from the regional-chain customers.

It takes a total of 7 days for JO to receive the payments, process the deposit, and receive available funds. Bank X has offered a lockbox service that would reduce the total to 3 days. The cost for the lockbox would be a fixed charge of P 500 per month and P 50 per processed. *JO* currently pays P .05 per item deposited at its bank. Santos does not believe there will be any additional savings to be achieved if the company eliminates the internal processing of the customers' remittances. *JO* has an opportunity cost rate of 10% per annum.

a. If *JO* uses the lockbox, should they have both classes of customers send their remittances to the lockbox.

b. Should *JO* use the lockbox?

E.

The Greenmax Company makes payments by checks. The Bluemax Company, a supplier has requested that Greenmax allow Bluemax to debit their account 10 days after the invoice date. Greenmax pays Bluemax with a check mailed 30 days after the invoice date. It takes an average of 5 days for the check to the cleared through Greenmax account. The average payment to Bluemax is P 500. It costs Greenmax an average of P 10 to process the invoice through their accounts payable department and to issue a check. These costs would be eliminated by the proposed procedure. The opportunity costs of funds to Greenmax is 10%.

a. Should Greenmax accept Bluemax offer?
b. Greenmax has received a similar offer from Redmax Company. Payments to Redmax company average P 5,000. All other information is unchanged from the Bluemax., Should Greenmax accept Redmax's offer?

F.

Cash Conversion cycle.

Helix Company pays account pays accounts payable on the tenth day after purchase. The average collection period is 30 days, and the average age of inventory is 40 days. The firm currently spends about P 15 million on operating cycle investments. The firm is considering a plan that would stretch its accounts payable by 20 days. If the firm pays 12% for its financing, what annual savings can it realize by this plan? Assume no discount for early payment of trade credit and a 360-day year.

G.

Lockbox decision

Hyperion Corp., a firm that has an annual opportunity cost of 9% is contemplating installation of a lockbox system at an annual cost of P 90,000. The system is expected to reduce mailing time by 1 ½ days, reduce processing time by 1 ½ days, and reduce check clearing time by 1 day. If the firm collects P 300,000 per day, would you recommend the system? Explain.

H.

Malayan Industries, Inc.

The Malayan Industries,Inc. maintain an account with Bank of Malaya for collection in the southeastern marketing area. The bank handles collection of P 750,000 per day in return for a compensating balance of P 500,000.

The company is considering an alternative of opening two separate accounts in the southeastern area. It has been projected that total processing time could be reduced by 2 days if accounts are maintained in a Colony Bank and in an Freedom Bank, each requiring a P 500,000 compensating balance. Would you recommend two bank system to Malayan Industries, Inc.?

If Bank of Malaya offers to drop the required compensating balance in favor of flat fee, what is the maximum fee Malayan Industries should be willing to pay to leave its business with that bank?

I.

Union Enterprises currently has a centralized billing system . On an average 5 days are required for customer's mailed payments to reach the central location. An additional 2-days are required for processing payments before a deposit can be made. The firm has a daily average collection of P800,000. The company has recently investigated the possibility of initiating a lockbox system. Such a system would reduce the mailed payments period from five to three days. Further, processing time would be reduced by one day, because each lockbox bank would pick up mailed deposits twice a day.

a. Determine the reduction in cash balance that can be achieved through the use of a lockbox system.

b. Determine the opportunity cost of the present system, assuming a 7.5% return on short term instruments.

c. If the annual cost of the lockbox system will be P120,000, should such a system be initiated?

J.

Exant Technologies,Inc. expects to have P 2,500,000 in cash outlays for next year. The firm believes that it will have an opportunity interest rate of 12.5% and will incur a cost of P 150 each time it borrows (or withdraws). Cash outlays are expected to be steady over the year. Using the inventory model:

a. Determine the optimal borrowing or withdrawal lot size for the Exant Technologies, Inc.

b. What is the total cost for the use of cash needed for transactions demanded?

c. What will be the cash cycle for the firm (velocity)?

d. What will be the average cash balance for the firm?

Refer to the same problem (10) assume that the Exant Technologies,Inc. began the year with P 2,500,000 in cash.

a. How much would initially be invested in securities?
b. How much would be invested in securities after 113 days?

K.

The *Grander Company* is setting up a new account with Independent Bank. Grander Company plans to issue checks in the amount of P 1,000,000 each day and to deduct them from its own records at the close of business on the day they are written. On average, the bank will receive and clear the check at 5 P.M., the third day they are written; for example, a check written on Monday will be cleared on Thursday afternoon. The firm's agreement with the bank required it to maintain a P 500,000 average compensating balance; this is P 250,000 greater than the cash balance the firm would otherwise have on deposit. It makes a P 500,000 deposit at the time it opens the account.

a. Assuming that the firm makes deposits at 4 PM each day (and the bank includes them in that day's transactions) how much must it deposit daily in order to maintain a sufficient balance once it reaches a steady state? Indicate the required deposit on Day 1, day 2, day 3, if any, and each day thereafter, assuming that the company will write checks for P1,000,000 on day 1 and each day thereafter.
b. How many days of float does Grander have?
c. What ending daily balance should the firm try to maintain (1) on the bank's records and (2) on its own records?

SHORT-TERM FINANCING & ACCOUNTS RECEIVABLE MANAGEMENT

Problems:

Aggressive vs. Conservative financing strategy

1. ***Jade Company*** has forecast its total funds requirements for the coming year as shown in the following items:

Month	Amount	Month	Amount
January	8,400,000.00	July	6,800,000.00
February	6,500,000.00	August	5,500,000.00
March	5,000,000.00	September	5,000,000.00
April	5,500,000.00	October	6,300,000.00
May	6,900,000.00	November	6,400,000.00
June	7,000,000.00	December	7,800,000.00

a. Divide the firm's monthly funds requirement into a permanent and a seasonal component, and find the monthly average for each of these components.

b. Describe the amount of long-term and short-term financing that is used to meet the total funds requirement under: 1) an aggressive strategy; and 2) a conservative strategy. Assume that under the aggressive strategy, long-term funds finance permanent needs and short-term funds are used to finance seasonal needs.

c. Assuming short-term funds cost 10% annually and long-term funds cost 16% annually, use the averages in a to calculate the total cost of each of the strategies described in b.

d. Discuss the profitability-risk trade-offs associated with the aggressive strategy and the conservative strategy.

Cash Discount decision

2. The credit terms for each of four suppliers of ***Majal Enterprises*** are shown as follows:

Supplier	Credit Terms
X	1/10 net 55 EOM
Y	2/10 net 30 EOM
Z	2/20 net 60 EOM

Majal Enterprises requirements:

d. Determine the approximate cost of giving up the cash discount from each supplier

e. Assuming that the firm needs short –term financing recommend whether it would be better to give up the cash discount or take the discount and borrow from a bank at 15% annual interest. Evaluate each supplier separately using your findings in a.

f. What would be the fact and impact to the firm that could stretch its accounts payable (net period) by 20 days from supplier Z have on your answer in b relative to this supplier?

1. Permanent vs. Seasonal funds requirements

3. Manheim International Corp.s current fixed, and total assets for each month of the coming year are summarized as follows:

Month	Current Assets Assets a	Fixed Assets b
January	15,000.00	25,000.00
February	22,000.00	25,000.00
March	25,000.00	25,000.00
April	19,000.00	25,000.00
May	6,500.00	25,000.00
June	6,500.00	25,000.00
July	9,500.00	25,000.00
August	9,000.00	25,000.00
September	16,500.00	25,000.00
October	21,000.00	25,000.00
November	23,000.00	25,000.00
December	21,000.00	25,000.00

a. Divide the firm's monthly total funds requirement (total assets) into a permanent and a seasonal component.
b. Find the monthly average: permanent ;and seasonal funds requirements using your findings in a.

Aging Accounts Receivable

Collection of receivables is detailed by means of aging schedule , according to the length of time they have been outstanding. A simple aging receivables is as follows:

Age	% Accounts Receivable
0- 30 days	52
31-60 days	31
61-90 days	12
91-120 days	5
bad debts	
	100%

The schedule above states that 52% of the company's receivables on the date of analysis have been outstanding for 30 days or less. Similarly, 5% have been outstanding for 91-120 days; and any accounts older than 120 days are written off as bad debt.

Comparing aging receivable schedules for different period, the credit officer can get some idea of any changes in collection experience, additionally, he can determine those individual accounts requiring attention. Like the collection period, however, a weakness of the aging schedule is that it is influenced by changes in sales. For example, if in the month prior to the analysis sales were usually high, it is probable that an inordinately high percentage of accounts will be in the 0-30 days category –even though collection experience may not have improved at all.

Aging is a technique that indicates the proportion of the accounts receivable balance that has been outstanding for a specified period of time. It requires that the firm's accounts receivable be broken down into groups based on the time of origin. The breakdown is made typically every month basis going back 3 to 4 months.

Solutions

A. Azenith Company

To determine the average float for the month we find the total Peso,-days of float by multiplying the face amount times the number of days delay and taking the total.

Face Amount	Days delay	Amount X delay
100,000.00	4	400,000.00
150,000.00	5	750,000.00
50,000.00	3	150,000.00
75,000.00	6	450,000.00
		1,750,000.00

The next step is to divide the total by the number of days in the month to determine the average float over the month. Since January has 31 days, the average float is P 56,451.61. Multiplying this by the opportunity cost for the month gives P 56,451X .12 X 31/365 = P 575.34. Note that we could have also just taken the total Pesos-days of float for the month of 1,750,000 and multiplied by the daily opportunity costs rate of .12/365 and obtained P 575.34.

A. JJ Enterprises

The net benefits consist of the float benefits plus the gain on the earlier investment less the additional connected with the controlled disbursing account less the transfer costs.

Float benefits are :

Annual disbursement X Float gain X investment rate

(P 30,000 per day X 100 X 250 days) X (.5 days) X (.06/365) = P61,644

Additional investment benefits are :

Amount of the investment portfolio X incremental rate

(P500,000) X (.0025) = P1.250

C. Nero Company

a. Total foat = P 450,000 (4 days) = P 1,800,000

Cost = .15 (P 1,800,000) = P 270,000 per year.

b. Reduced expense of float = 0.15 (1.5 days) (P 450,000)

= P 101,250

Total reduced costs = P 101,250 + P 52,000

= P 153,250.

Maximum acceptable compensating balance

= P 153,/0.15

= P 1,021,666.60

D. JO Company

a. the savings achieved on each item sent to the lockbox will be the 4 days saved times the opportunity cost rate times the size of the remittance. The additional cost will be the difference between the deposit cost and the lockbox processing charge. For single-outlet greeting saves P 300 X 4 X 1/365 = P 0.33 for every check. For regional-chain customers JO saves P 2,500 X 4 X 1/365 = P 2.74. The additional cost per item processed is P .50 = P .45. Thus, if JO uses the lockbox, it is worthwhile to have only the larger checks sent to the lockbox. The smaller checks should be processed at the company.

b. The decision depends on whether the total savings from sending the larges checks to the lockbox out-weights the full cost of using the lockbox. The total opportunity cost savings for the month would be 2,500 X 4 X 1/365 X 2,000 = P 5,476.45. The total cost of using the lockbox for a month would be P 500 + 2,000 X P 0.45 = P 1,400. Thus, JO should use the lockbox to capture the net savings of P 4,076.45 per month.

E. Greenmax Company

a. Under the current system Greemax loses value from its account on day 35. They also incur internal costs of P10. for simplicity assume these costs are incurred on day 35 when the payment is made. Under the proposed payment terms Greemax will lose value of P 500 on day 10. To compare these two we take the present value (on day 10) of the payment on day 35. This is P 510/(1+.1X 25/365) = P 506.53. Under the proposed payment terms they will lose value of P 500 on day 10. Since they will be better off by P 653 with the payment terms. Greemax should accept Bluemax's offer.

b. The present value on day 10 for the payment of Redmax under the system is P 5010/1+.1X 25/365) = P 4,975.92. If Greemax accepts Redmax's payment terms it will lose value of P 5,000 on day 10. Since Greemax will be worse off by P 24.08. It should reject Redmax's offer of the new payment terms.

F.

Cash Conversion Cycle

Helix Company

Basic Data

Time component	Current	Proposed
Average payment period (APP)	10 days	30 days
Average collection period (ACP)	30 days	30 days
Average age of inventory (AAI)	40days	40 days

Cash conversion cycle (CCC) = AAI + ACP-APP

CCC current = 40 days + 30 days – 10 days = 60 days

CCC proposed = 40 days + 30 days – 30 days = <u>40 days</u>

Reduction in CCC 20 days

Annual operating cycle investment = P 15,000,000

Daily expenditure = P 15,000,000 / 360 = P 41,666.00

Reduction in financing = P 41,666 X 20 days = P 833,320.00

Annual Profit increase = .12 X P 833,320.00 = P 99,998.40

G.

Hyperion Corporation

Time reduction:

Mailing time 1 ½ days

Processing time 1 ½ days

Clearing time <u>1 day</u>

Total time reduction <u>4 days</u>

Float reduction:

4 days X P 300,00/day = P <u>1,200,000</u>

Gross annual benefit of float reduction :

.09 X P P 1,200,000 = P <u>108,000</u>

Because the annual earnings from the float reduction of P 108,000 exceed the annual cost of P 90,000, the proposed lockbox should be implemented. It will result in a net annual savings of P 18,000 (P 108,000 earnings – P 90,000 cost).

H. Malayan Industries, Inc.

a. Additional required balance = P 1,000,000-P500,000 = P 500,000

Funds free by earlier collection = 2(P750,000 = P 1,500,000.

The company should change to the two-bank, since it yields P 1,500,000-P500,000=P1,000,000 in release funds.

b. There is no fee that would make it worthwhile for Malayan Industries,Inc. to remain with Bank of Malaya simply because the subsequent freeing up of P500,000 in funds will still be less than the P 1,000,000 in released funds under the two-bank arrangement.

I

Union Enterprises

a. Total time saving = 3 days

Time saving X daily average collection = reduction in cash balance achieved

3 X P 800,000 = P 2,400,000

Reduction in cash balances is P 2,400,000

b. Opportunity cost of the present system is .075 X P 2,400,000 = P 180,000

c. Since the opportunity cost of the present system (P 180,000) exceeds the cost of the lock box system (P 120,000) The system should be initiated.

J.

Exant Technologies,Inc.

a. The optimal borrowing or withdrawal lot size for the Exant Technologies,Inc. is:

$$C = \sqrt{\frac{(2)(150)(2{,}500{,}000)}{.125}}$$

$$\sqrt{6000{,}000{,}000}$$

C = P 77,460

b. The total cost for the use of cash needed for transaction :

$$\frac{(150)(2{,}500{,}000) + (.125)(77{,}460)}{77{,}460}$$

=4,841 + 5,841 = P 9,682

c. Cash cycle will be :

2,500,000

77,460 = 32.27

Or 365

1. = 11.31 days

d. Average cash balance will be:

P 77,460/2 = P 38,730

a. Initial investment in securities will be:

P 2,500,000 – P 77,460 = P 2,422,540

a. Investment in securities after 113 days will be:

P 2,500,000 – (10+1) (P 77,460)
= P 1,647,940

K.

Grander Company

a. First, determine the balance on the firm's check book and the bank's records as follows:

	Firm's Check Book	Bank's Records
day 1: Deposit P500,000; write check for P 1,000,000	(500,000.00)	500,000.00
day 2: write check for P 1,000,000	(1,500,000.00)	500,000.00
day 3. write check for P 1,000,000	(2,500,000.00)	500,000.00
day 4: write check for P 1000,000;'deposit P1,000,000	(2,500,000.00)	500,000.00

b. The firm has 3 days of float; not until day 4 does the firm have to make any additional deposits.

c. As shown above. Grander should try to maintain a balance on the bank's records of P 500,000. On its own books it will have a balance of minus P 2,500,000.

Account Receivables

1. ***Ajax Technologies,Inc,.*** is considering a change in its credit policy from net 20 to 2/10 net 30. Its sales should increase from P 500,000 to P 700,000, its cost of goods sold will go from 55% to 50 % of sales. Miscellaneous administrative costs remain steady at P 40,000, but collection costs will increase from P 20,000 to P 30,000 and bad debt losses will go from 5 to 10% of its average accounts receivables. 40% of the customers are expected to take the discount. This company current has indebted for P200,000 at 5%, which include the financing costs for the funds currently tied up in receivables. If the balance in receivables increases or decreases with the new policy, the extra costs of funds tied up will be computed at the 10% estimated cost of the firm's new debt.

a. What is the likely receivables balance with each policy?

b. What will be the forecasted net income after taxes with each policy?

2. ***Fernex Canned Products,Inc.*** thought of tightening its credit policy. The credit manager proposed this change in credit policy to the Chairman asserting that the 90-day terms of their company with the 30-day terms of the industry. Fernex is selling P 1,600,000 a year and costs are 80% variable and P 10,000 fixed. On the basis of a survey of Fernex's customers, the credit manager expects the following relationships between germs and sales:

Policy	Terms	Annual Sales
A	90	1,600,000.00
B	75	1,500,000.00
C	60	1,450,000.00
D	45	1,425,000.00
E	30	1,350,000.00
F	15	1,300,000.00

If the opportunity cost of capital is 15%, which policy is to be adopted? Assume that the average collection period corresponds to the terms given.

3. ***Prexis Company*** has annual credit sales of P 2,400,000. Average collection period is of 2 months. Average selling price per unit is P 10 and the average cost per unit of P 8.60. Prexis can reduce the average collection period by one month by giving 2% cash discount as 50% of the customers will avail of this cash. The required return for Prexis is 20%. Should Prexis liberalize credit policy?

4. ***Meldex Enterprises*** had earnings per share of P 4 last year, and it paid a P 2 dividend. Total retained earnings increased by P 1.20 during the year, while book value per share at year-end was P 4 . Meldex has no preferred stock, and no new equity was issued

during the year. Meldex Enterprises's year-end debt (which equals its total liabilities) was P 12 what was the company's year-end debt/assets ratio?

5. ***Shellex Distribution Company*** has the following data:

Cash and marketable securities	100.00
Fixed Assets	283.50
Sales	1,000.00
Net Income	50.00
Quick ratio	2.0X
Current ratio	3.0X
DSO	40 days
ROE	12%

Shellex has no preferred stock – only equity, current liabilities, and long-term debt.

a. Find Shellex's accounts receivable; current liabilities; current assets; total assets; ROA; equity; and long-term debt.

b. You should have found Shellex's accounts receivable (A/R) = P 111.1. If Shellex could reduce its DSO from 40 days to 30 days while holding other things constant, how much cash would it generate? If this cash were used to buy back equity shares (at book value) thus reducing the amount of equity, how would this affect the ROE; ROA; and the total debt/total assets ratio?

SHORT -TERM FINANCING

Aggressive vs. Conservative Financing

1. Jade Corporation

Month	Total funds requirements	Permanent funds requirements	Seasonal funds requirements
	a	b	[(a)-(b)]
January	8,400,000.00	5,000,000.00	3,400,000.00
February	6,500,000.00	5,000,000.00	1,500,000.00
March	5,000,000.00	5,000,000.00	-
April	5,500,000.00	5,000,000.00	500,000.00
May	6,900,000.00	5,000,000.00	1,900,000.00
June	7,000,000.00	5,000,000.00	2,000,000.00
July	6,800,000.00	5,000,000.00	1,800,000.00
August	5,500,000.00	5,000,000.00	500,000.00
September	5,000,000.00	5,000,000.00	-
October	6,300,000.00	5,000,000.00	1,300,000.00
November	6,400,000.00	5,000,000.00	1,400,000.00
December	7,800,000.00	5,000,000.00	2,800,000.00
Monthly average		5,000,000.00	1,425,000.00

Represents the lowest level of total funds required over the 12-month period

Found by footing the monthly amount for 12 months and dividing the resulting totals by 12.

For the permanent funds requirement, 60,000,000/ 12=5,000,000 for the seasonal funds P17,100,000/12= 1,425,000.

b. aggressive strategy – application of this strategy would result in a perfect matching of long-term financing with the permanent funds requirement and short-term financing with the seasonal funds requirement. Thus, 5,000,000 of long-term financing and average monthly short-term financing of 1,425,000 would be used.

c. Conservative strategy - this application would result in enough long-term financing to meet all projected funds requirements; short-term financing would be used only to meet emergency or unexpected financial needs. In this case, 7,400,000 of long-term financing would be used to meet the peak funds requirement (during January) and no short-term financing would be used.

Aggressive strategy : Total cost = (5,000,000 X .16) + (1,425,000 X .10)

=800,000 + 142,500= <u>942,500</u>

Conservative Strategy: Total cost = (8,400,000 X .16) + (0 X.10)
= 1,344,000+0 = <u>1,344,000</u>

a. The aggressive strategy is more profitable because, as noted in c, its total cot is 1,425,000 compared to the cost of 1,344,000 under the conservative strategy.

The difference result because the aggressive strategy uses as much of the less expensive short-term (current liability) financing as possible , whereas the conservative strategy finances all needs with the more expensive long-term financing. Under the aggressive strategy, interest is paid only on necessary financing ; under the conservative strategy; interest is paid on unneeded funds. (For example, under the conservative strategy, interest is paid on 8,400,000 in July when only 6,800,000 of financing is needed.

2. **Majal Enterprises**:

Supplier	Approximate cost of giving up cash discount
X	1% X [360/(55-10)]=1%360/45=1%X8= 8%
Y	2% X [360/(30-10)]=2%X 360/20=2%X18 = 36%
Z	2% X [360/(60-20)] =2%360/40=2%X9 = 18%

Supplier	Recommendation
X	8% cost of giving up discount <15% interest cost from bank/therefore, give up discount
Y	36% cost of giving up discount <15% interest cost from bank; therefore, take discount and borrow from bank;
Z	189% cost of giving up discount>15% interest cost from bank; therefore, take discount and borrow from bank

3.

Manheim International Corp

Month	Current Assets Assets	Fixed Assets	Total Assets [(a)+(b)]
	a	b	c
January	15,000.00	25,000.00	40,000.00
February	22,000.00	25,000.00	47,000.00
March	25,000.00	25,000.00	50,000.00
April	19,000.00	25,000.00	44,000.00
May	6,500.00	25,000.00	31,500.00
June	6,500.00	25,000.00	31,500.00

July	9,500.00	25,000.00	34,500.00
August	9,000.00	25,000.00	34,000.00
September	16,500.00	25,000.00	41,500.00
October	21,000.00	25,000.00	46,000.00
November	23,000.00	25,000.00	48,000.00
December	21,000.00	25,000.00	46,000.00

Accounts Receivable

Ajax Technologies,Inc.

a. Likely receivables with net 20 would be P 33,333 and P 50,000 with 2/10 net 30.

b. P 75,500 with net 20 and P 127,500 with 2/10 net 30

	Net 20	2/10 Net 30	
Sales	500,000.00	700,000.00	
Cost of Goods Sold	275,000.00	350,000.00	(55% to 30% sales)
Administrative Cost	40,000.00	40,000.00	
Collection Costs	20,000.00	20,000.00	
Bad-debt losses	2,000.00	5,000.00	
Discounts taken	-	-	
EBIT	16,300.00	269,000.00	
Interest	12,000.00	14,000.00	
Taxes	75,500.00	127,500.00	
Net Income after Taxes	75,500.00	127,500.00	

Fernex Canned Products,Inc.

a. Current investment in receivables is:

b. = (30/360)(P 5,000,000)(.70) = P 291,666.67

Change in Policy	A	B	C	D
Incremental sales	600,000.00	400,000.00	500,000.00	700,000.00
Incremental cost	420,000.00	280,000.00	350,000.00	490,000.00
Incremental profit	180,000.00	120,000.00	150,000.00	210,000.00
Average receivables	700,000.00	1,000,000.00	1,354,167.00	1,800,000.00
Investment in receivables	490,000.00	700,000.00	947,917.00	1,260,000.00
Incremental investment	198,333.33	210,000.00	247,917.00	313,083.00
Required return	39,667.67	42,000.00	89,583.00	62,617.00

Determine the marginal profitability from relaxing the credit policy first from the present policy to policy A and then from policy A to policy B and comparing the marginal profitability to the required rate of return (20%) on additional investment in receivables.

Policy A should be adopted and credit terms should not be relaxed as far as policy B is concerned for the marginal benefit is positive in moving from the present policy to policy A but negative in going from policy A to policy B. Table 1 gives the solution.

Annual sales	3,000,000.00	3,240,000.00
Turnover of receivables	6	4
Level of receivables after	3000000/6=	3,240,000/ 4=
change in credit policy	500,000.00	810,000.00
Additional receivables	300,000.00	310,000.00
Add'l investment in receivables above present investment (Cost per unit/selling price per unit) in Additional receivables	210,000.00	
Additional investment in receivables		217,000.00
Required return on additional investment (20%)	42,000.00	43,400.00
Addl sales above present sales(units)	60,000.00	
Addl sales above policy A sales(units)		24,000.00
Profitability of additional sales	180,000.00	72,000.00
Bad debt losses (percent of annual sales)	90,000.00	194,440.00
Addl bad debt losses above present losses	24,000.00	
A losses (90,000)		104,400.00
Profitability of additional sales less additl bad debt losses	114,000.00	(32,400.00)
Profitability of additional sales less additl bad debt losses,oresent policy to policy A	114,000.00	
Profitability of additional sales less addl bad debt losses policy A to policy B		(34,400.00)

Required return on additional investment	42,000.00	43,400.00
	72,000.00	75,800.00

Prexis Company

Reduction on investment in receivables	172,000.00
(P 200,000 X P 8.60/10)	20%
Required return on investment	34,400.00
Opportunity saving	
Opportunity cost of discount	
(P 2,400,000 X .02 X .05)	24,000.00
Net Savings	10,400.00

Meldex Enterprises

Meldex paid P 2 in dividends and retailed P 2 per share. Since total retained earnings rose P 1.2 there must be 6,000,000 shares outstanding. With a book value of P 40 per share, total equity must be P 40 (0.6) = P 24. Since Meldex has P 12 of debt, its debt ratio must be 33.3 per cent.

Debt/Assets = Debt/ Debt+Equity = P 12/ P12 +P 24 = 0.333 = 33.3%

Shellex Distribution Company

a. Begin writing down the relevant definitional equation, and start filling in figures :

1. DSO = Accounts Receivable / Sales/360

40 = Accounts Receivable/ P 1,000/360

A/R = 40 (P 2.778) = P 111.1

2. Quick ratio = Current assets – Inventories/ Current liabilities = 2.0

<u>Cash and marketable securities + A/R</u> =
Current liabilities 2.0

a. = P 100 + P 111.1/ current liabilities

Current liabilities = (P 100+P 111.2)/2 = p 105. 5 million

3. Current ratio = current assets/ current liabilities = 3.0
= current assets/ P 105.5 = 3.0
Current assets = 3.0 (P 105.5) = P 316.5
4. total assets = current assets + fixed assets
= P 316.5+ P 283.5 = P 600
5. ROA = Profit margin X Total assets turnover
= net income/ sales X sales/total assets
= P 50/P 1,000 X P 1,000/P 600
= 0.05 X 1.667 = 0.0833 = 8.33%
6. ROE = ROA X Assets/ Equity
12.0% = 8.33% X = P 600/equity

Equity = (8.33%)(P600)/ 12.0% = P 416.60

7. Total assets = total claims = P 600
Current liabilities+long-term debt+ equity = P 600
P 105.5 +long term debt + P 416.5 = P 600
Long term debt = P 600+P105.5- P 416.5 = P 78
Equity is as follows:
ROE = net income/ equity
12.0% = P 50/equity
Equity = P 50/0.12
= P 416.67

We could have gone on to find current liabilities and long-term debt.

1. **Jones & James, Inc**

Sources		Uses	
Funds provided by operations			
net profit	172		
Depreciation	189	Addition to fixed asset	474
	361	Increase, accounts receivable	182
Increase, accounts payable	2147		
Increase, accruals	88	Increase, inventories	251
Increase, bank borrowings	135		
Decrease, cash	109		
Total sources	907	Total uses	907

b. Statement of Cash Flows for Jones & James, Inc. (in thousands)

Cash flows from operating activities	
Net earnings	172
Adjustments to reconcile net earnings to cash provided by	
Depreciation	189
Changes in assets & liabilities	
Accounts receivable	(182)
Inventories	(251)
Accounts payable	214
Accruals	88
	230
Cash flows from investing activities	
Investment in fixed assets	(474)
Cash flows from financing activities	
Increase(decrease) short-term borrowings	135
Increase(decrease)in cash and cash equivalents	(109)
Cash and cash equivalents at beginning of year	140
Cash and cash equivalents at end of year	31

c. The company has had substantial capital expenditures and increases in accounts receivable and inventories. To finance this growth which is greatly in excess of the growth in equity base, the company has leaned on the trade, has increased its accruals, and has increased its bank borrowings significantly. This has not been enough; there was a substantial draw down of the cash position. The financing is short-term in nature, but it is being used mostly for long-term build-ups in assets.

2. **S & S Milling Company**

	Nov.	Dec	Jan	Feb	Mar	Apr
Sales	500	600	600	1000	650	750
Collections, current month's sales			120	200	130	
Collections, previous month's sales			420	420	700	
Collections, previous 2 months'sales			50	60	60	
Total cash receipts			590	680	890	
Purchases		360	600	390	450	
Payment for purchases			360	600	390	
Labor costs			150	200	160	
Other expenses			100	100	100	
Total cash disbursements			610	900	650	

Receipt less disbursement (20) (220) 240

b.

	Jan	Feb	Mar
Additional borrowings	20	220	(240)
Cumulative borrowings	420	640	400

The amount of financing peaks in February owing to the need to pay for purchase made the previous month and higher labor costs. In March, substantial collections are made on the prior month's billings, causing a large net cash inflow sufficient to pay off the additional borrowings.

c. Pro forma balance sheet, March 31 (in thousands)

Cash	50	Accounts payable	450
Accounts receivable	620	Bank loan	400
Inventories	635	Accruals	212
Current assets	1,305	Current liabilities	1,062
Net Fixed Assets	1,836	Long-term debt	450
		Common stock	100
		Retained earnings	1,529
Total assets	3,141	Total liabilities & equity	3,141

Accounts receivable = Sales in March X .9 + Sales in February X .1

Inventories = P 545 + Total purchase January through March – Total sales January

Through March X .6

Accounts payable = Purchases in March

Retained earnings = P 1,439 + Sales-Payment for purchases –Labor costs and

-Other expenses, all for January through March

3.

a. SGR = .75(.04)(1.6667) / .6667 –[.75(.04)(1.6667)] = 8.11%

1. **Wallex Technologies,Inc.**

Wallex Technologies, Inc. paid P 2 in dividends and retained P 2 per share. Since total retained earnings rose by P 12 million, there must be 6 million shares outstanding. With a book value of P 40 per share, total common equity must be P 40 (6 million) = P 240 million. Since Wallex has P 120 million of debt, its debt ratio must be 33.3 percent:

Debt / Assets = Debt / Debt+Equity = P 120million / P 120million + P 240million = 0.333 =33.3%

2. **Kerdex**: In answering questions like these, always begin by writing down the relevant definitional equations, then start filling in numbers. Note that the extra zeros indicating millions have been deleted in the calculations below:

1. DSO = Accounts Receivable / Sales/ 365

40.55 = A/R / P 1,000/ 365

A/R = 40.55 / (P 2.7397)

= P 111.1 million

2. Quick Ratio = Current assets – Inventories / Current liabilities = 2.0

= Cash & marketable securities + A/R / Current liabilities = 2.0

2.0 = P 100+P 111.1 / Current liabilities

Current liabilities = (P 100+P 111.1)/2 = P 105.5million

3. Current ratio = Current assets/ Current liabilities = 3.0

= Current assets / P 105.5 = 3.0

Current assets = 3.0 (P105.5) = P 31`6.5 million.

4. Total assets = Current assets + Fixed assets

= P 316.5 + P 283.5 = P 600 million

5. ROA = Profit margin x Total assets turnover

= Net income/ Sales X Sales/ Total assets

= P 50/ P 1,000 X P 1,000 / P 600

=0.05 x 1.667 = 0.0833 = 8.33%

6. ROE = ROA x Assets / Equity

=12.0% = 8.33% x P 600/Equity

Equity = (8.33%)(P 600) / 12.0%

= P 416.50 million.

7. Total assets = Total claims = P 600 million

Current liabilities + Long-term debt + Equity = P 600 million

P 105.5+Long-term debt+ P416.5 = P 600million

Long0-term debt = P 600 – P 105.5- P416.5 = P 78 million

We find equity as follows:

ROE = Net income / Equity

12.0% = P 50/Equity

Equity = P 50/0.12

= P 416.67 million (rounding difference)

We could have gone on to find current liabilities and long-term debt.

Kerdex's average sales per day were P 1,000/365 = P 2.7397 million. Its DSO was 40.55, so A/R = 40.55 (P 2.7397) = P 111.1 million. Its new DSO of 30.4 would cause A/R = 30.r(P 2.7397) = P 83. million. The reduction in receivables would be P 111.1-P 83.3 = P 27.8 million, which would equal the amount of cash generated.

New equity = Old equity – Stock bought back

P 416.5 – P 27.8

=P 388.7 million

Thus, new ROE = Net income/ New equity

= P 50/P 388.7

=12.86%(versus old ROE of 12.0%)

New ROA = Net income / total assets – reduction in A/R

= P 50/P 600 – P27.8

= 8.74% (versus old ROA of 8.33%)

The old debt is the same as the new debt.

Debt = total claims – Equity

= P 600 – P 416.5= P 183.5 million

Old total assets = P 600 million

Therefore, debt/ old total assets = P 183.5 / P 600 = 306%

While new debt / new total assets = P 183.5/P 572.2 = 32.1%

3 *Eastwood Products,Inc.*

CL = P 2,000,000; Inv. = P 1,000,000

4. Bread & Butter Enterprises

A/R = P 800,000

5. Brad & Saints Ltd.

D/A = 58.33%

6. D & D Dealers

S/TA = 5; TA/E = 1.5

7. Brewer Corporation

Net profit margin = 2%; D/A = 40%

8. Percy & Tom Company

P262,500; 1.19x

9. Kent & Haley Corporation

Sales = P 2,592,000; DSO = 36.33 days

10. AS Corporation

TIE = 3.86x

11. Jeff & Company

Current ratio = 1.98 x' DSO = 76 days; Total assets turnover = 1.7x; Debt ratio = 61.9%

12. Lance Industries, Inc.

A/P = P90,000; Inv. = P 90,000; FA =P 138,000.

APPENDIX D

1. Jade Industries, Inc.

Solution:

Jade Industries, Inc.

a. Payback period:

Project A: P 28,500 / P 10,000 = 2.85 years.

Year	Cash inflows (CF)	Cumulative Cash inflows
1	11,000.00	11,000.00
2	10,000.00	21,000.00
3	9,000.00	30,000.00
4	8,000.00	38,000.00

2 + P 27,000-P21,000 / P 9,000 = years

2+ P 6,000/ P 9,000 = 2.67 years

b. Net Present Value 9NPV)

Project A : NPV = (P 10,000 x PVIF 14%, 4 years) – P 28,500

= (P 10,000 x 2.914) – P 28,500

= P 29,140 – P 28,500 = P 640

(calculator solution = P 637.12)

Project J:

Year	Cash inflows (CF) (1)	PVIF (2)	Present Value at 14% [(1)x(2) (3)
1	11000	0.877	9,647.00
2	10000	0.769	7,690.00
3	9000	0.675	6,075.00
4	8000	0.592	4,736.00
present value of cash inflows			28,148.00
minus initial investment			27,000.00
Net present value (NPV)			1,148.00

(Calculator solution = P 1,155.18)

c. Internal rate of return 9IRR)

Project A : P 28,500 / 10,000 = 2.850

PVIFA *IRR, 4 yrs* = 2.850

From table:

PVIFA *15%, 4 years* = 2.855

PVIFA*16%,4 years* = 2.798

IRR = 15% (2.850 is closest to 2.855)

(Calculator solution = 15.09%)

Project J : P 11,000+P 10,000+P9,000+P8,000 / 4

= P 38,000 / 4 = P 9,500

PVIFA *k,4 yrs* = P27,000/P9,500 = 2.842

K – 15%

Try 16%, because there are more cash inflows in early years.

Year	Cash inflows (CF)	PVIF	Present Value at 16% [(1)x(2)	PVIF 17%	Present Value@17% [(1)x(4)]
	(1)	(2)	(3)	(4)	(5)
1	11000	0.862	9,482.00	0.855	9,405.00
2	10000	0.743	7,430.00	0.731	7,310.00
3	9000	0.641	5,769.00	0.624	5,616.00
4	8000	0.552	4,416.00	0.534	4,272.00
present value of cash inflows			27,097.00		26,603.00
minus initial investment			27,000.00		27,000.00
Net present value (NPV)			97.00		(397.00)

IRR = 16% (rounding to nearest whole percent)

(Calculator solution = 16.19%)

d.

	A	J
Payback period	2.85 years	2.67 years
NPV	640.00	1,148.00
IRR	15%	16%

Preferred project

Project J is recommended because it has the shorter payback period and the higher NPV which is greater than zero, and the larger IRR, which is greater than the 14% cost of capital.

	NPV	
Discount rate	Project A	Project J
0%	11,500.00	11,000.00
14	640.00	1,148.00
15	0	
16		0

(P 10,000+P 10,000+P10,000+P10,000)
-P 28,500=P 40,000-P 28,500= P 11,500
(11,000+P10,000+P9,000+P8,000)
-P27,000=P38,000-P27,000=P 11,000

From the NPV profile that follows, it can be seen that if the firm has a cost of capital below *approximately 6%(exact value is 5.75%), conflicting rankings of the projects would exist using the NPV and IRR decision techniques, because the firm's cost of capital is 14%, it can be seen in part d that no conflict exists.*

Solution Guide : Depreciation

1. Age of asset (1/1/79 to 1/1/84) = 5 years
Annual depreciation on cost (P 240,000/ 5) = 48,000
Original life (1,200,00/ 48,000) = 25 years
Answer A
Appraised value P 1,80,000
Less : Accumulated depreciation per appraisal
(1,800,000/20 x 5) = <u>450,000</u>
Sound Value P 1,350,000
Answer A
Condition percent (1,350,000 / 1,80,00) 75%

Age of asset 5 years

Remaining life per appraisal 20 years

Remaining life / total life per appraisal = 15/20 = 75%

2. Age of asset (1/1/74 to 1/1/84) = 10 years

Life per appraisal = Age of asset/ percentage of Accu.Depn. = 10/25% or 40 years

	Cost	Appraised Value	Appreciation
Building	6,000,000.00	9,000,000.00	3,000,000.00
Salvage Value	600,000.00	600,000.00	
	5,400,000.00	8,400,000.00	3,000,000.00
Accumulated Depreciation			
(6Mx2%x10)	1,200,000.00		
(8,400,000 x 25%)		2,100,000.00	900,000.00
	4,200,000.00	6,300,000.00	2,100,000.00

Depreciation:

On cost (4,200,00 / 30)	140,000.00
On appreciation (2,100,00 /30)	70,000.00
Total	210,000.00

3. Accumulated depreciation on cost (500,000/10) 50,000

Age of asset (200,000/50,000) 4 yrs

	Cost	Fair Market Value	Difference
Machinery	500,000.00	1,000,000.00	500,000.00
Accum.Depreciation	200,000.00	500,000.00	300,000.00
Balances	300,000.00	500,000.00	200,000.00

Accumulated depreciation (500,000/ 4) = 125,000

Life (1,000,000/125,000) = 8 years

Remaining life (8 /4) = 4

Depreciation (300,000/4) =	75,000.00
Difference(appreciation) (200,000/ 4)	50,000.00
	125,000.00

4. Original Cost (100,000/10) 90,000
litigation cost (30,000/10 x 12) 3,600
13,600
Total life 120 months
From May 6, 1982 to Dec. 31, 1983 20 months
Remaining life -1/1/84 100 months
Ans: A
5. 1984 Amortization (16,000/4) P 4,000
Useful life 8 years
1980 to 1983 4 years
Rem life 4 years
Ans. C
7.

Selling Price of Machine		20,000.00
Cost	28,000.00	
Annual depreciation (28,000-3000 =		
25,000 x 3.75(1/1/86to10/01/89)	9,375.00	18,625.00
Gain on sale of machine		1,375.00
Proceeds of insurers 2,500.00		
Book Value of Equipment		
Cost		7,000.00
Annual depreciation (70,000-1000/5) = 1,200x2.75 =		3,300.00
(7/1/86 to 3/31/89)		3,700.00
		(2,500.00)
loss upon retirement of equipment		1,200.00

8. Cost P 50,000
Salvage Value 5,000
Depreciation cost 45,000
<u>Depreciation rat</u> 5/15

Depreciation 1st year P 15,000
Depreciation for 1988 (15,000 x 6/12) P7,500
b. Depreciation 1/1/89 – 6/30/89 (15,000 x 6/12) = 7,500
Depreciation 7/1/89 – 12/31/89 45,000 x 4/15 x 6/12 6,000
Depreciation 1989 <u>13,500</u>
<u>C</u> Cost 50,000

Depreciation rate 1st year (1/5 x 2) 40%

Depreciation rate- 1st year <u>20,000</u>
d. Depreciation for 1988) 20,000 x 6/12 10,000
c. Cost 50,000
Accumulated depreciation 10,000
40,000 x 40% = <u>16,000</u>
9.

Book Value of old truck	33,000.00
Market value	30,000.00
Lower figure	30,000.00
Cash paid	35,000.00
market value of old truck	30,000.00
Cost of new truck	65,000.00
Gain or Loss	
Market value of old truck	30,000.00
Less: Book value	33,000.00
Indicated loss	(3,000.00)

If the asset are similar, any indicated loss should be recognized.

10.

Book value of old equipment	2,000.00
Trade-in value	3,000.00
Lower figure	2,000.00
Cash Paid	43,716.00
Less: Insurance	976.00
	42,740.00
Add: Book value of old equipment	2,000.00
cost of new equipment	44,740.00
Trade-in Value	3,000.00
Less: Book Value	2,000.00
Indicated loss	1,000.00

11.

Cost of land and building	220,000.00
Mortgage loan	200,000.00
Book Value	420,000.00
Multiply by	25%
	105,000.00
Landscaping	6,000.00
Total cost of land	111,000.00
Book value of land/bldg	420,000.00
multiply by	75%
	315,000.00
add: remodeling/painting	95,000.00
remodeling cost	(6,000.00)
Cost of building	404,000.00

Problems Solving: Capital Budgeting

Solutions

1. GE Enterprises

	Present Machine	New Machine
Annual revenue	2,295,000.00	2,565,000.00
Annual cost of operations	945,000.00	864,000.00
Pre-tax cash flow	1,350,000.00	1,701,000.00
Annual depreciation	162,000.00	216,000.00
Taxable income	1,188,000.00	1,485,000.00
Income tax	380,160.00	475,200.00
Net income after-taxes	807,840.00	1,009,800.00
Add: After tax flow depreciation	162,000.00	216,000.00
	969,840.00	1,225,800.00

The cash flow may also be determined by adding earnings after taxes to the depreciation. The depreciation expenses did not result in any outflow of cash, so at the end of the year, the firm would have P 600+P3,000 of increased cash inflow from operating the machine.

2.

The Raven Industries, Inc

Calculations of net initial outlay	
Outlays:	
Purchase price	116,000.00
Inflows:	
Salvage value of old machine	14,000.00
Tax savings @32% on short -term capital loss	4,480.00
Net initial outlay	97,520.00

Calculations of differential cash flows:

	Book Profits	Cash Flow
Savings		
Cash benefits	66,000.00	66,000.00
Costs:		
Increased depreciation expense (P26,000-7,000)	21,000.00	
Net savings before taxes	45,000.00	66,000.00
Taxes (32%)	14,400.00	14,400.00
Net cash flow		51,600.00

In addition, there is a P 18,000 cash flow at the end of year four from sale of new machine.

Period	Cash Flow	
	97,520.00	
1	51,600.00	
2	51,600.00	
3	51,600.00	
4	69,600.00	51,600+18,000

3.

L&M Poly Vinyl Inc.

Calculating the initial cash outlay

Outflow:	
Cost of the new machine	100,000.00
Transportation cost	40,000.00
Additional working capital	10,000.00
Total outflow	150,000.00
Inflow	
Salvage value of old machine	16,000.00
Tax savings(Dep)(20,000-8,000)	12,000.00
Net initial outlay	122,000.00

Depreciation of new machine:

P 140,000-{P 40,000)/5 = P 20,000

Annual after-tax cash flows:

	Present Machine	New Machine
Annual revenue	120,000.00	180,000.00
Cash expense	60,000.00	80,000.00
Earnings before taxes	60,000.00	100,000.00
Depreciation	8,000.00	20,000.00
Taxable income	52,000.00	80,000.00
Taxes (32%)	16,640.00	25,600.00
Net income after taxes	35,360.00	54,400.00
Add back depreciation	8,000.00	40,000.00
Cash flow after taxes	43,360.00	94,400.00
Book value		40,000.00
Cash value	10,000.00	50,000.00
Gain(loss)	10,000.00	10,000.00
Tax savings (add. Taxes)	(3,200.00)	3,200.00

Plus cash received	10,000.00	50,000.00
Net cash value	6,800.00	46,800.00
Return of working capital		10,000.00
Annual inflow	34,000.00	60,000.00
Final year cash flow	40,800.00	116,800.00

Cash flow stream:

	New Machine	Existing Machine	Differential
Year			
0	122,000.00		122,000.00
1	60,000.00	34,000.00	26,000.00
2	60,000.00	34,000.00	26,000.00
3	60,000.00	34,000.00	26,000.00
4	60,000.00	34,000.00	26,000.00
5	115,000.00	39,000.00	76,000.00

4.

AJAM Industries, Inc.

Initial cash outlay is 75,620 as in the following:

Outflows		
Cost of machine	85,000.00	
Installation fee	7,500.00	
Transportation fee	6,000.00	
Installation cost		98,500.00
Increased taxes		
(P38,500-35,000)(.32)		1,120.00
Increased in inventory		14,500.00
		114,120.00
Inflows:		
Salvage value of old machine		38,500.00
Net initial outlay		75,620.00

Calculations of depreciation for new machine

New machine purchase price	85,000.00	
Installation gee]	7,500.00	
Transportation fee	6,000.00	
Total depreciable value	98,500.00	
Less: Salvage value		
Divided by expected life	98,500.00	10 years
Equals: annual depreciation	9,850.00	

5.

The Birchstock Industries

a.

Year	Cash Flow	Cash Flow	Discount Factor(15%)	Pr Va
0	(700,000.00)	100,000.00	(700,000.00)	
1	(1,000,000.00)	0.86957	(869,570.00)	
2	250,000.00	0.75614	189,035.00	
3	300,000.00	0.65752	197,256.00	
4	350,000.00	0.57175	200,112.50	
5-10	400,000.00	2.1638*	865,520.00	
			(117,646.50)	

*5.0188 for 10 years - 2.8550 for 4 years

As the net present value is negative, the project is unacceptable

b. IRR = 13.20%

c. The project would be acceptable

d. Payback period = 6 years:

-P 700,000- P 1,000,000+P 250,000+ P 300,000+ P 350,000+400,000+P400,000 = 0

1. Incremental cash inflows:

	1	2
Savings	120,000.00	120,000.00
Depreciation,new	96,000.00	153,600.00
Depreciation, old	15,000.00	15,000.00
Incremental depn	81,000.00	138,600.00
Profit before tax		
(1)-(4)	39,000.00	(18,600.00)
Taxes (34%)	13,200.00	(6,324.00)
Operating cash		
flow (1)-(6)	106,800.00	126,324.00
Salvage value		
x(1-34)		

Net cash flow	106,800.00	126,324.00

Incremental cash outflow:

Cost –Sale of old machines – Tax savings on book loss

P 480,000-P 70,000-.32(120,000 -70,000) =581,600

b. Net present value of P 581,600 outflow and the cash inflow on line 9 above at 14 percent =

Project	Investment Required	Present Value Future cash Flows	Net Present Value
1	200,000.00	290,000.00	90,000.00
2	115,000.00	185,000.00	70,000.00
3	270,000.00	400,000.00	130,000.00
1 and 2	315,000.00	475,000.00	160,000.00
1 and 3	440,000.00	690,000.00	250,000.00
2 and 3	385,000.00	620,000.00	235,000.00
1,2 and 3	680,000.00	910,000.00	230,000.00

Projects 1 and 3 should be chosen, as they provide the highest net present value

3. a

Year	Cash Flow	Investment	Net Cash Flow	Present Value of Net Cash Flow
1	2,300,000.00	1,000,000.00	1,300,000.00	1,101,698.00
2	2,645,000.00	1,000,000.00	1,645,000.00	1,181,406.00
3	3,041,750.00	1,000,000.00	2,041,750.00	1,242,670.00
4	3,498,013.00	1,000,000.00	2,498,013.00	1,288,450.00
5	4,022,714.00	1,000,000.00	3,022,714.00	1,321,259.00
6	4,626,122.00	1,000,000.00	3,626,122.00	1,343,224.00
7	5,320,040.00	1,000,000.00	4,320,040.00	1,356,147.00
8	6,118,046.00	1,000,000.00	5,118,046.00	1,361,605.00
9	7,035,753.00	1,000,000.00	6,035,753.00	1,360,821.00
10-25	8,091,116.00	1,000,000.00	7,091,116.00	8,253,350.00
				19,810,630.00

b. The maximum price that is justified is approximately P 19.8 million. It should be noted that these calculations use present-value tables. For cash flows going from years 10 to 25, we subtract the discount factor for 9 years of annuity payments., 4.303 (Table of annuity) from that for 25 years, 5.4669. The difference 5.4669 – 4.3030 = 1.1639 is the discount factor for cash flows for an annuity starting in year 10 and going through year 25. If a present-value function of a calculator is used, a slightly different total may be given due to rounding in the present-value tables.

APPENDIX B TIME VALUE OF MONEY

1.

Solution :

Using equation 15. The compound value of an annuity is:

10

P 100,000 = AΣ (1+.10)^{10}

i=1

P 200,000 = A (15.9373)

A = P12,549.18

2

Solution:

The solution require the use of equation – 11 to find the effective rate:

(a) (1+ 0.08/2)^2 = 1.0816 effective rate = 8.16%

(b) (1+ 0.08/4)^4= 1.0824 effective rate = 8.24%

(c) (1+ 0.08/12) ^{12} = 1.0830 effective rate = 8.30%

3.

FV_n = P 50,000 (1.7908) = P 89,540.00

Next, determine how much the additional P 30,000 will amount in ten years. Using equation 15:

FV_a = P 30,000 (13.1808))

= P 395,424.00

The total of the two figures is P 484,964.00

4.

Solution:

Let x equal the amount of the loan. Then 10x is the annual interest payment. Since interest rate for 3 years will be subtracted from the total loan, the interest will be 3x.

x- .3x = P 100,000

.7x = P 100,000

X = P 142,857

The total loan would be P 142,857. Yearly interest at 10% would be P 142,857. The effective rate of interest is therefore;

P 142,857 = 1.43 = 143%

P 100,000

5.

Solution

The sinking fund is a typical application of a compounded annuity. The interest factor in the 15 year row in the future value of an annuity table is 25.1290

P 1,000,000 = annuity x 25.1290

Annuity = P 1,000,000 P 39,698.29

25.190 =

Norseman will have to put P 39,698.29 into the sinking fund each year.

6.

Solution:

The problem may be solved in two parts: First, compute for the next five years by using equation

PV_n _ (A) (ADF I,n)

PV_n = (P 500,000) (3.6048)

Pv_n = P 1,802,400

Next, determine the present value P 250,000 at the end of 6th year by using equation -14:

PV = (FV_n.)(DF I,n)

= (P 250,000)(.50663)

= P 126,658

7.

Solution

The present value of a perpetual stream is the annual flow divided by the discount rate. Using equation 20 :

(a) P 1,000 / 0.08 = P 12,500

(b) P 1,000 / .10 = P 10,000

8.

Rich Bank's effective annual rate is 8.24 per cent

Effective annual rate is 8.24 %:

$$\text{Effective annual rate} = [\,1 + I_{nom} / m\,]^m - 1.0$$

$$= [\,1 + 0.08 / 4]^4$$

$$= 1.0823\text{-}1$$

$$= 0.0824 = 8.24\%$$

Now *Millionaire Bank* must have the same effective annual rate:

$$[\,1 + 1/ 12\,]^{12} - 1.0$$

$$= 0.0824$$

$$[\,1 + I / 12]^{12} = 1.0824$$

$$1 + = I / 12$$

$$1 + = i / 12 = 1.00662$$

$$i/12 = 0.00662$$

$$I = 0.07944$$

$$= 7.94\%$$

Thus, the two banks have different quoted rates: Rich Bank's quoted rate is 8 per cent, while Millionaire Bank's quoted rate is 7.94 per cent; however, both banks have the same effective annual rate of 8.24 %. The difference in their quoted rates is due to the difference in compounding frequency?

9.

City Bank:

FV_3 = $ 10,000 x FVIF4%/3 yrs. = $ 10,000 x 1.125 = <u>$ 11,250</u>

Town Bank

FV_3 = \$ 10,000 x FVIF 4%/2.2 x 3 yrs. = \$ 10,000 x FVIF 2%,6 yrs.
= \$ 10,000 x 1.126 = \$ 11,260

Avenue Bank

FV_3 = \$10,000 x FVIF 4%/4, 4x3 yrs. = \$ 10,000 x FVIF 1%, 12 yrs.

B.

City Bank: k EAR = $(1+4\%/1)^1-1 = (1+.04)^1 - 1 = 1.04 = .04=$ 4%

Promdi Bank: k EAR = $(1+4\%/2)^2-1 = (1+.02)^2 -1 = 1.0404$ $-1= .0404 = 4.04\%$

Town Bank: k EAR = $(1+4\% /4)^4 -1= (1+.01)^4-1=1.0406-1 =$ $.0406 = 4.06\%$

c.

Mark should deal with Town bank. The quarterly compounding of interest at the given 4% rate results in the highest future value as a result of the corresponding highest effective annual rate.

d.

Avenue Bank

FV_3 = \$ 10,000 x FVIF 4%, 3 yrs. (continuous compounding)

= \$ 10,000 x $e^{.04x3}$= \$ 10,000 x e^{12}

= \$ 10,000 x 1.127497

= \$ 11.274.97

This alternative is better than Town bank, because it results in a higher future value because of the use of continuous compounding, which with otherwise identical cash flows always results in the highest future value of any compounding period.

10.

Annuity A looks more attractive than annuity B. The fact that annuity B's cash flows occur at the end of the year (an ordinary annuity) while annuity A's cash flows occur at the beginning of the year (an annuity due) favors annuity B, because its beginning of year cash flows will have more time to compound than the end-of-year cash flows of annuity B. On the other hand, it would seem that the extra $1,000 per year in cash flow from annuity B ($ 10,000 for annuity B and $ 9,000 for annuity A) would outweigh the benefit of annuity A's longer compounding period. As noted in what follows, only after making necessary computations can the more attractive annuity be determined.

b.

Annuity B (annuity due)

FVA_6 = $ 9,000 x $FVIFA_{15\%, 6\ yrs.}$ X (1+ .15)

= $ 9,000 X 8.754 X 1.15 = $ 90,603.90

Annuity B(ordinary annuity)

FVA_8 = $ 10,000 X $FVIFA_{15\%, 6\ yrs.}$

= $ 10,000 X 8.754 = $ 87,540

c.

Annuity A is more attractive, because its future value at the end of year 6, FVA_6 of $ 90,603.90 is greater than annuity B's end of year- 6 future value, FVA_6 of $ 87,540.00. The subjective assessment in answer a was incorrect. The benefit of receiving annuity B's cash flows at the beginning of the year more than offset the fact that is cash flows are $ 1,000 less than those of annuity B, which has end-of-year cash flows. The high interest rate of 15% added to the attractiveness of annuity A (the annuity due), because each of its cash flows earns at this rate for an extra year, thereby enhancing its future value.

COST OF CAPITAL

1.

Solution:

The cost of debt is:

a) K_d = P 15 / P 112 = 13.39% (before tax)

b) K_d = k_i (1-t) P 109

c) K_d = 15(1- .40) / P 109 = 9 /P109 = 8.26% (after tax)

2.

An issue of 12% preference shares, value of P 2100.00 has a current shares price of P 88,00 ex –dividend. Compute the cost of these preference shares for the company.

Solution:

The cost of these preference shares to the company is:

K_p = 12 / P 88 = 13.64%

3.

3.

In 2002, Zenrex Industries sold preference shares for P 70 per share. Zenrex paid a yearly dividend of P 8.60 per share. Zenrex received P 72 for each share. Determine the cost of the 2002 issue of preference.

Solution:

The cost of Zenrex is

k_p P 8.60 / P 72 = 11.94%

4.

Alchester's market price is P 27 per share. If the dividend is P 3.50 and has been growing at an average rate of 4%, What is the cost of equity?

Solution:

The cost of equity is determined as follows:

k_e = P 3.50 / P 27+ .04 = .13+.04 = .17 = 17%

5.

A dividend of P2.40 per share is about to be paid by AS *Powers Company and has a current share price of P 20.50 the expected future growth in dividends is estimated at 12%. Find the cost of equity.*

Solution:

The current ex –dividend price of equity is = P 20.50 – P 2.40 = P 18.10

k_t *= P 2.40 (1+.12) / P 18.10 + .12 = 26.85%*

6.

a.

Cost of debt, k, (using approximation formula)

1+ $1,000 -$N_d$

n

k_d = N_d + $1,000

2

1 = .10 x $1,000 = $ 100

N_d = $ 1,000 - $ 30 discount - $20 flotation cost = $ 950

N = 10 years

$ 100 +$ 1,000 - $ 950

10

K_d = ____________ = $ 100 + $ 5 = 10.8%

$ 950 + $ 1,000 $ 975

2

(Calculator solution = 10.8%)

K_j = kd x (1-T)

T = .40

K_j = 10.8% x (1-.40) = 6.5%

Cost of preferred stock, k_p

$K_p = D_p / N_p$

D_p = .11 x $100-$4 flotation cost = $ 96

K_p = $11 / $ 96 = 11.5%

Cost of retained earnings, k_r

$K_r = k_s = D_1 + g$

P_0

+ $ 6 / $ 80 + 6.0% = 7.5%—6.0% = 13.5%

Cost of new common stock, k_n

$k_n = \underline{D_1 + g}$

N_n

D_1 = $ 6

N_n = $ 80-$4 underpricing - $4 flotation cost = $ 72

G = 6.0%

K_n = $\underline{\$6}$ + 6.0% = 8.3%+6.0% = 14.3%

$ 72

b.

(1) Breaking point, BP

$BP_{\text{common equity}} = \underline{AF_{\text{common equity}}}$

$W_{\text{common equity}}$

$AF_{\text{common equity}}$ = $ 223,000

$W_{\text{common equity}}$ = 45%

$BP_{\text{common equity}}$ = $\underline{\$ 225{,}000}$ = $ 500,000

.45

(2)

WACC for total new financing < $ 500,000

Source of Capital	Weight	Cost	Weighted cost [(1)x(2)]
	(1)	(2)	(3)
Long-term debt	0.40	6.5	2.6
Preferred stock	0.15	11.5	1.7
Common stock equity	0.45	13.5	6.1
Totals	1		10.4

weighted average cost of capital = 10.4%

3.

WACC for total new financing > $ 500,000

Source of Capital	Weight	Cost	Weighted cost [(1)x(2)]
	(1)	(2)	(3)
Long-term debt	0.40	6.5	2.6
Preferred stock	0.15	11.5	1.7
Common stock equity	0.45	13.5	6.4
Totals	1		10.7

weighted average cost of capital = 10.7%

c.

IOS data for graph

Investment opportunity	Internal rate of return (IRR)	Initial Investment	Cumulative investment
D	16.5%	200,000.00	200,000.00
C	12.9	150,000.00	350,000.00
E	11.8	450,000.00	800,000.00
A	11.2	100,000.00	900,000.00
G	10.5	300,000.00	1,200,000.00
F	1.1	600,000.00	1,800,000.00
B	9.7	500,000.00	2,300,000.00

Leverage

Tetular Corporation

1.

$Q = FC / P - VC$

$= \$ 250{,}000 / \$ 7.50 - \$ 3.00$

= $ 250,000/ $ 4.50

= 55,556 units

b.

	———————————————- +20%————	
Sales (in units)	100,000.00	120,000.00
Sales revenue(units x $7.50/unit)	750,000.00	900,000.00
Less: Variable operating costs (units x $ 3.00/unit)	300,000.00	360,000.00
Less: Fixed operating costs	250,000.00	250,000.00
Earnings before interest and taxes (EBIT)	200,000.00	290,000.00
	————————————	+45%———-
Less: Interest	80,000.00	80,000.00
Net profits before taxes	120,000.00	210,000.00
Less: Taxes (T =.40)	48,000.00	84,000.00
Net profits after taxes	72,000.00	126,000.00
Less: Preferred dividends (8,000 shares x $5.00/	40,000.00	40,000.00

share)		
Earnings available for common	32,000.00	86,000.00
Earnings per share (EPS)	32,000/20000=$1.60share $ 86,000/20,000 = $ 4.30/share	
	'———————————	169%,———

c.

DOL = % change in EBIT / % change in sales = +4%/+20% = 2.25

d.

DFL = % change in EPS / % change in EBIT = +169%/ +45% = 3.76

e.

DTL = DOL x DFL

= 2.25 x 3.76 = 8.46

Using the other DTL formula:

DTL = % change in EPS / % change in sales

8.46 = % change in EPS / +50%

% change in EPS = 8.46 x .50 = 4.23 = + 42.3%

Newton Electronics

Sources of capital	Plan A (bond)	Plan B (stock)
Long term debt	$60,000 of 12% annual interest	$ 50,000 @12% annual interest
Annual interest	.12x$60,000 = $ 7,200	.12 x $ 50,000 = $ 6,000
Common stock	10,000 shares	11,000 shares

a.

	Plant A (bond)		Plan B (stock)	
EBIT	30,000.00	40,000.00	30,000.00	40,000.00
Less: Interest	7,200.00	7,200.00	6,000.00	6,000.00
Net profits before taxes	22,800.00	32,800.00	24,000.00	34,000.00
less: Taxes (T = .40)	9,120.00	13,120.00	9,600.00	13,600.00
net profits after taxes	13,680.00	19,680.00	14,400.00	20,400.00
EPS (10,000 shares)	1.37	1.97		
(11,000 shares)			1.31	1.85

Coordinates

	EBIT	
	30,000.00	40,000.00
Financing Plan	Earnings per share (EPS)	
A(Bond)	1.37	1.97
b (Stock)	1.31	1.85

c.

The bond plan (Plan A) becomes superior to the stock plan (plan B) at around $ 20,000 of EBIT, as represented by the dashed vertical line in the figure in b. (graphical illustration)

3.

4.

Netzel Milk Corporation

Capital Structure debt ratio	Expected earnings per share	Required return, ks	Estimated share value [(1)/(2)]
0%	3.12	13%	24
10	3.90	15	26
20	4.80	16	30
30	5.44	17	32
40	5.51	19	29
50	5.00	20	25
60	4.40	22	20

b.

Using the table in a:

1. maximization of EPS; 40% debt ratio, EPS = $ 5.51/ share (see column 1)

2. maximization of share value: 30% debt ratio, share value = $ 32.00(see column 3)

c.

recommend 30% 30% debt ratio, because it results in the maximum share value and is therefore consistent with the firm's goal of owner wealth maximization.

5.

6.

7.

Valentine Shoes

a. Earnings per share (EPS) = <u>$ 2,000,000 earnings available</u>

500,000 shares of common outstanding

= $ 4.00/share

Price earnings (P/E) ratio = $<u> 60 market price</u>

$ 4.00 EPS

= 15

b.

Proposed dividends = $ 500,000 shares x $ 2 per share = $ 1,000,000

Shares that can be repurchased = $ 1,000,000 / $ 62 = 16,129 shares

c.

After proposed repurchase

Shares outstanding = 500,000 – 16,129 = 483,871

EPS = $ 2,000,000 / 483,871 = $ 4.13 /share

d.

Market price = $ 4.13/share x 15 = $ 61.95/share

e.

the earnings per share (EPS) are higher after the repurchase, because there are fewer shares of stock outstanding (483,871 shares versus 500,000 shares) to divide up the firm's $ 2,000,000 of available earnings.

f.

In both cases, the stockholders would receive $ 2 per share - $ 2 cash dividend in the dividend case or an approximately $2 increase in share price ($60.00 per share to $ 61.95 per share) in the repurchase case. The $ 0.05 per share ($2.00-$ 1.95) difference is due to rounding.

8.

Arab Manufacturing Corporation

The formula for the degree of operating leverage may be used but the expected approach would be to calculate numerically the percentage changes by varying the number of units sold.

Units sold	3,000,000.00	3,000,001.00	4,000,000.00	4,000,001.00
Revenue	9,000,000.00	9,000,003.00	12,000,000.00	12,000,003.00
Fixed costs	3,000,000.00	3,000,000.00	3,000,000.00	3,000,000.00
Variable costs	5,400,000.00	5,400,001.80	7,200,000.00	7,200,001.80
Operating profit	600,000.00	600,001.20	1,800,000.00	1,800,001.20

at 3,000,000 units

Change in operating profit, % = change in profit/ P600,000

change in sales, % = change in sales / P 9,000,000

degree of operating leverage = change in operating profit, % / change in sales, %

= change in operating profit x P

9,000,000 / change in sales x P 600,000

15 (change in operating profit) / (change in sales)

degree of operating leverage = 15 (1.2) / (3.0) = 6

at 4,000,000 units, using the same relationships - change in operating profit x P 12,000,000 / change in sales x P 1,800,000

degree in operating leverage = 6.67 (change in operating

profit) /
(change in
sales)
= 6.67 (1.2)
.(3.0) = 2.67
thus, the
degree of
operating
leverage
depends on
the level of
output.

9.

The breakeven in units will be :

= P 3,300,000 / P 3 – P 1.70

= 2,538,460 units

At 4,000,000 units, operating profits are P 1,800,000. At the new cost level:

Operating profit = 4,000,000 (P 3.00 – P 1.70) – P 3,300,000 = P 1,900,000

10.

SunSung Electronics Corporation

a.

Breakeven units = P 200,000 / P 10 –P 4 = 33,333 units

b.

desired calculations are shown below. Because of the existence of fixed expenses, net income will change at a greater rate then the rate of change in sales. This magnification of the rate of change of net income causes the net income to sales ratio to change. Finally, it should be noted that the degree of operating leverage is greater near the breakeven point and diminishes as sales move away from that point.

	Sales	Variable Expense	Fixed Expenses	Net Income	Percentage change in Net Income	Net Income to Sales	D C le
10%	500,000.00	200,000.00	200,000.00	100,000.00		20.00	3
10%	550,000.00	220,000.00	200,000.00	130,000.00	0.30	23.60	2
10%	605,000.00	242,000.00	200,000.00	163,000.00	25.40	26.90	2
10%	665,000.00	266,200.00	200,000.00	199,300.00	22.30	30.00	2
10%	732,000.00	292,820.00	200,000.00	239,230.00	20.30	32.70	1
-10%	500,000.00	200,000.00	200,000.00	100,000.00		20.00	3
-10%	450,000.00	180,000.00	200,000.00	70,000.00	(30.00)	15.60	3
-10%	405,000.00	162,000.00	200,000.00	43,000.00	(38.60)	10.60	5
-10%	364,500.00	145,800.00	200,000.00	18,700.00	(56.50)	5.10	1
-10%	328,050.00	131,220.00	200,000.00	(3,170.00)	(117.00)	(1.00)	6

11.

	Plan A All Equity	Plan B Half Equity & Debt
EBIT	250,000.00	250,000.00
Interest		187,500.00
EBIT	250,000.00	62,500.00
Taxes (32%)	80,000.00	20,000.00
EAT	170,000.00	42,500.00
No. of shares'	6.80	12,500.00
EPS	6.00	3.40

The interest of P 187,500 was obtained by multiplying P 1,250,000 by 15%. The number of shares was determined by dividing the amount to be financed using equity share price, i.e., P 100 per share.

Thus, when half equity or P 1,250,000 was used, the number of shares is P 1,250,000 / P 100 = 12,500 shares.

12.

Dan Dimasupil

The firm's pretax operating return on assets (P 5millin . P20million = 25%) exceeds the interest rate on debt (15%) Therefore, an increase in leverage will increase expected EPS and ROE.

	No leverage	25% debt	50% debt
Assets	20,000.00	200,000.00	200,000.00
Debt		50,000.00	100,000.00
Equity	200,000.00	150,000.00	100,000.00
Interest (15%)	-	7,500.00	15,000.00
EBIT	50,000.00	42,500.00	35,000.00
Taxes (50%)	25,000.00	21,250.00	17,500.00
EAT	25,000.00	21,250.00	17,500.00
No.of shares	10,000.00	7,500.00	5,000.00
EPS	2.50	2.83	3.50
ROE	12.50	14.17	17.50

EPS are not in thousands

c.

	No leverage		25% debt		50% debt	
	Bad Year	Good Year	Bad Year	Good Year	Bad Year	Good Year
EBIT	20,000.00	80,000.00	20,000.00	80,000.00	20,000.00	80,000.
Interest(15%)	-	-	7,500.00	7,500.00	15,000.00	15,000.
EBT	20,000.00	80,000.00	12,500.00	72,500.00	5,000.00	65,000.
Tax (50%)	10,000.00	40,000.00	6,250.00	36,250.00	2,500.00	32,500.
EAT	10,000.00	40,000.00	6,250.00	36,250.00	2,500.00	32,500.
No. of shares	10,000.00	10,000.00	7,500.00	7,500.00	5,000.00	5,000.0
EPS (Php)	1.00	4.00	0.83	4,833.00	0.50	6,500.0
ROE(%)	5.00	20.00	4.17	24.17	2.50	22.50

Summarizing the results ; In terms of impact on EPS:

	Type of Year		
	Bad	Expected	Good
No leverage	1.000	2.500	4.000
25% debt	0.833	2.833	4.833
50% debt	5.000	3.500	6.500
In terms of impact on ROE			
no leverage	5.00	12.50	20.00
25% debt	4.17	14.17	24.17
50% debt	2.50	17.50	32.50

13.

a. For debt financing
b. Total debt interest= 0.15 (P 50 million)+0.12(P60million) = P14,700,000
c. Shares issued = 4,000,000

(in thousand)

EBIT	20,000.00	75,000.00
Interest	17,400.00	14,700.00
EBT	5,300.00	60,300.00
Taxes	2,650.00	30,150.00
EAT	2,650.00	30,150.00
EPS	0.6625	7.5375

For equity financing:

Interest = 0.12 (P60million)

=P 7,200,000

Total Share = New shares + existing shares

Total shares = (P 50million /P 20)+4,000,000

= 6,500,000

(in thousand)

EBIT	20,000.00	75,000.00
Interest	7,200.00	7,200.00
EBT	12,800.00	67,800.00
Taxes	6,400.00	33,900.00
EAT	6,400.00	33,900.00
EPS	0.9846	5.2154

a. the answer depends on the expected level of EBIT and its variance. At higher EBIT, debt produce higher EPS.

Author

Artusard Renault is a lecturer-teacher of various subjects in college such as Accounting, Finance, Taxation, Basic law, Political Science,, Public & Fiscal Admin. He is a Business Accountancy graduate and finished MBA. He also finished Bachelor of Laws and a Barrister. It is a pen name of *Artemio Saguinsin,* the original author.

About the Author

The author is a book author-writer, researcher, lecturer-teacher, religion and spiritual enthusiast. He has been publishing a lot of titles about his profession in business and law. Hence, a number of religion books for guidance and education for populace from various denominations.

Read more at https://tinyurl.com/arenault.

www.ingramcontent.com/pod-product-compliance
Lightning Source LLC
LaVergne TN
LVHW090258210926
848480LV00001B/62